Eighteenth-century British Literature and Postcolonial Studies

Suvir Kaul

Edinburgh University Press

© Suvir Kaul, 2009

Edinburgh University Press Ltd
22 George Square, Edinburgh

www.euppublishing.com

Reprinted 2010

Typeset in 10.5/13 Sabon
by Servis Filmsetting Ltd, Stockport, Cheshire, and
printed and bound in Great Britain by
CPI Antony Rowe, Chippenham and Eastbourne

A CIP record for this book is available from the British Library

ISBN 978 0 7486 3454 5 (hardback)
ISBN 978 0 7486 3455 2 (paperback)

The right of Suvir Kaul
to be identified as author of this work
has been asserted in accordance with
the Copyright, Designs and Patents Act 1988.

Contents

Series Editors' Preface   vii
Acknowledgments   viii
Timeline   x

Introduction: 'Towards a Postcolonial History of
    Eighteenth-century English Literature'   1
    Postcolonial Studies and Empire Today   1
    Nation-formation and Empire in the Eighteenth Century   4
    Territory, Trade Routes, War and 'Great Britain'   15
    Print and Public Culture   18
    Literary Creativity, Literary Criticism, Postcolonial
      Criticism   22
    Plan of the Book   26

1   'Theatres of Empire'   35
    Davenant, the Revival of Performance, and the Thematics
      of Empire   36
    Aphra Behn, Colonial Self-making, and the Uncertain
      Consolations of Romance   50
    Civil Tragedy, Commercial Humanism, and Colonial
      Consciousness   56

2   'The Expanding Frontiers of Prose'   61
    Yariko and Inkle and the Staging of Polite Culture   64
    Crusoe the Merchant-adventurer – and Friday   67

3   'Imaginative Writing, Intellectual History, and the Horizons of
       British Literary Culture'   84
       The Spectator, Print Culture, and the Circulation of
           International Value   87
       The Languages of National Difference: Becoming
           Roderick Random   95
       Luxury, Commercial Society, Enlightenment
           Historiography   108

4   'Perspectives from Elsewhere'   120
       Lady Mary Wortley Montagu and her Turkish
           Embassy Letters   123
       Johnson's *Rasselas*: Philosophy in an 'Oriental' Key   126
       Phillis Wheatley: Literacy, Poetry, and Slavery   133
       Ukawsaw Gronniosaw: Writing in Another Voice   143

Conclusion: 'Gazing into the Future'   155
       Literary Transport: to India and the South Seas   156

   Bibliography   166
   Further Reading   181
   Index   185

Eighteenth-century British Literature and Postcolonial Studies

Postcolonial Literary Studies

Series Editors: David Johnson, The Open University and Ania Loomba, University of Pennsylvania

Published titles:

Eighteenth-century British Literature and Postcolonial Studies,
Suvir Kaul
Victorian Literature and Postcolonial Studies, Patrick Brantlinger

Forthcoming titles:

Medieval Literature and Postcolonial Studies, Lisa Lampert-Weissig
Renaissance Literature and Postcolonial Studies, Shankar Raman
Postwar British Literature and Postcolonial Studies, Graham MacPhee

Series Editors' Preface

Postcolonial Literary Studies foregrounds the colonial and neo-colonial contexts of literary and cultural texts, and demonstrates how these texts help to understand past and present histories of empires. The books in the series relate key literary and cultural texts both to their historical and geographical moments, and to contemporary issues of neo-colonialism and global inequality. In addition to introducing the diverse body of postcolonial criticism, theory and scholarship in literary studies, the series engages with relevant debates on postcolonialism in other disciplines – history, geography, critical theory, political studies, economics and philosophy. The books in the series exemplify how postcolonial studies can re-configure the major periods and areas of literary studies. Each book provides a comprehensive survey of the existing field of scholarship and debate with a time line, a literature survey, discussion of key critical, theoretical, historical and political debates, case studies providing exemplary critical readings of key literary texts, and guides to further reading. At the same time, each book is also an original critical intervention in its own right. In much the same way that feminism has re-defined how all literary texts are analyzed, our ultimate aim is that this series will contribute to all texts in literary studies being read with an awareness of their colonial and neocolonial resonances.

D. J. and A. L.

Acknowledgments

David Johnson and Ania Loomba asked me to write this book and helped shape its concerns and final form. I am grateful for the opportunity to think about the interlocking cultures of 'English Literature' and 'Great Britain' in the eighteenth century for a series that will map similar issues across a range of literary-historical fields.

A section of this book was presented to the Penn Eighteenth-century Reading Group, and I wish to thank in particular Stuart Curran, Toni Bowers, Joe Drury, Anna Foy, Michael Gamer, John Richetti, and Chi-ming Yang. I also presented sections to the English Department at Cambridge University (thanks to Philip Connell and Priyamvada Gopal), the Department of English and Comparative Literary Studies at Warwick University (thanks to Karen O'Brien), the English Department at the University of Delhi (thanks to Sambuddha Sen), the English Departments at National Taiwan University (thanks to Charles Shepherdson and Liang-ya Liou) and at National Central University, Taiwan (thanks to Lili Hsieh), at the 'Master Narratives' conference hosted by the Center for Cultural Analysis and the English Department at Rutgers University (thanks to John Kucich), as the Robert J. Kane Lecture to the English Department at Ohio State University (thanks to Roxann Wheeler and David A. Brewer), and at the 'Eighteenth-century Cosmopolis' Conference at SUNY Stonybrook (thanks to Kathleen Wilson). I am grateful to colleagues at each of these venues whose comments (and hospitality afterwards!) energized the process of research and writing.

David Alff interrupted his graduate studies at Penn to read and comment upon the entire manuscript, for which I am very grateful. Kim Gravenor, a Penn undergraduate, helped draft the Timeline, sorted out bibliographical details, and chased down typos. I remember fondly the largely anonymous staff in the Rare Books Room at the British Library (where I wrote much of this book), who create the smooth flow of volumes that sets an unattainable standard for the movement of ideas and prose!

*

This book says thank you to three men, each of whom I called *Bhai*:

N. G. K.

A. K. P.

and

A. S. A.

*

Timeline

Date	Historical Events	Literary and Other Publications
1642	Charles I captured. Queen Henrietta Maria and Charles, Prince of Wales, escape to France	John Denham, *Cooper's Hill*
1642–6	Civil War	
1649	Charles I beheaded	Gerard Winstanley, *The True Levellers' Standard Advanced*
1649–60	The Commonwealth Interregnum	
1650		Andrew Marvell, 'An Horatian Ode upon Cromwell's Return from Ireland'
1652	Merchants Daniel Edwards and Thomas Hodges establish the first London coffee house	
1652–4	First Anglo-Dutch War	
1654–60	Anglo-Spanish War	
1655	English fleet repulsed from Hispaniola but takes Jamaica	
1656		William Davenant, *The Siege of Rhodes, Part 1* (Part 2 performed between 1657 and 1659)

1658	Oliver Cromwell dies; succeeded by his son Richard	
1658–9		William Davenant, *The History of Sir Francis Drake.*
1660	Charles II restored to the throne. Royal Society established. Royal African Company granted royal charter	
1665–7	Second Anglo-Dutch War	
1666	Great Fire of London	John Bunyan, *Grace Abounding to the Chief of Sinners*
1667		John Dryden, *Annus Mirabilis*, John Milton, *Paradise Lost*
1670		John Locke, *An Essay on Human Understanding*, John Dryden, *The Conquest of Grenada*
1672–4	Third Anglo-Dutch War	
1672		John Dryden, *Amboyna or The Cruelties of the Dutch to the English Merchants, a Tragedy*
1673		Richard Ligon, *A True and Exact History of the Island of Barbadoes*
1675		William Wycherley, *The Country Wife*
1676	Bacon's rebellion in the Viriginia Colony	William Wycherley, *The Plain Dealer*, Sir George Etherege, *The Man of Mode or Sir Flopping Flutter*
1677		Aphra Behn, *The Rover*
1683	Ottoman Empire loses the Battle of Vienna	
1685–8	Charles dies; succeeded by his brother James II	

1688	James flees to France and is deposed. His daughter Mary and her husband William, Prince of Orange, are invited by Parliament to share the crown	Aphra Behn, *Oronooko* and *The Widow Ranter, or The History of Bacon in Virginia*
1689		John Locke, *Two Treatises of Government*
1694	Mary dies. William III sole ruler	
1697–1703		William Dampier, *A New Voyage Round the World* and *A Voyage to New Holland*
1698		Ned Ward, *Trip to Jamaica*
1700		William Congreve, *The Way of the World*
1702	William dies; succeeded by Anne (Mary's Anglican sister)	
1702–13	War of the Spanish succession	
1704		Joseph Pitts, *A True and Faithful Account of the Religion and Manners of the Mohammetans, with an Account of the Author's Being Taken Captive*
1707	Act of Union between England and Scotland	George Farquhar, *The Beaux' Stratagem*
1708		John Philips, *Cyder*
1711–14		Addison and Steele's *Spectator* papers
1712		Edward Cooke, *A Voyage to the South Sea and Round the World* and Woodes Rogers, *A Cruising Voyage Round the World*

1713	Peace of Utrecht	Alexander Pope, *Windsor-Forest*
1714	Anne dies, succeeded by George I (of Hanover)	Bernard Mandeville, *The Fable of the Bees*, Alexander Pope, *The Rape of the Lock*
1715	Jacobite Rebellion	
1718		Susanna Centlivre, *A Bold Stroke for a Wife*
1719	Riots against Indian silks and calicoes	Daniel Defoe, *Robinson Crusoe*
1720	South Sea Bubble	William Pitts, *The Jamaican Lady*
1721–42	Robert Walpole Prime Minister	
1722		Penelope Aubin, *The Nobles Slaves*, also translates *The History of Genghizcan the Great First Emperor of the Antient Moguls and Tartars*
1724–6		Daniel Defoe, *A Tour Through the Whole Island of Great Britain*
1726		George Berkeley, 'On the Prospect of Planting Arts and Learning in America,' Jonathan Swift, *Gulliver's Travels*
1726–30		James Thomson, *The Seasons*
1727	George I dies; succeeded by George II	
1728		John Gay, *The Beggar's Opera*, Edward Young, *Ocean, An Ode*
1729		James Thomson, *Britannia: A Poem*

1730		Charles Hayes, *The Case of the Royal Africa Company*
1731		George Lillo, *The London Merchant*
1735		Thomas Blackwell, *Enquiry into the Life and Writings of Homer,* Samuel Johnson, *A Voyage to Abyssinia by Father Jerome Lobo*
1735–6		James Thomson, *Liberty*
1737		Alexander Pope's imitation of *The First Epistle to the Second Book of Horace*
1739–44	War of Jenkins' Ear	
1740		Samuel Richardson, *Pamela,* John Dyer, *The Ruins of Rome*
1740–4	George Anson circumnavigates the globe	
1742		Henry Fielding, *Joseph Andrews*
1745	Jacobite rising in support of Bonnie Prince Charlie	
1748		Richard Walter and Benjamin Robin's compilation of Admiral George Anson's *A Voyage Round the World in the Years MDCCXL, I, II, III, IV,* Samuel Richardson, *Clarissa,* Tobias Smollett, *Roderick Random*

1749		Henry Fielding, *Tom Jones*, William Collins, 'Ode on the Popular Superstitions of the Highlands of Scotland, considered as a Subject of Poetry'
1752		David Hume, 'On Commerce' and 'Of National Characters,' Christopher Smart, *The Hop-Garden*
1754	Anglo-French war begins in North America	
1755	Lisbon earthquake	
1756		John Henry Grose, *Voyage to the East Indies*
1756–63	Seven Years' War	
1757	Battle of Plassey consolidates East India Company power in India	John Dyer, *The Fleece*
1759	British Museum opens	Laurence Sterne, *The Life and Opinions of Tristram Shandy, Gentleman*, Samuel Johnson, *The History of Rasselas, Prince of Abyssinia*
1760	George II dies; his grandson crowned George III	James McPherson, *Fragments of Ancient Poetry*, Oliver Goldsmith *Citizen of the World* (1760–1) Briton Hammon, *A Narrative of Uncommon Sufferings and Surprizing Deliverance of Briton Hammon, A Negro Man*

1763	Treaty of Paris ends Seven Years' War	Hugh Blair, *A Critical Dissertation on the Poems of Ossian, the Son of Fingal*, Bishop Percy, *Five Pieces of Runic Poetry*, Lady Mary Wortley Montagu, *Letters of the Right Honourable Lady M—y W—y M—e, Written, during her Travels in Europe, Asia and Africa, To Persons of Distinction* (written in 1716–18)
1764		James Grainger, *The Sugar Cane* and *An Essay on the more Common West-India Diseases; and the Remedies which that Country itself produces. To which are added Some Hints on the Management, &c. of Negroes*
1765	Riots against the importation of French silk	Oliver Goldsmith, *The Traveller, or A Prospect of Society*
1766		Jemima Kindersley, *Letter from the Island of Teneriffe, Brazil, the Cape of Good Hope, and the East Indies*
1767		Adam Ferguson, *An Essay on the History of Civil Society*, Richard Jago, *Edge-Hill*

1768		John Fielding, *Extracts from such of the Penal Laws, as Particularly relate to the Peace and Good Order of this Metropolis*
1768–71	Captain James Cook's first voyage	
1770		Oliver Goldsmith, *The Deserted Village*
1771		Tobias Smollett, *The Expedition of Humphrey Clinker*, Henry Home, *Origin of the Distinction of Ranks*
1772	Lord Mansfield issues judgment barring slave-owners from forcibly deporting slaves from Britain	Samuel Foote, *The Nabob*
1772–6	Cook's second voyage	
1773		James Burnett, *Origin and Progress of Language*, Phillis Wheatley, *Poems on Various Subjects, Religious and Moral*
1774		James Gronniosaw, *A Narrative of the Most Remarkable Particulars in the Life of James Albert Ukawsaw Gronniosaw, An African Prince, Written by Himself*
1775	American Revolution begins	
1776		Adam Smith, *The Wealth of Nations*
1776–9	Cook's third voyage; he is killed in Hawaii	

1777		John Gilmore, *Jamaica, a Poem: In Three Parts*, William Robertson, *History of America*
1780		James Dunbar, *Essay on the History of Mankind in Rude and Civilized Ages*
1781	Discovery of Uranus by William Herschel	
1783	Peace treaty signed in Paris between Great Britain and the United States	Hugh Blair, *Lectures on Rhetoric and Belles Lettres*
1784		Richard Jago, *Poems, Moral and Descriptive*
1787	Warren Hastings impeached	
1789		Gustavus Vassa, *The Interesting Narrative of the Life of Olaudah Equiano, or Gustavus Vassa The African. Written by Himself. 2 vols.*

'Towards a Postcolonial History of Eighteenth-century English Literature'

Postcolonial Studies and Empire Today

In recent years, apologists for the power of the United States (and of its client states in Europe, including Great Britain) have sought to rehabilitate empire as a form of international government. Their arguments justify wars led by the United States in places like Iraq and Afghanistan, and claim more generally that the world is populated by a large number of failed states which should be taken over and governed by the United States and its allies in the interests of managing global resources and preserving order. Some of these ideologues are not shy of describing such intervention as a new colonialism, a label hard to avoid given that most of these so-called failed states were, till forty or fifty years ago, colonies of one or the other European empire. In their view, colonialism has undeservedly been given a bad name, and contemporary western regimes should not shirk from renewing their historical responsibility to supervise lesser nations and peoples.[1]

As revivalists of Anglo-American imperialism, they are particularly irked by the social scientific and humanistic research which has examined the record of modern empire and shown that European nations exploited vast swathes of the globe economically, while subjecting its colonial populations to brutal and corrupt rule. Scholars have detailed the racist foundations of such rule, explained its dehumanizing powers, and demonstrated the connections between the political-economic, legal, and pedagogic practices enforced by European nations in their colonies and those that continue to exacerbate divides in once-colonized nations today. For the proponents of empire, such revisionist and anticolonial scholarship is anathema, as they argue that economic relations between colonizer and colonized are equitable, or at least mutually beneficial, and their view of European empire emphasizes a benign colonial administration devoted not to revenue extraction but to the amelioration of local social wrongs. European or Anglo-US empire is, for them, justified on economic and political grounds, but also because its practices are ideologically and ethically legitimate.

Postcolonial scholarship has been a powerful intellectual resource for the delegitimation of the ideologies and self-justification of modern empires. While anti-imperialist historians and critics of empire in Europe throughout the twentieth century pointed to the material brutalities of colonial rule, postcolonial scholars have added to such critiques by developing insights first articulated by nationalist thinkers and activists who laid the intellectual and cultural grounds for self-determination and independence. For them, the desire to renew a sense of the nation (or in some cases, to construct the idea of nationhood for the first time) was a crucial element of anti-colonialism. To do so, they had to reject ways of thinking derived from imperialist notions of racial and cultural and religious difference and imposed upon them by imperial rule. Anti-colonial nationalism was thus often a cultural nationalism devoted to the molding of an independent citizenry from long-colonized subjects.

This is a project postcolonial scholarship has espoused too, with one major difference: postcolonial critics have noted that national elites were quick to determine the leadership and priorities of both anti-colonial movements for independence and then of the newly-independent nation. In doing so, they adopted many of the legacies and institutions of colonial rule, and thus maintained many of the economic and social divides (within and across nations) enforced by colonialism. Thus political economists and historians have pointed to the many structures of colonial governance, including institutions of trade, finance, and development, that continue to structure postcolonial societies, and indeed to provide the framework for globalization today. We live, they argue, in a neocolonial rather than in a postcolonial world, and our intellectual activity must derive its priorities accordingly.[2]

This insight into the powerful afterlife of colonialism has led literary and cultural critics to pay renewed attention to the history of modern imperialism, in order to understand better the making of both the cultures of the colonized and the cultures of the colonizer. Hence postcolonial scholars (such as the Subaltern School of historians) have re-thought conventional historiographical assumptions while examining the relationship between colonial rulers, nationalist elites and those marginalized *within* the colonized and the postcolonial nation. In such historiography, colonialism is depicted as a process that enriches the colonizing metropole but also small sections of colonized elites, while reinforcing exploitative relations at large amongst colonized peoples. These local elites are then beneficiaries of what is most appropriately termed the 'transfer of power' between colonial and postcolonial rulers at the moment of independence.

Secondly (and this is important for the purposes of this book), postcolonial scholars have turned their attention to processes of nation-formation within *colonizing* nations, and have pointed to the mutual reinforcement provided by internal and international developments in the making of modern European nation-states. This approach to nation-formation in Europe refuses the blinkered historiographical assumption that nationalism is a process of self-construction at work only in once-colonized nations that needed to articulate legitimate political and cultural grounds for their independence. On the contrary, postcolonial scholars who study metropolitan national cultures emphasize the role played by military coercion, economic exploitation, and cultural incorporation in the internal making of the imperialist nation-states of Europe, and argue that the historical force of colonialist practices is also at work in the domestic political and economic consolidation of the nation.[3]

Thus, for example, Great Britain comes into being in the eighteenth century as an Anglocentric nation that incorporates Ireland and Scotland at the same time, and employing many of the same methods, as it becomes an empire overseas. This historical claim distinguishes postcolonial scholarship from other more descriptive studies of empire: it understands that many of the attributes of modern European societies derive from the political-economic, social, and cultural developments that also shaped the colonial and commercial expansion of European power across the globe.[4] Indeed, it argues that the uncompensated extraction of colonial resources and labor as well as the genocidal replacement of native populations by Europeans in different parts of the world was crucial to the economic success and the domestic political and cultural consolidation of European colonial nations. Most historical accounts of these nations, or indeed traditional celebrations of the modern European nation-in-the-making, insulate the glories of national achievement from the barbarities of empire. Culture – the arts, literature, architecture – and the life of the mind are in particular held by many scholars to be inviolate, to be spheres of creativity separate from the buccaneering energies of armed trade and territorial conquest. Postcolonial criticism refuses to occlude these connections, and demonstrates instead the worldly ambitions of art and writing in the age of empire.

This book, as an exercise in the postcolonial interpretation of literary culture in late seventeenth- and eighteenth-century England and Britain, will argue that these literary texts are a wonderful archive for any analysis of the connections between the idea of 'English Literature' (that is, a national literature), nation-formation, and the making of the British empire.[5] My focus on the place of imaginative writing in the reciprocal formation of British nationalism and empire will emphasize subject-formation, that is, the making of the ideological and aesthetic codes that define ideals of masculinity and femininity in this period. These ideals are arrived at by juxtaposing stories and characters – whether in poems, plays, non-fiction prose, or the novel – from within and without the British Isles in order to explore normative definitions of gender, family relations, sexual practice, class behavior, and racial being. I will show that this literary corpus enables us to draw models of idealized or denigrated individual and collective subjectivities, and thus to understand that representations of domesticity, nationalism, or internationalism in eighteenth-century Britain articulated ideas of class, gender, and racial difference derived from accounts of the other worlds being brought into its ambit by exploration, trade, and colonization. Whenever feasible, I will also comment on civic and governmental institutions, from coffee houses to joint stock companies to the military, which were important to the consolidation of Great Britain – the empire and the nation.

Nation-formation and Empire in the Eighteenth Century

The study of imaginative writing in England and Britain in the late seventeenth and eighteenth century ought to be central to our understanding of colonial discourse more broadly. This is because many of the cultural formations, knowledge systems, and governmental and civic institutions crucial to modern European empires either originated in, or were developed to functional efficiency in, this period. Indeed, the very form of the modern European nation-state – centralizing in its political and administrative functions, internationalizing in its economic and territorial ambitions, self-aggrandizing in its cultural and ideological formations – is a product of international competition in trade and territories. In the case of Britain, success in such ventures demanded not only great naval ingenuity and military prowess, but also domestic systems that integrated more forcefully otherwise autonomous political entities in the provinces (Ireland, Scotland, even Wales), as well as their agricultural and manufacturing practices and populations, to create a national economy and demography robust enough to support overseas ambitions. An England-centric Great Britain was brought into being in these years, with London increasingly its administrative, financial, scientific, and cultural hub, even when provincial capitals like Edinburgh and to a lesser extent Dublin became centers of political and intellectual activity in the second half of the eighteenth century. In these 100 years and more, the conglomeration of multi-lingual and distinct communities in Ireland, Wales, Scotland, and England were brought within a more clearly-defined national ambit. This did not mean the loss of local cultures (though some inevitably disintegrated) as much as a realignment of power in which regional distinctions became markers of a provincial, and even backward, identity as English modes of behavior and standards of correctness became the currency of the nation.

For political theorists and humanists in early modern England, the idea, or perhaps the ideal, of a territorial empire had a venerable history, with the Greek city-states of Sparta and Athens, the Macedonian empire under Alexander, and particularly the Roman empire (which included large parts of Britain for almost four centuries from 43 AD to 425 AD) being invoked as instances of imperial success. In the case of Rome in particular, its territorial conquests were seen as the basis of the civilization to which it lent its name and laws. In this understanding, Augustus Caesar's rise to power in 27 BCE inaugurated the Pax Romana, which, for almost two centuries to come, linked – administratively and commercially – vast areas around the Mediterranean, and to the north and east of Italy. Augustan Rome also suggested a remarkable instance of the coincidence of arts and arms that was to define imperial civilizations: any city that could boast poets like Virgil, Horace, Ovid, and Propertius (and a patron like Maecenas, whose name became synonymous with the sponsorship of poets), historians like Livy, and architecture that had declined into the magnificent ruins that defined classical achievement (including obelisks brought as tribute from Egypt), embodied an inheritance claimed by many historically-literate Britons.[6]

For eighteenth-century historians, the rise and fall of territorial empires was one way of understanding the large movements of human history. Indeed ideas of *translatio imperii et studii*, the transfer of imperial authority and of knowledge, were central to English neoclassical historiography. In the sixteenth and early seventeenth centuries, the Spanish colonization of the Americas confirmed this model of territorial conquest, but in the later seventeenth century the Dutch rise to commercial power suggested seemingly more pacific forms of international trade. However, warfare was never far away: in 1619 and 1623, the Dutch and English East India Companies battled each other over the spice trade in Batavia and the Molucca Islands, which proved to be a prelude to the three Anglo-Dutch wars that were fought in 1652–4,

1665–7, and 1672–4 for control over the sea lanes in the Baltic and in the English Channel. Contemporary empires outside Europe loomed large too, as the Ottomans, the Mughals, and the Qing dynasty in China offered compelling instances of political centralization and enormous wealth. Trade brought some of the riches of these empires into British homes, and, along with travelogues (whose witness was often unreliable or occasionally forged), whetted competitive ambitions.

Travelogues combined instrumental aims (they exhorted their readers to overseas trade and settlement and provided useful information, including beautiful illustrations of flora and fauna); ethnographic interests (they described other peoples and social formations, always in comparative terms, and usually to emphasize the distinction of Christian Europe); and literary agendas, in that they also sought to entertain and to generate patriotic ideas of national greatness. In 1598, when the Dutch Jan Huygen van Linschoten's *Itinerario* (1596) was translated into English, the prefatory address to the reader explained the need for the translation by saying that it was recommended by Richard Hakluyt, the great contemporary collector of travel accounts and propagandist for English overseas enterprise ('a man that laboureth greatly to aduance our *English* Name and Nation'), and because it would serve the following purposes:

> I doo most hartely pray and wish, that this poore Translation may worke in our *English Nation* a further desire and increase of Honour ouer all *Countreys* of the *World*, and as it hath hitherto mightily aduanced the Credite of the Realm by defending the same with our *Wodden Walles* (as *Themistocles* called the Ships of *Athens*:) So it would employ the same in forraine partes, as well for the dispersing and planting true Religion and Ciuill Conuersation therein: As also for the further benefite and commodity of this Land by exportation of such thinges wherein we doe abound, and importation of those *Necessities* whereof we stand in Neede: as Hercules did, when hee fetched away the Golden Apples out of the Garden of the Hesperides; & Iason, when with his lustie troupe of courageous *Argonautes* hee atcheiued the *Golden Fleece* in *Colchos*.[7]

These are high ambitions for English merchant-adventurers: they need to match the deeds of Hercules and Jason, mythic hero and imperial voyager, but also to learn, from Linschoten (and presumably others like him), the sea-faring and trading expertise of contemporary Portuguese and Dutch traders.[8]

Over the course of the sixteenth and seventeenth centuries, English merchants and colonial prospectors developed, in occasionally faltering but increasingly successful ways, the ship-building, navigational, and commercial expertise that allowed them to move from the margins to the center of European overseas trade.[9] They were helped along in this project by the sustained volume of translations of travelogues and ship's logs and journals from Portuguese, Dutch, French (and from Arabic via these languages and Latin), and by a number of important travelogues produced by Englishmen who traveled to the Ottoman courts, India, north and north-west Africa, and the Americas.[10] Recent scholarship has restored for us the political and economic urgency of such writing, and we need to keep in mind that this body of instruction was well known to the commercial and political elites of late seventeenth- and eighteenth-century Britain. Certainly these texts, as well as poems, plays, and some prose fiction, confirmed the English in their sense of being a great trading nation and a potentially great colonial power, and if there was a gap between discursive ambition and historical reality, merchant-adventurers, backed by the state, were urged to reconcile the two. That is, even when it was clear that England, and Britain, was by no means the commanding commercial or military power in Europe, or that Britain and its monarchs did not possess the riches of the Ottomans, the Mughals, or of China or Japan, literary writing in a variety of forms argued that Britain had a divine or civilizational mandate to assume global authority or even dominance.[11]

The 'propagandist' role played by travelogues that encouraged commerce and settlement (for its own sake or because it would enhance trade), was from its very inception interwoven with the ethnographic elements of such writing. Everywhere travelers went they described the landscapes they traversed, the produce and goods available (and how to price and bargain for them), and the people they met or heard about, and in doing so they assembled a complex world-picture. Many of these texts contained maps and illustrations, which ranged from fruits and flowers to landscapes to families, ritual occasions, forms of labor and assembly, village views, and, where appropriate, maps of port towns and cities. What is impressive today is how the bulk of such description was crafted from what can only be understood as an early colonial perspective, that is, even before European traders and colonists were able to establish their dominance over trade routes or territories, their accounts of non-European cultural and social formations worked hard to suggest European superiority.[12] Not on all fronts of course, particularly when traders or ambassadors were reduced to the position of favor-seekers in the opulent courts of Asia or the Ottoman kingdoms, but even as they acknowledged the wealth and power of these states, they described moral degeneracy, political absolutism, or inhumane social practices, and, most importantly, argued these conditions to be *definitive* of these nations (see Matar 1999).[13] Both in these descriptions, or even when they wrote about groups of hunter-gathers or pastoralists, the terms of superiority were supple, and could be based on comparative accounts of religious beliefs, political systems, the organization of labor and productivity, forms of consumption (food, clothing, domestic and public ornamentation are prominent), gender relations, or cultural practices. For all the individuality and specificity of these accounts of people from East Asia and the Spice Islands to the Americas (and that specificity is not to be discounted), we find a remarkable accretion of repeated tropes, metaphors, images, modes of description.[14] By the eighteenth century, and in some cases, well before, the ways of seeing that we associate with colonialism and imperialism are convincingly in place (see Pratt 1992; for analyses of earlier travelogues, see Fuller 1995).

Scholars have shown how this flood of travelogues, and the ways of seeing they enabled, provide a fecund archive in which to delineate contemporary collective desire and anxiety.[15] These texts, that is, have been seen as a literary repository, and not only because playwrights, poets, and writers of prose fiction drew upon them, but because they too reveal the rhetorical and psychological complexities we look for in literary texts. Travel writers were popular beyond their print runs, by which I mean that their observations percolated into magazines, newspapers, personal correspondence, and along with historical geographies (world histories), and illustrated maps, played a crucial role in defining British attitudes to non-European peoples globally.[16] 'Attitudes' is too narrow a word here; much more was at stake. These accounts of different parts of the globe, along with details of their flora, fauna, and horticultural potential, came to constitute the forms of modern knowledge, and were crucial to the development of economic, anthropological, and historiographical paradigms with which to understand nature and culture across the globe. Much of this discussion is beyond our purview here, but one eighteenth-century example of such world-systematizing ambition can be discussed briefly.

In 1705, John Harris, a Fellow of the Royal Society, compiled voyages that he was certain would be of use to Englishmen. The title page of the 1744 edition suggests the ambition of the enterprise (after Harris's death in 1719, John Campbell added to and revised the compilation):[17]

Navigantium atque Itinerantium Bibliotheca.

OR, A

COMPLETE COLLECTION

OF

VOYAGES and TRAVELS.

CONSISTING OF ABOVE

Six hundred of the most AUTHENTIC WRITERS,

BEGINNING WITH

Hackluit, Purchass, &c. *in* English;

Ramusio, Alamandini, Carreri, &c. *in* Italian;

Thevenot, Renaudot, Labat, &c. *in* French'

De Brye, Grynaeus, Maffeus, &c. *in* Latin;

Herrera, Oviedo, Coreal, &c. *in* Spanish;

And the Voyages *under the Direction of the*

EAST-INDIA COMPANY *in* HOLLAND,

in Dutch.

Together with such Other

HISTORIES, VOYAGES, TRAVELS, OR DISCOVERIES,

As are in GENERAL ESTEEM;

Whether published in *English, Latin, French, Italian, Spanish, Portuguese, High*

And *Low Dutch*, or in any other *European* Language.

Containing whatever has been observed Worthy of Notice in

EUROPE, ASIA, AFRICA, and AMERICA;

IN RESPECT TO THE

Extent and Situation of EMPIRES, KINGDOMS, PROVINCES, &c.

THE

CLIMATE, SOIL, and PRODUCE, whether Animal, Vegetable, or Mineral, of Each COUNTRY;

LIKEWISE THE

RELIGION, MANNERS, and CUSTOMS of the several INHABITANTS, their Government,
Arts and Sciences, Publick Buildings, Mountains, Rivers, Harbours, &c.

ILLUSTRATED BY

Proper CHARTS, MAPS, and CUTS.

TO WHICH IS PREFIXED

A Copious INTRODUCTION, comprehending the RISE and PROGRESS
of the ART OF NAVIGATION,

And its successive Improvements; together with the *Invention* and *Use* of
the LOADSTONE, and its *Variation*.

Originally published in Two VOLUMES in FOLIO,

By JOHN HARRIS, D.D. and F.R.S.

Now Carefully REVISED,

With LARGE ADDITIONS, and Continued down to the PRESENT
TIME;

Including Particular ACCOUNTS of the

MANUFACTURES and COMMERCE of Each COUNTRY.

LONDON:

Printed for T. WOODWARD, A. WARD, S. BIRT, D. BROWNE, T.
LONGMAN, R. HETT, C. HITCH, H. WHITRIDGE,
S. AUSTEN, J. HODGES, J. ROBINSON, B. DOD, T, HARRIS, J.
HINTON, and J. RIVINGTON.

M.DCC.XLIV.

To handle these volumes today is to note not only their sheer program-
matic scope and the care that is lavished upon their presentation, but also
the unusual collective of booksellers who published them.

A Royal Warrant granted the publishers full rights for fourteen
years, thus making their expenditure worthwhile. Their joint financ-
ing and marketing functions parallel the efforts of the merchants and
merchant companies Campbell celebrates in his dedication 'TO THE
MERCHANTS OF *GREAT-BRITAIN*.' British merchants are 'the
greatest and most considerable Body of Men undignified with Titles,'
and their profession, Trade, has 'Divine Favour' enough to overcome
the 'Separation of Mankind' caused by the 'Confusion of Tongues.'
Campbell's effusive compliments accompany a rudimentary model of
human socio-economic development: agricultural societies grew out of
'natural Instinct,' but human rationality produced Trade. Thus those
nations who were best able to develop the 'Art of Navigation' became
dominant globally, and he offers as a historical maxim *'That whoever
was Master at Sea, must be Master at Land likewise.'* Tyre in the past
and Holland in the present day are for him examples that trade can
enrich an entire country, and Britain itself is an instance that Trade
benefits all the nation, and that the interests of 'Land and Trade [are]

reciprocal, or rather the self-same Thing.' Overseas trade is crucial, for 'though Labour may improve, though Arms may extend, yet Commerce only can enrich a Country.' Further, commerce is understood to be a self-correcting system ('the evils created by Trade, are corrected by Trade') which leads to a more equitable distribution of fortunes and a greater regard for 'Liberty,' for only those who possess the latter can be certain to retain the property they gain via trade. Finally, Campbell generates a miniature version of the four-stages theory of social development when he writes:

> on the Whole, we may safely affirm, that the greatest Differences between Nations, arise chiefly from the Degrees, and the Nature of their Commerce, and according as it is, either little or large, extended or confined; the People are Civilized or Rude, Rich or Poor, Powerful or Weak, Brave or Base, and finally, Free or Slaves: So from Reason we ought to judge and so from Experience it appears.

The 'Preface' to these volumes is particularly noteworthy in that it develops a theory of reading to go with its account of the world voyagers have made available. Campbell remarks that the 'peculiar Pleasure and Improvement that Books of Voyages and Travels afford, are sufficient Reasons why they are as much, if not more read than any one Branch of polite Literature,' and asks why this should be the case. His answer is that such reading combines 'Amusement with Instruction,' and 'keeps alive that Thirst of Inquiry, which we are apt to lose, when too closely constrained to severer Studies.' Equally, 'a modern Reader of Travels becomes, without Travel or Fatigue, better acquainted with the true State of Things, and the real Condition of the Universe, and its Inhabitants, than the wisest of the antient Philosophers with all their Study and Thinking.' 'This Kind of Knowledge,' he goes on to add, 'of all others most opens and inlarges the Mind.' Harris recognizes that most readers will not have the time required to work their way through the by now enormous library of voyages, and offers his volumes as an attempt to collect the 'best Writers' and to digest them for 'general Use' and draw them 'into a Body in a natural and easy Order,' such that each work illuminates those that came before and prepares the grounds for the next. Thus will emerge 'a System of this Sort of Literature as regular and useful, and, at the same time, as pleasant and entertaining, as could be expected.' Harris's editorial principle – the creation of 'a System of this Sort of Literature' for the general reader – reminds us that his efforts are part of the new worlds of publishing and reading in the eighteenth century, of polite writing and its consumers.

There is of course no contradiction between these readers and those Campbell addresses at the end of his 'Introduction':

> We have Commodities, we have Manufactures, we have Shipping, we have Seamen, we have Merchants, what can we possibly want, if we have the Will to employ those as we ought? Methinks I hear some modern Sceptick cry, This is very fine, indeed; but where, which Way shall we search; would you have us Freight and Man our Ships, and then turn then [sic] a-drift, in Hopes that Chance may bring them to some new World? No, the following Sheets will shew, that the Means of Finding are very well known, that the Methods of extending Commerce are natural and easy, and which is more, in a Manner certain; so that there is no need of employing Chance, the very Skill we have, will do the Business.

Readers are now understood as consumers and as opinion makers, which is why Harris embeds this appeal into a longer celebration of commerce as it links different parts of the globe. The voyages Harris and Campbell collect made possible this world of beatific and mutual enrichment, and also allow contemporary scholars to aspire beyond earlier limits to knowledge (as Campbell wrote in the 'Preface': 'what way so likely to convey universal Knowledge, as exhibiting a complete View of the Universe?'). And now, these new volumes, weighty with their exhibition of the 'Universe' as with their aspiration to 'universal Knowledge,' embody in themselves the attractions and excitement of commodity culture, global knowledge, and national power.[18]

Both promoters of trade and proponents of new forms of knowledge and intellectual procedure drew upon these reports of the world, whose authenticity or scholarly probity were often contested by others with differing political or philosophical commitments. In an analysis of John Locke's extensive reading of travelogues, Daniel Carey has followed debates at Oxford in the seventeenth century and states that despite 'misgivings raised by some over the merit of travel accounts, an important group of Oxford-based geographers and historians accepted the conclusions offered by travelers and re-circulated them in their work.' Geographers 'customarily adopted the moral conclusions made by travelers, supplying rapid, if highly unsympathetic summaries of human character,' especially those that confirmed the superiority of European (or English) religion, arts, and civility. More considered responses were possible: Locke's treatises on government, on religious belief, and on human nature drew extensively on the testimony of travelers, and while he was aware of the probability of error or exaggeration, the form remained for him 'a useful historical resource' whose claims could be cross-checked by 'cumulative investigation,' and the critical skills of learned but sympathetic readers. Indeed Locke wrote that such writing contained 'a very good mixture of delight and usefulness' (Carey 2006: 100–1, 120, 114). Locke's writing is only one instance of a larger intellectual and cultural phenomenon: by the eighteenth century, almost all debates in political theory and law, in theological disputation and the history of religion, in botany and biology, in poetics and literary history, drew upon the witness of merchants and the naturalists who traveled with them, as did the creative arts from painting to fiction. The world of the intellectual and the reader were thus made systematically international, and included the 'old' world and the 'new.'

In any case the Royal Society wanted to systematize the kinds of information that it exhorted travelers to collect.[19] As it sought to create a repository of scientific, maritime, ethnographic, and geographical information that would help commercial travelers find and negotiate their way across the world, it sought to weed out the unscrupulous and largely unverifiable testimony of earlier voyagers. In *Philosophical Transactions* 11 (2 April 1666), Robert Boyle suggested observational protocols that would stabilise reportage. He asked for anthropological, commercial, and metallurgical data in addition to the climatic and geographical information seamen were to record. Lands encountered were to be described and their features, as well as their agriculture, mapped. Grain, fruit and vegetables were to be catalogued, as well as the 'particular Arts and Industries [by which] the Inhabitants improve the Advantages, and remedy the Inconveniences of their Soyl.' Timber trees, especially those 'whose wood is considerable,' are to be noted, and animals (both wild and domesticated) described, as are minerals, metals and mining operations.[20]

> Boyle also called for a 'careful account . . . of the *Inhabitants* themselves,' both *Natives* and *Strangers*, that have long been settled there: And in particular their Stature, Shape, Colour, Features, Strength, Agility, Beauty (or the want of it) Complexions, Hair, Dyet, Inclinations, and Customs that seem not due to Education. As to their Women (besides the other things) may be observed their Fruitfulness or Barrenness; their hard or easie Labour, *&c.* And both in Women and Men must be taken notice of what diseases they are subject to . . .

'To these General Articles or Inquiries,' Boyle wishes to add further '*Inquiries* about *Traditions* concerning all particular things, relating to that Country, as either peculiar to it, or at least, uncommon elsewhere.' Being concerned that such inquires will require more 'Learning or Skill' than the answerer might possess, Boyle recommends that to such inquiries be 'subjoined *Proposals* of ways, to enable men to give Answers to these more difficult Inquiries.' Boyle does not elaborate on the nature of the '*Proposals*' that will allow those questioned to respond in ways intelligible to their interlocutors, but his recommendation makes clear that both the questions, and the appropriate form and terms of the answers, are to be defined by the English voyager and observer. The problem of cultural difference and mistranslation is here intuited, and then, at the level of observational protocol, solved.[21]

Accounts of voyages and travels became crucial to both specialized and polite knowledge (see Marshall and Williams 1982). Literary texts in this period are littered with caricatures of loony philosophers and antiquarians whose speculations are fueled by trivia from across the globe, but far more substantial and institutionalized forms of knowledge were based on reports of the world provided by traders and colonists.[22] Details of the globe and its people percolated into all manner of conversations, adding layers to the historical information and lore already in circulation. Accompanying these inflows of information – and often acting as their immediate motivation – were the quantities of material objects imported into Britain. A vogue in chinoiserie and in Chinese aesthetics resulted as china crockery and decorative objects altered the look and feel of British homes and landscaped gardens (see Porter 2001).[23] Spices from India and south-east Asia, tea from China, chocolate from America, and sugar from Caribbean plantations flavored tastes; imported cottons, calico, silks and textile dyes altered clothing; rum and tobacco offered addictive pleasures; and the procurement and supply of these commodities energized trade.[24] Precious and semi-precious stones and worked metalware were rendered more valuable for their distant origins. And the 'foreignness' of these imports was kept in view by a number of protests (which included riots against silk and calicoes in 1719) against their import by domestic manufacturers threatened by their cost and quality.[25]

Proponents of trade and plantation insisted that all Britons benefited from their goods and profits. The author of *The Case of the Royal African Company of England* argued that '*there is not a Man in this Kingdom, from the highest to the lowest, who does not more or less partake of the Benefits and Advantages of the* Royal African Company's FORTS *and* CASTLES *in* Africa' (*The Case of the Royal African Company* 1730: 31).[26] While this was an opinion contested by some who feared the unsettling domestic impact of imported luxuries and fortunes, or those political economists who argued against monopolies granted to the trading companies, or the few Christian moralists upset about the inhumanity of the slave trade and forced labor, the majority of writers who considered these issues either celebrated the refinements of civil society supposedly enabled by commercial power or restricted their ire to satires of over-consumption, particularly of female consumers. But there was no gainsaying the fact that these consumer comforts came at a price: the expansion of British commerce and colonies in the eighteenth and nineteenth centuries led to a nearly continuous series of wars with a succession of European and non-European powers. Accordingly, almost regardless of the particular ministry in power, English and British state policies made exportable military and naval firepower the *sine qua non* of national glory, and a crucial component of domestic and foreign policy.

Territory, Trade Routes, War and 'Great Britain'

English kings had previously ruled over territories in France after Norman rule was established in England, and had control over large areas in Ireland from the late twelfth century. Under the patronage of Elizabeth and James I after her, tenuous settlements were established in North America, and English sea-captains like Sir Francis Drake had profited from raids on Spanish shipping and settlements in Florida and the West Indies. Elizabeth encouraged the formation of trading companies that would do business in the Levant and with the Islamic kingdoms of Turkey and Morocco, and in the East Indies, and over the course of the seventeenth century, these Mediterranean and Asian ventures allowed England to develop an understanding of itself as an aspiring and occasionally successful global trading power. There were of course several moments when the course of true trade (or indeed colonization in Ireland or the Americas) did not run smooth, since Englishmen not only competed with European competitors but faced armed opposition by local forces and navies across the globe. Nevertheless the lure of large profits, and of settlement, was robust and energizing even in the face of setbacks. Spain's trans-Atlantic colonies and trade were a reminder of riches to be gained, and one of Cromwell's first forays after he consolidated power in England, Ireland and Scotland was his 'Western Design,' a plan to dislodge the Spanish from Hispaniola (and to force Spain to allow English merchants to trade in the Caribbean). As it happens, in 1655, the English fleet was repulsed from Hispaniola but took Jamaica, and thus added to the British presence on the smaller islands of Barbados, Montserrat, Nevis and St Kitts. Even though this was considered a failed expedition, with its leaders jailed once they returned to London, it made clear that European rivalries were going to be fought in places and trade routes across the Atlantic and elsewhere. In the second half of the seventeenth century, then, England was committed to protecting and expanding its seaborne commerce, its trans-Atlantic settlements, its trading 'factories' in India and elsewhere, all in the face of Spanish, Dutch, and French competition.

Britain's key competitor in the eighteenth century was France, and historians have argued that the patriotic sentiments generated by the wars fought against France were central to British nationalism.[27] Anglo-French rivalry derived both from balance of power concerns within Europe, and, increasingly, from competition for territories and trading monopolies overseas. Or perhaps it is more accurate to say that all balance of power concerns in Europe now involved territorial holdings and trading monopolies around the Mediterranean, in the Americas including in the Caribbean, on the coast of Africa, in India, and in south-east Asia. In this period, Britain would consolidate and then lose its territories in North America, when thirteen colonies confederated themselves as the United States of America and declared their independence in 1776. However, large parts of Canada had previously come under British control as part of the Treaty of Paris at the end of the Seven Years' War (1756–63), a war that at one point or another involved virtually every European nation, with battles and skirmishes in Europe, North America, India, the Caribbean, the Philippines and off the African coast. British successes resulted in the dislodging of the French as a colonial power in North America and their restriction to commercial activities alone in India. The East India Company established significant territorial control in the province of Bengal in 1757, and thus laid the grounds for its transformation from trading company operating under the aegis of the Mughal emperor, to a sovereign military, administrative and revenue-collecting authority. The Treaty of Paris also added to Britain's possessions in the Caribbean, on the Mediterranean, and on the west coast of Africa, and confirmed Britain as the dominant European overseas power. (The geopolitical consequences of the Seven Years' War should not be underestimated, for even as Britain lost a substantial empire across the Atlantic two decades later, its settlements in Asia, Africa, and the Pacific continued to expand.)

If Gallophobia, and warfare against competing European powers, helped consolidate a sense of doughty Englishness, the 1707 Act of Union between England and Scotland brought to the fore the need for a different, more inclusive, definition of a 'Briton,' that is, the national subject of the new political entity of Great Britain. This composite nation was itself the result of a long history of wars and tenuous political alliances between its constituents, but by the early eighteenth century, the

English were entrenched in Ireland and dominant over Scotland. Much in this history militated against any easy idea of Britishness. Ireland had long been treated as an island to be Anglicised and brought under English control, and some analysts of later English colonial practices have argued that their early plantations in Ireland (where English farmers were settled onto lands seized from the Irish) were testing grounds for the racist expropriation of land and labor that would define their presence in the Americas and in Asia.[28] In the middle of the seventeenth century, Cromwell consolidated his rule in England in part because of his bloody and successful Irish campaigns, including his destruction of the Scottish armies backing Charles II (1649–52).[29] The English Protestant supremacy in Ireland was confirmed by the success of William of Orange's armies in 1689–91, and Ireland was thereafter ruled from London.[30]

Scotland was never colonized in the same way as Ireland, but, in 1707, Scottish Lowland elites, unable to develop independent overseas trade or settlements, moved to become junior partners in a British union, and in doing so, made Scotland a prime source of the manpower required to settle, work, or police British territories and interests across the globe. After each of the two failed Jacobite uprisings in 1715 and 1745, but particularly after the latter, the clan system of the Scottish Highlands was disbanded, and large numbers of Scots emigrated (often under conditions of indenture) or joined the British army, and thus, even as they were denied rights at home, became loyal soldiers of the British Empire. By the second half of the eighteenth century, in the contrast between the modernizing commercial and civil society of the Lowlands and the 'archaic,' underdeveloped and increasingly exploited Highlands, Scotland reproduced internally key features of the divide in socio-economic and cultural power between itself and England.

The paragraphs above are a quick reminder of significant political and military milestones in the making of the nation and the empire. If there is any one historical point here, it is that 'Great Britain' came into being as much from its territorial and trading successes overseas as it did from the consolidation of the Three Kingdoms, and particularly of England and Scotland. These became reciprocal processes: international commercial and colonial gains offered prospects for all those who functioned under the aegis of Britain, and Great Britain achieved stability as a nation in spite of war against the Scots in 1715 and 1745. Having stated that, it is important to remember also that both these nationalizing and internationalizing processes were uneven and significantly contested, in war, in political negotiations, in print, in Parliament, and on the street.[31] People did not lose their provincial identities easily, or cease to identify as English or Scottish or Welsh even as the idea of the Briton was given a fillip by wars and conquests fought in the name of the nation.[32] Nor is this surprising, if only because of great disparities across the isles, which refracted identification with any nationalizing political icon, including 'Britannia' or 'John Bull.'

Great Britain was an uneven promise for those increasingly marginalized, whether Scottish highlanders, Irish crofters, Welsh peasants or even the dispossessed and the poor in England who chose to emigrate as indentured labor or ended up pressganged or transported. Dispossession and displacement caused the poor to experience the growth of commercial society, enclosure, and overseas endeavors differently from those poised to benefit immediately from these processes, but the latter too were divided about the proper national policies to further their prosperity. Since politics and policy decisions in London were divided along party lines and lobbied by differing economic interests, decisions about alliances or warfare in Europe, the Americas, and Asia, negotiations for trade routes and regulations in waters near and far, appropriate fiscal and administrative procedures, were all debated at length, and passionately, and often on behalf of some sub-national interest. Operations in non-European theaters had a differential impact on domestic and overseas populations, particularly since the latter had a sharper sense of their own needs, and were not loathe to contest or ignore Parliamentary policy. A loose constellation of 'Britons' fought those they displaced (native Americans, the French, and the Spanish in the Americas, local rulers and traders in Asia and Africa), those they enslaved (on the West African coast, in the Caribbean and North America), but equally, in North America in 1776, others like themselves who no longer wished to be governed by the British monarch and parliament.[33]

Print and Public Culture

Nation-formation and empire-building are rough, demanding, and unforgiving processes, centered on coercion and the violent rearrangements of power, and such violence was certainly a feature of the experiences of Britons in this period. Central to both nation-formation and empire-building are the institutions of the state, institutions which range from the fiscal and administrative to the juridical and pedagogic, dedicated both to the construction of civil and military apparatuses and of the citizens who people them. Historians have detailed the many administrative and logistical innovations that characterized eighteenth-century British society and enabled it to efficiently pursue its provincial and expansionist goals (see Brewer 1989).[34] However, as theorists of national identity have been at pains to show, the modern nation is also characterized by an enormous and vital non-state apparatus of citizenship, civic being, and sociality that encourages particular ways of being in the world. This was very much the case in eighteenth-century Britain too, particularly in the development of a vibrant, inventive, and contentious print culture that mapped models of individuality, family networks, social practices, class relations, as well as hierarchies of cultural and human development within and without the nation. [35]

Indeed it can be argued that no 'institution' was more crucial to the self-regulating, self-improving, elite conception of the British nation than that of print culture, with the accompanying development of a putatively disinterested mode of writing increasingly understood as 'Literature.'[36] The polyphonic play of voices and positions in print, and the seeming sublation or resolution of such contention into a realm of aesthetics and literary performance suggested an ethical and cultural achievement that emphasized Britain's right to export its civilities alongside its systems of governance and its commerce. (It is important however to keep in mind that very little writing – as reviews and rebuttals remind us – was in practice understood to be non-partisan or disinterested, but the whole added up to a demonstration of exemplary national self-correction.) By the end of the century, as Paul Keen suggests, there was 'a growing consensus about Britain's imperial status which insisted on the literary republic as a disinterested sphere of learning whose merits partially justified and partially helped to fine-tune the development of emergent geopolitical formations' (Keen 1995: 235).

Debates about normative ideas of social being, citizenship and the nation were central to the history of nation-formation and empire I have sketched above, and even when this contemporary history was not elaborated as the frame for these discussions, its shaping presence can be found in any number of crucial asides, seemingly throwaway remarks, undeveloped allusions, or unsubstantiated assertions about peoples and places not British.[37] For instance, when James Thomson writes, in his anthem to British power, 'Britons never will be slaves,' his refrain derives its ironic force and resonance from the British trans-Atlantic slave trade and its colonial plantations in the Caribbean and North America, even though he calls no attention to this world (see Kaul 2000). As I will go on to show in this book, an enormous volume of writing in this period engaged with – in varying detail and method – ideas of nationalism and of internationalism; engaged, that is, in discussions about the desirability, feasibility, and ideal forms of nation and empire. This conversation, in its varied literary, imaginative, ethnographic, and even 'scientific' dimensions, shaped not only British attitudes to domestic and foreign social formations, and indeed British subjectivity itself, but also (given British holdings and influence overseas) shaped the cultures and consciousness of millions of non-British subjects of the empire. And this long conversation – or more particularly, its eighteenth-century variations – is the subject of this book.

This is an appropriate place in which to note a powerful but not unsurprising irony: as several commentators have shown, after the Union, Scottish writers and philosophers played a disproportionate role in denominating and crafting the culture of the nation, that is, of Great Britain (as opposed to England).[38] Robert Crawford argues that as mid-century Scottish 'improvers' like Adam Smith tried to rid their urban elites of the localisms of speech and writing that marked their provinciality, they produced courses in rhetoric and belles lettres that are the first formal attempts to bring together, in an institutional and proto-disciplinary format, exemplary instances of English literary practice, thus precipitating the idea of 'English Literature' itself (Crawford 1992; see also Crawford 1998). Clifford Siskin writes that the Scottish Enlightenment grew out of the need to develop the idea of *culture* itself as the medium that would register provincial differences while accommodating them within the more totalizing script of British nationalism (Siskin 1998). The cultural and ideological consolidation (however partial and contested) of the Union, that is, did not simply flow outwards via a series of aesthetic mandates or intellectual performances from the English metropolis to its provincial capitals; rather, provincials actively defined Britishness on their own, perhaps more accommodating, terms.

Manuscripts and books played a powerful role in defining, legitimizing or questioning (occasionally with transformatory effects) social institutions and hierarchies in early modern Europe. The tales and ideas contained in them were crucial to any sense of community, whether religious or civil, even when feudal social formations constrained literacy. The pace of learning quickened alongside the forms of commercial growth that inaugurated capitalism in England – the need for skills like accountancy, record-keeping, and letter-writing gave impetus to literacy and numeracy, while also creating communities of people whose self-understanding included a developed sense of functioning in a world larger than that of their immediate village or parish.[39] The growth of overseas plantations, colonies, and trade rendered these communities more visible and more powerful economically. They also became important consumers of the new print culture that came into being in the last years of the seventeenth century, and which expanded exponentially (particularly in London) in the early eighteenth century. This print culture was made feasible by technology that allowed the manufacture of cheap printed products, and the new volumes of printed matter encouraged the generic creativity that began to define the concerns and characteristic formats of newspapers, periodicals and journals, travelogues, conduct manuals, anthologies of poetry, and the misshapen forms of imaginative storytelling that we know today as the novel.[40]

Well into the eighteenth century, British writers and commentators on literature worked with a sense that the corpus of materials in the English language was impoverished when compared with its classical Graeco-Latin forebears or even with the achievements of modern poets and philosophers writing in French or German.[41] One important way in which poets, playwrights, and writers of prose combated this feeling of cultural provinciality was by including in their writing references to illustrious predecessors whose work they invoked for its imaginative or formal powers. Thus Shakespeare's genius, Jonson's polish, Waller's correctness of tone and diction, or Milton's sublimity were woven into an uneven and as yet unfolding historical narrative about the rise of English 'sons of letter'd fame,' that is, as milestones of *national* literary achievement, to be compared favorably with the best of the Ancients and the European Moderns.[42] Such references were not isolated or idiosyncratic; they are acts of 'canon-formation,' part of the self-reflexive celebrations (and debates) that added up to a national literature in English.[43] Indeed 'English Literature' itself, as a specialized body of imaginative writing with its own, increasingly visible, regulatory institutions of commentary and criticism, and its own canon, is brought into being in this period. As poets are anthologized, and their 'Lives' written, as their corpus, and that of playwrights, is standardized and stabilized, as different 'schools' are identified and influences outlined, as the first national literary histories are planned and written, the boundaries between 'literature' and other sorts of writing are demarcated and made central to critical evaluation.[44]

This process, as scholars of literary history have shown, is also deeply interconnected with the crafting of a nationalist cultural repository for Great Britain, and the making of a literary culture self-confident enough to support its imperial ambitions, or, more occasionally, to contest them.[45] Pope's view that the working coincidence of 'arts' and 'arms' spells out the glorious achievement that is empire runs as a forceful undercurrent in the ebb and flow of English letters through the century, even if the precise relation between arts and arms in the making of national glory is debated, as is the proper relation between writers and the state. Many writers lived in close financial or cultural alliances with men in power, and others aspired to such relations of patronage, which meant that a great deal of literary production is partisan in its motivations and in its account of individuals or of the nation. Even when writers were not explicitly partisan in their concerns, but took upon themselves the exploration of ideas or emotions or the telling of stories not directly connected to a political point-of-view, their themes and formal experiments are self-consciously transnational, and to that extent, caught up in defining properly English subjects. This is as true when Pope translates Homer or when he, in the *Essay on Criticism*, 'englishes' elements of Boileau's *Art poétique* (1674) (which was itself a redaction of Horace's *Ars Poetica*), as it is when Defoe shipwrecks Robinson Crusoe on an uninhabited island in the Caribbean in order to explore the shaping force of colonial experiences on English subjectivity.[46] The ideal attributes of the British subject, male and female, are constantly embodied, debated and given to revision depending on the party and class affiliations of the writer, and indeed the stories they choose to tell, for notions of subjectivity are derived from the changing contrast between British men and British women; between the aristocracy, the country gentry, manufacturers, and tradesmen; between English gentlemen and their domestic inferiors, whether the Irish, the Scots, the peasantry or the urban poor; between the British and their European rivals, and, importantly for this book, between the British and the non-European peoples they encountered or imagined, enslaved or colonized, emulated or feared.

Literary Creativity, Literary Criticism, Postcolonial Criticism

Postcolonial critics share with historicist literary critics the belief that the most rewarding readings of literary texts are arrived by paying careful attention to the relation between a text and its historical moment. An analysis of this relation does not simply involve a study of the themes of the text – that is, what the text is 'about' – or of the stories the text chooses to feature. (The analysis of content is in any case a vexed business; what the author chooses to leave out, or to downgrade in significance, can be very important in understanding how the text comes to terms with the history it makes available.) Historicist literary readings must also take into account the formal arrangements – genre, style, idiom – that individuate any text and ask how the individuality of each text is at the same time a measure of its engagement with its historical moment, and thus with developments in cultural and social history. At its best, postcolonial criticism demands similar attentiveness to form, theme, and historical location, with the proviso that the historical framework of explanation is not limited by, and internal to, the nation.

On the contrary, postcolonial scholars understand that, from the seventeenth century onwards, the growth of the English economy and power were coterminus with, and dependent upon, the expansion of trade and colonies overseas, with the result that any analysis of national culture and literary production in this period must be located in an international, or more precisely, a colonial frame.[47] The outer horizon of imaginative possibility – the limits of innovation – broadened as the globe was brought increasingly into view, and the overarching view was that of a colonizing power. Imaginative writing of all kinds became crucial for the detailing of novel experiences across the globe, and doing so in ways that made them comprehensible within the cultural and moral codes that defined Englishness. Over time, and with increasing self-confidence, writers accounted for all manner of differences – religious, ethnic and racial, social and cultural, political and economic – by creating complex, and increasingly racist, hierarchies of human achievement, with the English, the 'lords of human kind,' at the very pinnacle.[48] Understood in these terms, English literary practices in the eighteenth century constitute a rich canon of colonial discourse, and postcolonial criticism offers particularly important insights into this literary history.

In this section, I will sketch some of my key literary-critical methods and literary-historical assumptions. These ideas have been debated at complex length by literary theorists, and I will not revisit those debates here. I will however provide a brief theoretical explanation of the multiply-mediated links between authorial subjectivity, literary creativity, and the world the text makes available as well as the history within which it comes into being, if only because such a 'theory of the text' is important to the literary criticism and literary history practiced in this book. First, a literary text is defined by its form, that is, the elements of genre that it orchestrates into its own composition, thus simultaneously locating itself vis-à-vis a history of prior practices and individuating itself via innovations that themselves reshape that history. For instance, an eighteenth-century poet who chose to write a sonnet could invoke the Petrarchan precedent (with its *abba abba cdecde* rhyme scheme and its shift of theme in the last six lines) or the Spenserian (three quatrains and a couplet, in the rhyme scheme *abab bcbc cdcd ee*), or the Shakespearean example (in the rhyme scheme *abab cdce efef gg*, in which the closing couplet often contains a surprising turn). Literary innovation is always enabled (and also contained) by the conventional practices it sees as precedents, and the history of formal innovation becomes one way in which we can track the patterns of continuity and change we describe (in this instance) as the history of the sonnet.[49] The same model holds when we write a broader history of poetry, or, more ambitiously, narrate literary history – particular accretions of formulaic practice might define one historical moment just as insistent breakaways from such formulae define another. Part of my argument in this book will be that key innovations, or retreats from innovation, in the eighteenth century are fueled by the desires and fears that marked English expansionism.[50]

Literary forms mutate throughout the century, and in many cases such changes indicate to us shifts in British priorities in the formation of social and cultural norms adequate to the exercise of international power. A form might come to be defined closely with the class concerns of its major practitioners, as was the case with the staging of aristocratic and military heroism (most often located in venues outside of England) in Restoration heroic drama or indeed in comedies like Behn's *The Rover* (1677). These plays celebrated the return of a Stuart monarchy in 1660, reasserted Cavalier values, and also reminded their audiences that England under Charles II possessed precisely the right aristocratic leadership with which to wrest control of foreign spaces from the Spanish or the French. Not surprisingly, the passing of the Stuarts from power also saw the virtual demise of that form of playwriting. English ambition did not cease – it transmuted into a less bellicose form, as when in *The London Merchant* (1731) George Lillo offered the merchant Thorowgood as the new national hero. (Thorowgood manages the defence of his nation as ably as he shepherds the work-habits and ethics of its apprentices and workers.) The georgic poem, domesticated in England in poems that celebrated rural labor and productivity as the cornerstones of national prosperity, took a remarkable turn with James Grainger's *The Sugar-Cane* (1764), which claimed for slave owners and plantations in the Caribbean the same cultural and ethical legitimacy that defined agricultural communities in Britain.

Or, as happened with the novel, a literary genre might retract from experiment, innovation and messiness into a more safe and domestic mode. Early English novels traveled, which is not surprising given that the form itself adapted storytelling techniques from Asia and other parts of Europe. *Oroonoko* is located in Surinam, Robinson Crusoe travels to the islands of the Mediterranean and the Caribbean (and farther afield in Asia in sequels), Roxana's adventures lead her to France and to America, and Lemuel Gulliver wanders in fantasy lands anchored off Asia or

Africa. Over the course of the century, while the novel never quite loses its global compass, and is populated by characters from a wide range of professions and classes, it does increasingly become the form that champions domestic interests and values, particularly those espoused by the more substantial merchants and country gentry of England.[51] The benign mix of individualism, nuclear family values, social stability, moral centeredness, and cultural improvement that the novel helped consolidate produced its own representational and narrative conventions, which relegated into subsidiary genres (the 'Oriental tale,' criminal biographies, the Gothic) the more outlandish and enterprising elements of the early novel.[52] The 'rise' and disaggregated growth of the novel, that is, can also be better understood by taking seriously the important role played by such imaginative prose in stabilizing and normalizing English world-views, if only by devising distinct generic forms for the separation and better management of the mess of information and stories filtering in from the contact zones of the world (see, for instance, Ballaster 2005).[53]

Literary creativity engages past literary practices as much as those that characterize the present, which is to say that writers always work with a sense of what has come before as well as of what is *au courant* (if only because they want to sell books and influence or entertain people). The creative dialogue that ensues has allowed historians to catalogue trends in productivity, both at the epiphenomenal level of fashion or vogue and as movements that achieve staying power and define their cultural moment and shape what comes after. The literary text thus inhabits a very supple temporality as it converses with the past, debates issues in the present, and, equally importantly, imagines a different future. This last element – sometimes identified as utopian – derives great force from the psychic and social desires that grant acts of writing their particular creative intensity. To write is to intervene in or to reinvent difficult situations, and thus to make things better, or so the author believes, and this motivation is as true of the lyricist who imagines a space whose isolation will bring to fruition the reverie he engages in or the loss he feels, as it is of the playwright who produces a play satirizing corruptions that she believes are vitiating the social order. To write is to explore and to imagine differences of all kinds, whether these be ranges of emotion, varieties of individual or collective being, or provincial, national, or international identities. Each act of literary creativity does not do all this at once, but a surprisingly large number of texts (as this book will argue) derive their affective and ideological power by orchestrating a variety of characters and experiences in ways that encourage the local to resonate with that which lies elsewhere. The compressed power of the literary text then lies precisely in its ability to move its readers into spaces not their own, and then perhaps to offer compensatory resolutions of the dissonances that result.

This is very much the case with the late seventeenth- and eighteenth-century texts I will discuss here. As overseas expansion played an increasingly important role in the British economy, social system, and culture, newspapers, journals, travelogues, and all manner of imaginative writing were informed by, and contributed to, ideas of nation and empire.[54] My focus will be on the myriad details in each literary text (and on repeated patterns in clusters of texts) that move English, and British, readers into arenas of experience far removed from England or even provincial Britain, such that these faraway spaces precipitate challenges that redefine the British subject, even as they typically reduce other people and places to a subordinate status in relation to Britain and Britons. As they do so, they also – this too is a feature of plot, range of character, and the particularities of experience represented in such writing – produce an internally differentiated system of socio-cultural, political, and ethical values that maps Britain itself, showing how provincial ways of being lag behind (or occasionally contribute usefully to) the norm that is defined by elements of London-based and English life. In this view, to read eighteenth-century British imaginative writing is to limn the contours of English Literature and the British nation as each is defined vis-à-vis cultural, political, and economic formations elsewhere. The book that follows will thus argue that even as literary critics must elaborate on the thematic and formal features of any text – its literariness, that is – they must also pay systematic attention to the textured world it weaves. Only such criticism can be adequate to the world-creating ambition of writers. This last describes not only authors like John Dryden, Aphra Behn, Henry Fielding, or Oliver Goldsmith, but also authors like Anne Finch or Thomas Gray or William Cowper, whose literary personae and practices were far more self-effacing. They were all, to borrow a phrase from Goldsmith, 'citizens of the world' that commerce and colonization was bringing into view, and our assessment of their achievements would do well not to diminish that self-understanding.

Plan of the Book

Chapter 1, 'Theaters of empire,' examines the revival of performance and theater exemplified in *The History of Sir Francis Drake* (1658–9) and *The Siege of Rhodes*, Part 1 (1656) and 2 (1657–9), each of which is an instance of – in different theaters of the world – the seventeenth-century vogue for plays about overseas conquest and the rise and decline of empires. I move then to a discussion of Aphra Behn's *The Widdow Ranter, or, The History of Bacon in Virginia. A Tragi-comedy* (1688–9), to examine the comedy of colonial self-making.

Chapter 2, 'The expanding frontiers of prose,' argues that the early prose narratives that led to the novel traveled the globe while developing their plot lines and their cast of characters. I pay particular attention to Richard Steele's 1711 retelling of the tale of Yariko and Inkle in *The Spectator* to suggest the myriad ways in which stories of miscegenation in faraway lands defined the sensibility and concerns of London drawing rooms. I then move to a longer consideration of Robinson Crusoe, who illustrates the material travails (and successes) and psychological dramas of English merchant-adventurers.

Chapter 3, 'Imaginative writing, intellectual history, and the horizons of British literary culture,' spends time in the cosmopolitan world of *The Spectator*, in part to suggest the power of print culture in London and in Britain more generally. I then analyse Tobias Smollet's *Roderick Random* (1748) to emphasize the difficult relations between Scottish and English modes of being in the composite imperial culture of Great Britain. I conclude with a section on the importance of ideas of commercial society to Enlightenment historiography, especially those explanations of historical transition that were developed by Scottish commentators. Chapter 4, 'Perspectives from elsewhere,' is concerned with the writing of four very different people whose attitudes to cultural geography were at odds with the conceptions of peoples and places fostered by British nationalism and empire: Lady Mary Wortley Montagu (in her letters about Turkey), Samuel Johnson (in *Rasselas*), Phillis Wheatley (in her poems), and Ukawsaw Gronniosaw (in his memoirs dictated to an amanuensis).

In the 'Conclusion,' I point to the increasing importance of India and the South Seas to British imperialism and cultural creativity, and end with a brief reading of the young John Keats finding in George Chapman's translation of Homer a poetic elevation that parallels the expansive possibilities that astonished the Spanish conquistadors when they first gazed upon the Pacific. It perhaps bears stating that a book of this length cannot attempt to be comprehensive, and I hope that readers will find in the analyses of individual texts ideas that can be generalized across the 100 years and more of literary and political history included here. I should explain, however, the absence of any sustained analysis of poetry: my book *Poems of Nation, Anthems of Empire: English Verse in the Long Eighteenth Century* covers this ground much more effectively than a chapter might here, and I refer readers to it for a parallel argument about the interplay of poetic forms and nationalist debates in this period (see also Kaul 2008).

Notes

1. A representative instance is Niall Ferguson (Ferguson 2003: 54). A recent member of the 'celebrate English-speaking Empire' brigade is Andrew Roberts; in his prolix *History of the English-Speaking Peoples since 1900*, he offers this anodyne summary of British (and US) imperialism: 'Ever since the mid-1830s, the English-speaking peoples had considered it their civilizing mission to apply – with varying degrees of force – their values and institutions to those areas of the world they believed would benefit from them' (Roberts 2006: 6).
2. For a recent discussion of the issues and debates that characterize such scholarship, see Loomba et al. (eds), *Postcolonial Studies and Beyond*.
3. Scholarship like that of Hilary Beckles has shown that labor conditions and poverty within Britain generated the forms of un-free labor crucial to tobacco and sugar plantations in British West Indian colonies. White indentured labor was 'instrumental in the transformation of the West Indian frontier into an ideal mercantile construct – the jewel in the crown of the English seaborne empire' (Beckles 1989: 172); African slave labor served the same purpose after 1660.
4. For instance, Janet Sorensen argues that we 'simply cannot talk about national notions of linguistic identity outside of political and linguistic relations of empire' (Sorensen 2000: 223).
5. In practice, this book will deal with literature between 1660 and 1776. These dates are conventional in demarcating 'Restoration and Eighteenth-century Literature,' but they are also of political interest to students of English nationalism (the return of the monarchy) and of English colonialism (the breaking away of key American colonies).
6. English literary responses to Augustan power were complicated, if only because the Emperor represented an unacceptable authoritarianism (see Weinbrot 1978 and Erskine-Hill 1983). For instance, Alexander Pope's *First Epistle to the Second Book of Horace Imitated* (1737) both emulates and satirizes Augustus's legacy, particularly in his prefatory comments (Pope 1961: 634–5).
7. John Wolfe, 'To the Reader,' in John Hvighen Van Linschoten, *His Discours of Voyages into yᵉ Easte & West Indies* (1598), quoted in Kamps and Singh (2001: 6).
8. At an earlier moment in this address, the translator-publisher makes a distinction between 'Poeticall Fictions, and vain Fables,' and the writing of travelers that

   > being neither coniured out of hell, nor rapt into the heauens, but of their own honourable disposition and instinct of Nature, haue not only compassed Sea and Land in their own persons to learne and beholde *Nations, Realmes, Peoples & Countries* unknown, for the augmentation of their owne priuate skill and cunning, but also haue committed their knowledge and labours to writing for the propagation of the seruice and glorie of God in *Pagan* and *Heathen* places, and the great pleasure, profit & commodity of their *Countrymen*. (Kamps and Singh 2001: 6)

   This passage summarises the reasons why travel writing was understood to be of consequence to seaborne exploration, trade, and colonization.

9. England was in many ways a latecomer to the trade routes, and had little access to the overland routes that had fertilized European economies (and enriched their art and culture) from the fifteenth century onwards (see Brotton 2002).

10. In the case of Asia, Donald F. Lach and Edwin J. Van Kley write that what 'began as a stream of information in the sixteenth century became a virtual deluge during the seventeenth' (Pagden 2000: 243). Lach has provided massive documentation of the enormous impact on Europe of ideas of and from Asia in *Asia in the Making of Europe*.

11. Robert Markley shows that English (and European) poets, geographers, travelers, and historians produced ' a variety of compensatory strategies to deal with Europe's marginalization in a global economy dominated by the empires of the Far East' (Markley 2006: 3).

12. In the particular instance of 'Renaissance' Europe, Jerry Brotton argues that Europeans were far more caught up with systems of exchange with the Islamic world than they acknowledged (Brotton 1997: 9).

13. Matar argues that, in the seventeenth century, precisely 'because the Muslims were beyond colonial reach, Britons began to demonize, polarize, and alterize them' (Matar 1999: 12). Matar believes that literary and theological texts were crucial to this modern process, which is true, except that these texts are also replete with evidence of Islamophobia that goes back several hundred years, and particularly to the Crusades. It is thus more accurate to suggest that the 'imperial' forms of such demonization drew upon, and rendered more urgent, longer histories of cultural and religious differentiation. Matar develops his arguments in *Britain and Barbary*.

14. Travel writers had few qualms about repeating, without attribution, entire passages from previously published texts. In one wonderfully ironic instance, Fisher shows that the Indian Dean Mahomed based some of his observations of Surat and Bombay on John Henry Grose's *Voyage to the East Indies* (1766) and Jemima Kindersley's *Letters from the Island of Teneriffe, Brazil, the Cape of Good Hope, and the East Indies* (1766). He points out that such copying was a feature of travel writing (Fisher 1996: 232–3).

15. Peter C. Mancall's comment on Hakluyt is representative: in the *Principal Navigations*, Hakluyt allowed readers access to vital parts of the early modern world, and also 'formulated plans for the expansion of the English realm. In the process, he created a language to justify overseas expeditions and colonization. Later that language became part of the foundation of the British Empire, an entity that did not exist during Hakluyt's lifetime' (Mancall 2007: 305).

16. For example, Matthew H. Edney details the overlap between British commercial and administrative interest in India and British cartography – these maps suggest increasing knowledge as well as increasing power (Edney 1997: 2).

17. The English ur-text of such editorial and national ambition is Richard Hakluyt's *The Principal Navigations, Voyages, Traffiques and Discoveries of the* English Nation, *made by Sea or over-land, to the remote and farthest distant quarters of the Earth, at any time within the compasse of these 1600 yeres* (1598–1600). As the title-page of the 1599 edition announces, Hakluyt's volumes included '*many notable monuments and testimonies of the ancient forren trades, and of the warrelike and other shipping of this Realme of England in former ages.*'

18. Travelogues, geographies, histories of non-European states, and accounts of the necessity of global trade proliferated: this includes books by Peter Heylyn, William Dampier, Herman Moll (particularly his atlases), Thomas Mun, John Ogilby, Woodes Rogers, and Daniel Defoe. Perhaps the most popular travelogue was Richard Walter's and Benjamin Robins's compilation of Admiral George

Anson's *A Voyage Round the World in the Years MDCCXL, I, II, III, IV*, published in 1748.

19. In *Philosophical Transactions* 8 (8 January 1666), seamen 'bound for far Voyoges' (sic) are given a list of scientific observations to record in their journals, copies of which were to be turned over to various authorities for study. These observations range from marking latitude and longitude, charting tide and river flows, especially those near ports, mapping coasts and islands, making soundings to check depth and soil consistency, keeping records of weather patterns, all of which were designed in keeping with the Society's mandate to 'study *Nature* rather than *Books*' and thus to compose a natural history of the earth.

20. Boyle expands on these 'Articles of Inquiries touching Mines' in *Philosophical Transactions* 19 (19 November 1666). An expanded compilation of subjects for further inquiry was published in a handy duodecimo volume as *General Heads for the Natural History of a Country, Great or Small; Drawn out for the Use of Travellers and Navigators* (London, 1692). To Boyle's questions were added others 'By another Hand' to be asked by those traveling to 'the most noted Countries in the World'. Questions range from the commercial-artisanal ('What is the true way of Making and Colouring *China*-dishes, and how in *China* and *Japan* they make the Black Varnish.' [lacquer] 92) to speculations about natural wonders ('Whether it be true that the Locust of *Brasil*, called, *Caayra*, changeth in the *Spring*-Time into a Plant, and withers away like a Plant.' 107). Curiosity takes many forms, as in the desire to know 'Whether there grows a Wood in *Java* that naturally smells like Human Excrements; and if so what kind of Ground it grows in.' 93).

21. Boyle's law of cultural understanding, that (native) answers must conform to the parameters implied in the (European) question, is at work in most travelogues. For instance, Gordon Sayre identifies two 'colonial narrative genres' which overlapped in practice – the *récit de voyage* and the *mœurs des sauvages* – and argues that this overlap was ideologically crucial, as each explorer-ethnographer needed to 'both convey the knowledge he had learned from the Indians about America and deploy European knowledge to control his representation of the foreign culture' (Sayre 1997: 25).

22. Richard Grove's *Green Imperialism* is a wonderful account of the commercial, political, and scientific actions that resulted in modern systems for cataloging and managing nature. As Europeans expanded their control over the globe, they absorbed (often unattributed) lessons from local systems of knowledge, and colonial political control allowed scientists and administrators early experiments with botanical gardens, social forestry and water management. The essays collected in Schiebinger and Swan are also useful reading.

23. Robert Batchelor suggests that buyers of porcelain in England 'used them to create interior spaces that had not previously existed.' Local porcelain manufacturing in the 1740s and 1750s made it possible to use china to 'assemble an environment' that while familiar, was the product of 'globalization,' and which, in its growing familiarity, both gestured towards, and rendered invisible, processes of international exchange' (Brewer and Trentmann 2006: 111–12, 116).

24. Carole Shammas argues that 'the most striking development in consumer buying during the early modern period was the mass adoption by the English and the colonials of certain non-European groceries' (such as pepper, dried fruits, tobacco, sugar, tea, coffee, chocolate) (Brewer and Porter 1993: 178).

25. These public actions against imports confirmed xenophobic responses to foreigners, including, ironically, the Scots and Irish in England (see Statt 1995).

26. *The Case of the Royal African Company of England* makes an impassioned plea for public funds for the maintenance of English forts in Africa, as they enable the

export of slaves, without whose labor (the author argues) the West Indies and American plantations would collapse, shipping and navigation shrivel, customs and revenues shrink, and the price of land in Britain collapse! (Dabydeen 1985: 27).

27. For Linda Colley (1992), Gallophobia was central to British national self-definition. Critics have since argued for the importance of other axes of nationalist identification: James Shapiro details the role played by 'the Jewish Other' and argues further that a 'complex set of projections, one that include first and foremost the Irish as well as the Jews, the French, the Spanish, and the peoples colonized in these early years of the British Empire, collectively combine to redefine British and English identity' (Shapiro 1996: 207).

28. In this argument, the relation of England to Ireland and even Scotland in the early modern period is one of 'internal colonialism' (Hechter 1978). For English (and Scottish) colonization and settlement in Ireland, especially in comparison for similar efforts in America, see Canny 1988 and 2001. Thomas Scanlan emphasizes the importance of the English editions (published four times between 1583 and 1699) of Bartolomé de Las Casas's *Brevíssima relación de la destrucción de las Indias*, and of Hakluyt's *Discourse of Western Planting*, in forging an explicitly *nationalist* ideology of colonization that linked English policies in Ireland with those that encouraged their North American ventures (Scanlan 1999, especially 19–37).

29. Patricia Coughlan details contemporary English responses to Ireland in Healy and Sawday 1990.

30. This Irish history leads Luke Gibbons to argue that English, and then British, ideas of 'race and empire begin at home.' That is, 'both colonization and the animus against Catholicism were inherently bound up with the subjugation of the Celtic periphery – Gaelic Ireland and the Scottish Highlands – from the early modern period' (Gibbons 2004: 11).

31. For an analysis of debates and opinions (including street protests) in Scotland that led up to the Union, see Bowie 2007.

32. The poetry of Jacobitism is, in Murray G. H. Pittock's reading, a resonant archive of cultural resistance to national amalgamation (Pittock 1994).

33. Julian Hoppit states that 'England may have been at the heart of the British empire, and believed that empire was ruled over by its monarch, Parliament, and laws, but political and military dominance did not bring absolute control, even in the sphere of overseas trade where its grip was strongest' (Hoppit 2000: 247).

34. Patrick Brantlinger comments that it was 'the new financial institutions grounded in public credit and the national debt,' that led to the setting up of the Bank of England and 'laid the foundations of the modern British Empire' (Brantlinger 1996: 38–9).

35. For discussions on these topics, see Anderson 1991, and Habermas 1989.

36. Bruce McLeod writes that 'a great deal of [English] national culture during the seventeenth and eighteenth centuries was imbued with a geographical imagination fed by the experiences and experiments of colonialism.' He argues that the 'cultural imagination was never outside the geopolitical development of empire. Indeed . . . some of the great works of English literature are inconceivable without imperialism' (McLeod 1999: 8).

McLeod's generalization about writers and empire is worth quoting as a rebuttal to those critics who believe that postcolonial scholars do not respect the independence of the creative imagination: 'The authors I examine,' he writes, 'are not simply tools of empire, lauding Britannia's sway overseas.' They often combat its mismanagement abroad and at home, and 'they all exhibit an awareness of writing from within the 'fault-lines' of an imperial or colonial society. Put another way, they write from the interstices of empire, never comfortably at 'home' yet positioned socially so as to be particularly astute about the machinery and metaphorizing nature of empire' (McLeod 1999: 28).

37. Since much writing in this period elaborates normative models of English masculinity and femininity as well as codes of gender and class behavior for Britons as a whole, it is not surprising to find a range of insufficiently-Anglicized (and thus comic, pitiable, or disgusting) provincial Britons offered in salutary contrast to the idealized norm. Such characters play important, if not always developed, roles on the stage and in the novel, and range from Irish drunkards, incomprehensible Scotsmen, or slovenly county squires to full-blown protagonists like Roderick Random, who learns to integrate a provincial Scottish ethics into a metropolitan, Anglicized sensibility. Jewish and Muslim characters make similar if more occasional appearances. Everyday speech naturalized various 'outsiders' into figures of unethical practice: to be a Jew is to be usurious or duplicitous, just as sensuality and tyranny are figured as Muslim, or drunkenness as Irish or Dutch.

It is arguable that religious discourses (those that defined appropriate forms of Christian belief as well as those that defined Christians against non-Christians) were the most significant and contentious cultural determinant of the terms of national belonging, but this is not an area I investigate. The book that does so has not yet been written, but a particular set of anti-Semitic Christian beliefs and cultural practices are considered by Frank Felsenstein (1995). Felsenstein quotes Isaac Watts's song, 'Praise for the Gospel:' 'Lord, I ascribe it to thy Grace,/ And not to Chance, as others do,/ That I was born of *Christian* Race,/ And not a *Heathen*, or a *Jew*' (Watts 1715: 3). Watts's songs are full of such contrasts; in one, 'Praise for Birth and Education in a Christian land,' the child is grateful to be born in Britain, rather than in 'rich *Peru* with all her gold' or in the East or West Indies.

38. And not only writers and intellectuals – as John Robertson says, the 'numbers in which Scots merchants, soldiers and administrators contributed to – and benefited from – imperial activity in the eighteenth century were to ensure that the Empire acquired its "British" identity earlier and with fewer reservations than many of the domestic institutions of the newly unified state' (Robertson 1995: 3).

39. David Zaret argues that public communication ('appeals to public opinion') bame the basis of political formations and reflections during the two decades of the English Revolution (1640–60) and presaged the eighteenth-century expansion of the print public sphere (Zaret 2000: 6–7).

40. As Raymond Williams puts it, a 'new kind of middle-class reading public becomes evident' from the last decade of the seventeenth century. 'New forms of reading, in the newspaper, the periodical and the magazine, account for the major expansion, and behind them comes the novel, in close relation from its beginnings to this particular public' (Williams 1961: 161).

41. See Alok Yadav (2004). Carey McIntosh shows that ideas about linguistic refinement became central to the Scottish elaboration of the four-stages model of human development, in which the highest state of gentility was embodied in the cultural and aesthetic practices of the urban commercial classes of Scotland or England. (In this form of historical anthropology, the lowest contemporary condition was that of tribal peoples – still hunter-gatherers – without literacy). The 'New Rhetoric' propounded by improvers like Adam Smith and Hugo Blair made correct, more literary, articulation crucial to their ideas of class, provincial, and civilisational difference and hierarchy. In doing so, they located their pedagogy within the intellectual and philosophical framework enabled by empire (McIntosh 1998, especially 163–8).

42. The phrase 'the sons of letter'd fame' is Edward Young's, from his poem. *Imperium Pelagi* (1730). He calls upon them to inspire his decision to sing the 'Merchant,' who he sees as the new national hero who will rule the 'empire of the seas' of his title.

43. William St Clair has pointed to the role played by copyright restrictions and publishing cartels in determining the choice of poets in important collections in the eighteenth century (St Clair 2004: 122–39). We might note, however, that St Clair's conclusions are narrowed by his limiting himself to information about editorial and publishing decisions gleaned from analyses of book runs and prices. Canons emerge out of a much larger cultural conversation that includes comments by writers in prefaces or in the body of their work on those who came before, or even more bitingly, on their contemporaries; reviews in newspapers and journals; republication (including of selections or excerpts) in periodicals and anthologies; references (including in fiction) to family or public events that feature readings or performances; scholarly and dilettantish correspondence about the arts; and excerpts chosen for school texts, grammars, writing manuals and rhetorics.

44. Periodicals, magazines, and newspapers played a significant role in circulating poems and literary prose, and embodied the idea of discrimination and selection in the making of literary reputations. British literary periodicals also made clear their ambition to circulate the best writing for the cultural edification of their readers, and indeed for the crafting of readers into citizens.

45. Clement Hawes argues that because we 'find in the British eighteenth century the emergence of a democratizing public sphere that had not been fully coopted by the imperatives of a race-based imperial project,' we can locate in it examples of 'challenging intellectual positions' whose anti-imperialism (however qualified) allows us to define 'an *immanent critique* of the modernity we now inhabit.' He offers Swift and Johnson as exemplary of resistance to the 'global fashioning of imperial Britishness' (Hawes 2005: 205, 207).

46. The general point here parallels McLeod's argument that writers like Defoe and Jonathan Swift in *Gulliver's Travels* 'use colonial space to work through Britain's social and spatial challenges. And there was no better place than the colonies to find or set, and evaluate the objectification and negotation of sovereignty, social orders and boundaries' (McLeod 1999: 175). Swift and Defoe had very different, even opposed, ideas about the legality and necessity of British colonialism (not least because of Swift's Anglo-Irish concerns), but their imaginative worlds were inseparable from its contemporary practices.

47. John Brewer and Susan Staves tell us that historians in general 'are becoming increasingly conscious that early modern history must be understood not only as a history of nationalism in European nation-states and of various forms of enlightenment progress, but also as a history of European imperial projects' (Brewer and Staves 1995: 13). This conception is far from the norm yet, as most historians and literary critics of early modern Europe keep the history of 'imperial projects' at a sanitary distance from the events, texts, and people that they analyze.

48. The phrase is Goldsmith's, from 'The Traveller, Or A Prospect Of Society' (1765: l. 328). Victor Kiernan's *The Lords of Human Kind*, first published in 1969, still remains salutary reading in its wide-ranging account of the cultures of European imperialism.

49. Conventional practices are not only defined in terms of formal arrangements – if the early history of the sonnet was typically that of male poets writing poems of desire and seduction whose object is a woman, then that combination of poet, theme, and object of address also becomes the history of the form, and thus a history that both men and women poets register differently when they write.

50. John Barrell has argued that the literary desire to represent the increasing diversity of society 'necessitated the introduction of literary genres new to England,

among them, the periodical essay, the georgic poem, and the picaresque or comic epic novel offering a "panoramic" view of society.' Writers from Bernard Mandeville to Adam Smith were acutely aware that this diversity, including new forms of occupational specialization, followed from the expansion of overseas trade and colonies (Barrell 1983: 19–21). Efforts to realign relations between England and its provinces, including Ireland and Scotland, brought into general view recalcitrant political and cultural differences, thus confirming the problem of diversity that demanded innovative forms of representation.

51. John Richetti's *Popular Fiction before Richardson* (1992) remains a fine introduction to the proliferation of eighteenth-century English prose fiction from which the 'novel' emerged and against which it defined itself: these are stories of rogues and whores, travelers, pirates and pilgrims, lovers in travail, and white captivity in Barbary and elsewhere. Richetti notes (but does not make much of) the fact that many of these 'fantasy machines' travel in non-English or British locations (including fanciful and imagined spaces), in contrast to the primary fiction of Richardson and Fielding (Richetti 1992).

52. In his analysis of Defoe's criminal and pirate tales (each examples of very popular early eighteenth-century genres), Srinivas Aravamudan remarks, 'The novel as an illegitimate discourse that eventually legitimated itself is fundamentally and repeatedly associated with criminality in this period.' Piracy of one kind or the other both enabled and challenged early mercantilism, colonialism, and the book trade; Aravamudan suggests that Defoe's career as a writer shows how to capitalize on these 'business' practices and to re-narrativize them into normative moral and ideological codes (Aravamudan 1999: 100–2).

53. Ballaster argues that critical attention to the sub-genres of the oriental tale will allow us to see that the novel, far from turning inward to shore up a sovereign and imperial self, actually was willing to 'project outward, to imagine itself serially in the place of the "other", especially the eastern other' and to pleasurably abandon the 'sense of self to an other in a space in which such activity is virtually free of risk' (Ballaster 2005: 14). My sense of the 'evolution' of the eighteenth-century English novel differs in that I see novelistic and critical practices over that period putting in place hierarchical distinctions between the novel proper and secondary fictions such as oriental tales (as Ballaster herself notes in her discussion of Clara Reeve's and James Beattie's comments on the 'Romance,' (2005: 19)). These tales, like the Gothic stories that overlap with them, are the fantasy spaces that allow fevered cultural translations; the proper English novel retracts from such *frisson*.

In another matter, I am less sanguine than Ballaster about any abandonment of a British and Christian self 'to an other' in the writing and reading of fiction, if only because such instances of self-abandonment, or even seeming cultural reciprocity, are inevitably followed by narrative resolutions that reassert cultural authority or normative ethical and rational procedures that are identifiably English in origin or import. In that way, prose forms like the oriental tale develop codes of civility whose ideological import parallels that of the Anglocentric novel.

54. It is important to remember that eighteenth-century British epistemology and systems of knowledge are the product not only of all that was learned about and from places elsewhere, but also of all that was learnt and *repressed* in order to allow particular models of cultural and social distinction to emerge. For a wonderful instantiation of the politics of such cultivated ignorance, see Schiebinger 2004.

Chapter 1

'Theatres of Empire'

Imaginative writing in the cultures which now constitute 'Europe' has, almost from its inception, ranged far afield in order to enliven plots and offer novelties, as encounters with unknown peoples or societies intensify the challenges its protagonists must overcome. The travels of the seafarer Odysseus on his way back from the Trojan wars allow Homer's epic to take on board the strange and faraway, the demonic and the divine, the human and more-than-human, as it tells the most romantic (and to that extent domestic) of stories: the return of Odysseus to Penelope, his wife, and to Ithaca, his home. The classical epic, a form that features clashes between near-divine and divine figures and between rival kingdoms (if not broader cultural formations), is not alone in juxtaposing the domestic with spaces and peoples elsewhere. The clamor of marching armies and of world-creating struggles touches the muted celebrations of pastoral too: Virgil's *Eclogues* open with a tale of dispossession and exile, as Meliboeus is forced from his homeland because he has been dispossessed of his farm to resettle a soldier from the returning army of Octavian (later Augustus) after the battle of Philippi in 41 BCE (Alpers 1979: 66, 68). (It is also germane that Octavian came to absolute power in Rome by winning wars fought in Roman colonies across the Mediterranean.) Similarly, the classical Greek and Roman stage is criss-crossed by people and events whose origins, destinations, and adventures enable the theatre to imagine worlds far removed from Athens or Rome, even as the plays themselves enact ethical, religious, and social lessons to be learned by Athenians or Romans.

Early modern England saw a great expansion of literary ambition, particularly in verse and in the theater, as stories from, and of, cultures across the globe were rewritten to suit English audiences. This ambition crested in the remarkable range of Elizabethan and Jacobean drama, which brought home to London protagonists like Volpone, Othello, or Anthony and Cleopatra, or Tamburlaine, or Faustus, with cameo performances by the likes of Helen of Troy or the Duchess of Malfi, such that a catalogue of the memorable characters in this most English of theatres is virtually a catalogue of foreigners. Further, numerous and important plays explore military heroism and feature events and sites crucial to the making or decline of empires. The geographical and temporal sweep of such theatrical productivity suggests the influence of the transnational nature of medieval modes of storytelling (particularly the romance), and of Arab and European historians and writers of the lives of famous men, but the desire for the 'elsewhere' was also fueled by contemporary travelogues, or translations of travelogues written in Spanish and Portuguese. And not by travelogues alone, as Elizabeth's reign was defined by her victory over the Spanish Armada in 1588, the trans-Atlantic successes of her sea captains like Walter Raleigh and Francis Drake, and the quickening of trade and exploration as English sailors sought to compete with Spanish and Portuguese merchants in the Americas and in Asia. Elizabeth's militant anti-Catholicism and her diplomatic acumen (along with her cult of virginity and her literary sensibility) were celebrated in poem and pageant, till she became iconic of England's resources and self-confidence as an international sea power. In retrospect, we can see the mutually-reinforcing political and cultural achievements of Elizabethan England as an important step in the making of the imperial English identity that this chapter will explore.

Davenant, the Revival of Performance, and the Thematics of Empire

In mid-century, Cromwell's consolidation of English power in Scotland and Ireland and his 'Western Design,' his plan to challenge Spanish power in the Caribbean, both in effect extended Tudor policies. (Charles I's military ambitions had been largely confined to Europe.) Cromwell encouraged expeditions against Spanish possessions in the Caribbean: during the Anglo-Spanish War (1654–60) English ships raided Spanish treasure fleets, fought them for control of trade routes, and attacked Hispaniola (they were repulsed) and Jamaica (which they took). This quickening of military activity in the Caribbean revived Elizabethan representations of English naval skills and audacity, and served to shift attention away from unresolved domestic divisions precipitated by the dethroning and decapitation of Charles I. These stories circulated in print, but the London theatres, crucial spaces for the animation of international themes, were shut down for almost two decades under Puritan rule.

Thus, when William Davenant began reviving theatrical activity in London, it is scarcely surprising that he took his cues from adventures abroad. In several innovatory theatrical performances, which combined operatic elements, the tableaux-format of masques, and the poetic mode of nationalist panegyric, Davenant suggested that such performances were vital to England's understanding of heroism and national destiny.[1] And he does so, as Susan Wiseman argues, in a manner that displaces anxieties about the definition of English nationhood away from the 'civil, ideological and epistemological crisis' precipitated by the Civil War onto 'fantasies of colonial dominance' (Wiseman 1990: 190, 202). In the two plays I examine here, the first, *The History of Sir Francis Drake* (1658–9), allows for a decade and more of bitter divides between battling Monarchists and Republicans to be set aside in visions of Protestant English triumphs overseas. The second, *The Siege of Rhodes*, Part 1 (1656) and 2 (1657–9), returns to the scene of Ottoman triumph over a European and Christian outpost, and in doing so exemplifies the seventeenth-century vogue for plays about the rise and decline of empires, a vogue that developed as England built the resources to compete for trading routes and territories overseas. The themes and forms of Davenant's plays derive from his preoccupation with empire. Even more to the point here, the legitimacy offered by nationalistic explorations of the opportunities (and costs) of empire were crucial to the institutional and ideological grounds upon which theatre was revived in the last years of the Cromwellian interregnum.

In *Sir Francis Drake*, as Davenant returns to an Elizabethan hero and links that moment of national glory with the present, he suggests a continuity of English sea power. In doing so he re-introduces into literary circulation ideas that were to prove crucial to the development of an English apologetics for imperialism. In Davenant's entertainment, Drake is welcomed in Peru by the Symarons, described as 'a Moorish people' who have escaped enslavement by their brutal Spanish masters. In deference to Drake's renown, they offer their allegiance to the English queen. This ideologically crucial alliance is repeated when Drake, guided by the Symarons, encounters Peruvian villagers, who are also reverential enough about his reputation to welcome, rather than to resist, his forces (he does have to put on a semblance of an assault though, so as not to reveal their sympathy for the English to the Spanish). Davenant's representation of the progress of the English raiders makes clear the crucial difference between Spanish and English forms of colonial authority – the former is heartless and rapacious, the latter principled, honor-bound, and liberating. English honor is demonstrated not only in implied contrast to Spanish rule, but also in lessons Drake must teach Symaron soldiers who take a woman (a bride at that) prisoner on her wedding day. Drake declaims that 'the honour of my nation turns/ To shame, when an afflicted beauty mourns' (V, 109–10), and then chooses not to punish the offending soldiers as long as they learn that English values are centered around the protection of women in need. (This idea that English colonial control over native societies is legitimate because they act on behalf of oppressed native women becomes an ideological commonplace in the centuries ahead.)

Sir Francis Drake begins with the English reveling in their desire to take Spanish bullion, which Drake calls 'man's bright mistress, gold' (I. 86). However, late in the drama, when Drake rallies his men before their raid on the Spanish mule train, he sings a different, less materialistic, song:

> All I would speak, should tell you, I despise
> That treasure which I now would make your prize:
> Unworthy 'tis to be your chiefest aim.
> For this attempt is not for gold, but fame;
> Which is not got when we the reco [the mule train] get,
> But by subduing those who rescue it. (VI, 25–30)

Supplanting his desire for bullion is his thirst for 'fame,' which will be assuaged by defeating would-be Spanish rescuers who come to the aid of their mule train. This turn from the motivation provided by loot does rescue Drake from the taint of freebooting, but the invocation of the ethically and historically positive term 'fame' is a reminder of Davenant's determination to conclude his play in praise of the power of performance to commemorate and perpetuate national heroism. Thus, Drake's vision of the English future is based on their deeds being reported and circulated:

> Our dangerous course through storms and raging floods,
> And painful march through unfrequented woods,
> Will make those wings by which our fame shall rise.
> Your glory, valiant English, must be known,
> When men shall read how you did dare
> To sail so long and march so far,
> To tempt a strength much greater than your own. (VI, 104–10)

He imagines their welcome home, with bells ringing and streamers fluttering, 'Whilst cheerfully they sing/ Our story, which shall their example be/ And make succession cry, to sea, to sea' (VI, 118–20). At this moment there is no distinguishing the prophecies of Drake and Davenant, national hero and nationalist playwright, twin celebrants of England's prowess on sea and in song.

Theatrical performances are also good reminders that the making of a nationalist culture – particularly one that defines the nation in its encounters with peoples overseas – requires both scripts and institutions. That is, literary creativity of all kinds is enhanced by the creation of infra-structure devoted to it, whether this be a theatre or a press devoted to poetry or a critical journal that calls attention to new writing, or indeed sinecures that allow authors to be productive. Accordingly, Davenant's performances at Rutland House called attention to the materiality and quality of his staging, that is, to the spectacle made possible by the com-bination of moving flats and scenery, the sense of depth and movement enabled by a proscenium stage, and the painted riches on display. In his address 'To the Reader' attached to the 1656 edition of *The Siege of Rhodes,* Davenant laments the fact that his theatre is not larger, because it has 'hinder'd the splendor of our Scene.' 'It has been often wisht that our Scenes,' he writes, 'had not been confin'd to eleven foot in height, and about fifteen in depth, including the places of passage reserv'd for the Musick. This is so narrow an allowance for the Fleet of *Solyman* the Magnificent, his Army, the Island of *Rhodes*, and the varieties attending the Siege of the City.'[2] Davenant's complaint is not about verisimilitude but about a theatrical space and a richness of setting adequate to the grand scope of the events and personages he stages, and he solicits his audience for contributions to build a larger theatre. Davenant's argument for a more ambitious theatre reminds us that in the 1630s, he and set-designers like Inigo Jones had based their designs on Italian pageants, and that part of his project as an impresario, especially after the Restoration, was the recreation of an English theatre which, in its physical and infra-structural capacity, would be the equal of theaters in France or opera houses in Italy.[3] In his Rutland House theatre, Davenant's fusion of the material display fundamental to courtly masques and pageants with the plot-structures and characterization that defined the public theatres shut down during the Interregnum, ushered in the rich stage properties and complex genres of Restoration drama.

The Siege of Rhodes is important too as an instance of the remarkable number of seventeenth-century plays that feature protagonists and stage events crucial to the making or decline of historical empires ranging from the Roman to the Inca to the Ottoman. As Bridget Orr has shown, these plays engage energetically with the allure and corruptions of impe-rial power, and explore the proper ethical, political, and behavioral foundations of empire, such that both studies of success and of failure provide lessons for contemporary Englishmen and women (Orr 2001).[4] *The Siege of Rhodes* furthers the English fascination with the Ottoman Turks, their empire, political system, and (crucially) gender and sexual relations. The Ottoman empire challenged European nations, *in* Europe, for over two centuries till it lost the Battle of Vienna in 1683, and its imperial power was taken seriously throughout the eighteenth century. Anglo-Turkish relations in the early modern period were a shifting mix of political and trading alliances, economic competition, and cultural and religious polarization. Literary responses to this history ranged from envy to repulsion, particularly as regards the power of the Sultan (and Islamic rulers more generally), which was described as absolute (even when there was little or no functional difference between the practices of the English monarch and those of the Sultan). The harems of the Turkish nobility, to which no outsiders had access, added a titillating dimension to patriarchal power, and English drama repeatedly returned to Ottoman courts and harems as sites of political and sexual intrigue. In doing so, dramatic explorations of contrasting norms of patriarchal sovereignty also allowed for a voyeuristic unveiling of Turkish women. Plots often counterpose the demands of love and honor at a time of imperial crisis, all the while calling attention to Ottoman and English (or European Christian) differences in gender relations and political principles.

In the opening scene in *The Siege of Rhodes*, military symbols are symmetrically opposed: Western arms on 'the Right hand' and arms 'esteem'd in the Eastern countries' alongside 'an Antique Shield [with] the Crescent of the Ottomans' on the other. This opposition belies the drama of cultural similarity and difference that follows. Quite unusually, the Turkish Emperor Solyman, whose forces lay siege to, and ultimately defeat, the Christian defenders of Rhodes, is portrayed as honorable and principled, both in love and war. In this he is no different from Alphonso, a Sicilian visitor who stays on to defend Rhodes, and Ianthe his wife. All three are represented in the manner of protagonists in a courtly romance, who experience the joys and torments of romantic desire while attempting to remain steadfast to ethical norms. Yet this is not how Alphonso thinks of Solyman at the beginning of the play, when he decides to join battle against him and 'His cursed prophet and his sensual law' (I. i. 86). (The word 'sensual' here condenses two meanings, one which suggests that Islam – Muhammad's 'law' – is irreligious, and the other that Turks are defined by their sensuality, as evidenced by the multiple wives and harems of their nobility.) The line itself is repeated in chorus, and, as a Christian rallying cry, sets the stage for battle. Solyman's view of the Rhodians is no less damning. He thinks of Christians as 'oft misled by mists of Wine,/ Or blinder love,' as prey to adultery and 'ev'ry loud expensive Vice,' and as people who expend in strange ways the wealth they make 'by avarice.' However, their defence of the city forces him to a begrudging admiration of their courage (1, II, ii, 37–46).

Solyman's prejudices change too when he first encounters Ianthe, who has been taken prisoner by the Turks as she sails to Rhodes to join her husband. Ianthe refuses to unveil for her captors, saying that only her 'Lords dear hand this Vail should draw' (1. II, ii, 92). Solyman is first impressed that Ianthe would adventure to Rhodes to 'save her ruin'd Lord' (1, II, ii, 78), and even more that her refusal to unveil contravenes the behavior of other Christian wives who 'wear their faces free;/ Which they to more than Husband show' (1, II, ii, 88–9). He offers safe passage to her and Alphonso from Rhodes to Sicily, and she reciprocates by prais- ing his nobility and virtue. Solyman is so taken with Ianthe that he delays an all-out attack on Rhodes till a Turkish messenger is able to ensure that she and her husband leave. Meanwhile within Rhodes, assembled notables celebrate Ianthe's bravery in venturing there and her generous gift of jewels towards the costs of war, which they contrast with the parsimony of European monarchs, who have offered no help. Alphonso, however, is less celebratory, and expresses his misgivings about her journey to Rhodes, whose interrupted progress made him fearful and whose bravery outshines his own, but most of all about her encounter with Solyman. Her explanations of Solyman's generosity ('He seem'd in civil *France*,' (1, III, ii, 102)) leads Alphonso to call him a 'Christian Turk' (1, III, ii, 112), but once he learns that his wife has spent two nights at Solyman's court, Alphonso is tormented by jealousy, especially because he – as a man and a warrior – cannot understand why Solyman would give up what 'was his own by right of War' (1, III, ii, 125).

Davenant refuses neat polarities as he complicates his drama of Christian and Muslim, Sicilian and Turk, civil 'lover' and jealous husband, grateful captive and suspect wife. There are multiple inver- sions at work: Ianthe's veil is read as a symbol of *Christian* modesty, as is Solyman's civility. Alphonso reveals a jaundiced Christian mas- culinity as he doubts his wife and the 'wondrous Turkish chastity' (1, III, ii, 127) that allowed her to go free. When Ianthe learns of Alphonso's suspicions, she notes the irony: 'Could *Solyman* both Life and Honour give?/ And can *Alphonso* me of both deprive?' (1, IV, ii, 74–5). Solyman's magnanimity is confirmed when he hears that Ianthe and Alphonso have refused his offer of safe passage – he believes their 'vertue' has overcome his 'strength' (1, IV, i, 29–30) and gives instructions that they are not to be harmed in the assault on the city. At this stage of the play, Solyman's generosity and Ianthe's virtue are in stark contrast with Alphonso's suspicions – a plot contrivance which might be acceptable within the conventions of courtly romance, where only the nobility of the protagonists is at stake. However, this is a play that stages the Turkish victory over the Christian defenders of Rhodes in 1522, and the ethical and religious equivalences suggested here do not last long. The actions and speech of Roxolana, Solyman's wife, ensure that crucial forms of gender and political difference continue to demarcate Christian from Muslim, and keep alive key features of the cultural history of Anglo-Ottoman rivalry.

When Roxolana hears of Solyman's encounter with Ianthe, she fears he has lost his heart, and jealous herself, ventures to Rhodes to regain his favor. Her response parallels Alphonso's jealousy, and when Solyman meets her in Rhodes, he upbraids her for her fears. His response also makes clear her political power, or at least her power to make trouble. 'My War with *Rhodes* will never have success,' he says to her, 'Till I at home, *Roxana*, make my peace.' He bids her 'chide her Whisp'rers and your Spies,' and to be circumspect: 'Be satisfy'd with liberty to think/ And, when you should not see me, learn to wink' (1, V, iv, 19–24). European commentators on Turkey from Knolles onwards had emphasized the intrigues that allowed the Sultan's concubines to occasionally develop great power at the court, and the historical Roxolana was often identified as an instance of the grasping and ultimately destructive power of women in the Ottoman harems. In Part 2 of *The Siege of Rhodes*, Davenant stages an elaborate scene in which Roxolana browbeats one of Suleyman's Bassas, Rustan, who she believes has countermanded some of her orders regarding the sharing of spoils and the conduct of foreign policy. The scene ends with a long speech in which she describes the Turkish Bassas as 'Court-monsters' who 'sawcily believe, we Monarch's Wives/ Were but made to be Dress't/ For a Continu'd Feast,' and who think that, being mere women, they will not intervene in court matters (2, II, iii, 31–48). 'But they shall find,' she says

> I'm no *European* Queen,
> Who in a Throne does sit but to be seen;
> And lives in Peace with such State-Thieves as these
> Who Robb us of our business for our ease. (2, II, iii, 49–52)

Roxolana is true to her word, as we learn when a disturbed Solyman confides to his Bassas that she has, 'by ambitious strife/ To get unjust Succession for her Son,' campaigned to discredit 'the Heroique story of my Life' (2, II, i, 24–8). He speaks here as a wronged Sultan, but also portrays himself as an emasculated and suffering husband: far from finding in Roxolana the 'soft Bosom, where relea's'd from care/ I should securely rest from toils of Warr,' he seeks sleep in vain with 'a tempestuous Wife.' He mourns the irony that he, 'whose Banners brave/ The world, should thus to Beauty be a Slave' (2, III, i, 35–43). His complaints make explicit the always implicit contrast between the self-serving Roxolana and the dutiful Ianthe, who constantly acts on behalf of her husband or her people, particularly when Solyman welcomes Ianthe once again to his court, where she has been sent as an emissary to plead for the safety of the people of Rhodes. Solyman holds out hope of a reprieve, but demands that Ianthe spend the night in his camp, and sends her to Roxolana's tent. Roxolana is vexed enough to write to Alphonso alerting him to Solyman's pursuit of Ianthe, and also plots to murder Ianthe while she sleeps, though she is talked out of that by the eunuch Haly. In subsequent conversation about their husbands, Ianthe charms and befriends Roxolana, who contrasts Ianthe's commitment to, and happiness with, Alphonso with her own more tempestuous relation with Solyman.

In Act IV, scene iii, Solyman and Roxolana go over the grounds of their disaffection in great detail, and the scene allows each of them equal time to debate their grievances, both as lovers and as monarchs with opposed ideas about Solyman's successor. They part unreconciled, but not before Roxolana rails against the Turkish imperial system that kills off all rivals (and thus probably her child, who is a younger son) when the new Sultan comes to the throne. In the meantime, once Alphonso receives Roxolana's letter, he and the other Christian allies decide to storm Solyman's camp and rescue Ianthe, an attempt that fails and results in Alphonso's capture. Roxolana asks Solyman for the prisoner, but before she leads Alphonso to Ianthe, she (with what seems like gratuitous cruelty) torments Ianthe by telling her that Alphonso must die and that all the promises of friendship she had made to Ianthe were counterfeit. Ianthe offers to sacrifice herself for her husband, and Roxolana is once again impressed ('Are Christian Wives, so true, and wondrous kind?' (2, V, vi, 87)), and reveals her true plans, which are to give Alphonso to Ianthe. In this generous act Roxolana also proves herself to Solyman, who believes that her action demonstrates that she, being assured of his heart, can endure rivals (2, V, vi, 180–1). Solyman frees Alphonso and Ianthe, and tells her that as she has 'Conquer'd' him, she can set the conditions for the surrender of Rhodes (2, V, vi, 209–11). The play ends then, though not so much with the triumph of the Turks as with (in Solyman's closing words) the triumph of 'Love' over 'Jealousie,' and of 'Honour' over all else (2, V, vi, 214–23).

In the conclusion, Roxolana joins the gallery of courtly protagonists, and the play finds in the elevated pieties of romance a vocabulary of reconciliation that draws attention away from the historical moment and the victory of the Muslim Ottomans over Christian Rhodes. Critics have understood this conclusion, as well as the representation of Solyman's magnanimity and greatness, as evidence of Davenant's need to produce idealized representations of heroism and noble actions that would elevate his entertainment above the partisan politics that continued to polarize English monarchists and republicans in the last years of the Interregnum and even after the Restoration. Thus, it is argued, the plot-lines and characterization of gender and national difference, and of the costs of empire, intersect with, but are finally contained within, the conventions of heroic romance that suggest the shared nobility of people in high places.[5] However, Roxolana's assertiveness and intrigue leave an indelible imprint. The Christian heroine Ianthe, even at her most powerful, never threatens patriarchal authority, and is a consistent reminder to Davenant's audiences of feminine propriety. On the other hand, even when Roxolana is reconciled with Solyman, she stands for worryingly proud, demanding, and possibly emasculating, female power, and thus demarcates Turkish difference (she is no 'European Queen.'). For postcolonial critics, the contrast between Roxolana and Ianthe cannot be understood simply as a contrast between two models of feminine behavior (the difference between, say, Lady Macbeth and Lady Macduff in Shakespeare's *Macbeth*), but must be explained by the long history of antagonism and exchange between Christian Europe and Islamic Turkey, which yields to Davenant both the cross-cultural nobility of Solyman and Ianthe and the intractable difference of Roxolana.

The Siege of Rhodes also allows us to emphasize the capacity of theatrical texts, and literary texts more generally, to make available historical and social dynamics that (in retrospect at least) seem to be at odds with each other. The drama of empire, that is, does not only stage imperial triumphs, but also – importantly – includes critiques of such triumphalism. Theatre at its most compelling offers complex explorations of the burdens of empire even as its glories are enacted. As Solyman builds his empire though conquest, we encounter depictions of empire as bloody and cruel, and of the Emperor as trapped in a cycle of violence at home and abroad. When Roxolana attacks the Turkish policy that kills all rivals to the throne when a new Sultan takes over, Solyman defends the domestic system as a cruelty necessary to empire:

Those are the Secret Nerves of Empires force.
Empire grows often high
By rules of cruelty,
But seldome prospers when it feels remorse. (2, IV, iii, 341–4)

At another moment, Solyman ponders the continual costs of empire and the mentalities it breeds:

Of Spacious Empire, what can I enjoy?
Gaining at last but what I first Destroy.
Tis fatal (*Rhodes*) to thee,
And troublesome to me
That I was born to govern swarms
Of Vassals boldly bred to arms:
For whose accurs'd diversion, I must still
Provide new Towns to Sack, new Foes to Kill.
Excuse that Pow'r, which by my Slaves is aw'd:
For I shall find my peace
Destroy'd at home, unless
I seek for them destructive Warr abroad. (2, II, ii, 53–64)

Solyman's sentiments here can of course be read as applicable only to the Ottomans in their pursuit of empire, thus emphasizing a bloody history that differentiates them from Europeans.[6] However, these moments in *The Siege of Rhodes* also suggest an English concern with the domestic costs of empire. Indeed, the range of plays on the Restoration stage that explore similar sentiments suggests that such commentary on the history, psychology, and sociology of empires in the past answers an urgent contemporary English need to thrill to stories of empire's riches and pitfalls, excitement and perils.

The 'Englishness'of Davenant's drama is also indicated by the compliments he has other nationalities direct at the English contingent at Rhodes. The English fight 'merrily and fast' (1, II, i, 40), Alphonso says, and Pirrhus worries, as a Turkish attack is repulsed, that 'Those desp'rate *English* n'er will fly!/ Their firmness still does hinder others flight.' (All this is in contrast with the historical record, which suggests that the English redoubt at Rhodes was the first to fall.) Pirrhus's explanation for their bravery invokes a trope of chivalric romance – the English fight as if watched and praised by their 'Mistresses,' he thinks (1, IV, i, 37–40). This chivalric figure resurfaces when Alphonso hears that Ianthe is, mid-battle, guarded by the English: he is then certain of her safety, 'For what will not the English do/When Beauty is distress'd and Vertue too?' (1, V, i, 107–8). However, this sort of English boosterism is far from being the most prominent or interesting feature of the play – Davenant explores the larger logic of empire here, and only incidentally (if at all) asserts an English right to dominance. To note this is to make the larger critical point that postcolonial emphases on the cultures of empire are not derived from a narrow attention to only those texts in which English writers boost English claims to power overseas (at the expense of both European rivals and Native Americans or Indians or south-east Asians or Africans). Postcolonial critics understand the making of colonial discourse – that is, the forging of the languages and icons of imperial superiority – to be a complex, internally differentiated and confused process, in which the English fascination with stories of empire extends to empires outside of Europe, including the Ottomans and the Mughals against whom battles had been, and would be, fought. At this point in the seventeenth century, writers are fluid in their explorations of empires and imperial ways, and notions of Englishness as demanded by the exigencies of empire emerge as much by indirection as they do in more direct statements of character, ability and motivation. (As a point of comparison we might note that the more univocal and polarized understanding of the terms of English dominance emerge in the nineteenth century.)

Fluidity must not be confused with lack of purpose, though, and Davenant's drama does resonate with the many late seventeenth-century poems, plays, and prose tracts that rejoice in England's rise to maritime power, and which do so by also (somewhat self-servingly) celebrating the power of art to commemorate heroism or national achievement. But, as I have suggested, this chapter (or this book) is not simply about the images or ideas of English commercial and colonial power that are to be found in a variety of seventeenth- or eighteenth-century media. Celebrations of 'Gloriana' or of James I, or even of Charles I, as puissant monarchs of an ever-more powerful England are pervasive, whether they take the form of poems, portraits, or statuary. Indeed the literary and the performative occasionally fused into moments of great public import. As Paula Backscheider has shown in her study of the coronation rituals of Charles II, England's putative imperial might provided a recurrent rhetorical formula for the (re)legitimation of the monarchy. She quotes one of John Tatham's entertainments for the occasion, in which the Thames welcomes Charles as a 'Mighty *Monarch*! Whose Imperial Hand/ Quiets the Ocean, and secures the Land.' The Thames flows on:

> You are our *Neptune*, every Port, and Bay
> Your Chambers: the whole Sea is Your High-way.
> Though sev'ral Nations boast their Strength on Land,
> Yet You alone the Wat'ry World Command.' (Backscheider 1993: 16)

Well before England became the dominant European power overseas, literary propagandists fashioned the key tropes of seaborne dominance that would come to define English colonial and commercial power in the decades ahead.

Indeed, Robert Markley has argued that precisely because Englishmen were uncertain about their power abroad, and because they were often in competition with other better financed or organized European traders and colonists, English writers produced compensatory, even wish-fulfilling, testimonials to English civility, rectitude, and valor. Thus, English losses were also grist for this ideological mill, and were rewritten into instances of their ethical superiority as compared to their rivals or of the inherent nobility of their sailors and merchants when facing overwhelming odds. A single brief instance of such creativity must suffice here: John Dryden's *Amboyna or The Cruelties of the Dutch to the English Merchants: A Tragedy* (1672), which features his countrymen being captured and tortured by their Dutch commercial rivals. The immediate provocation for this play was the Third Anglo-Dutch War (1672–4), and Dryden returned, for propagandistic purposes, to a significant reverse suffered in 1623 by factors of the East India Company as they attempted to establish themselves on the Spice Island of Amboyna (now Indonesia).[7] Dryden simplifies the commercial and legal issues that precipitated the torture and execution of the Englishmen in order to produce, as Markley puts it, a 'mercantile morality play' that recasts 'England's humiliation on Amboyna as the martyrdom of national virtue, liberty, and nobility' (Markley 2006: 143–5, and 143–76 *passim*).

Dryden's tragedy emphasizes Dutch greed and violence, which destroys both virtuous Englishmen and Ysabinda, the Amboinese princess who has been wooed and won by the heroic Towerson. Dryden makes clear just what is at stake when Ysabinda is raped on the day of their wedding by Harman Junior, the son of the Dutch Governor, whose life Towerson once saved. (The play finds no room for Amboinese men, nor does it represent any of the local elites with whom Europeans traded, preferring instead to symbolize all that is attractive – and for the taking – about the island and its riches in the figure of Ysabinda.)[8] While Dutch perfidy contrasts with English steadfastness, events and conversations in *Amboyna* suggest that the Englishmen do not remain entirely untainted by the exploitative trade practices that characterize the Dutch. Towerson does claim that responsible ('moderate') trade ought to be pacific:

> what mean these endless jars of Trading Nations? 'tis true, the World was never large enough for Avarice or Ambition; but those who can be please'd

with moderate gain, may have the ends of Nature, not to want: nay, even its Luxuries may be supply'd from her o'erflowing bounties in these parts; from whence she yearly sends Spices, and Gums, the food of Heaven in Sacrifice: And besides these, her Gems of richest value, for Ornament, more than necessity. (I, i, 220–7)

However, the Englishman Beamont's attitudes to colonial possessions are not markedly different from those of the Fiscal (a Dutchman). We know this from the fact that the other woman character in this play, Julia, who is married to a Spaniard, Perez, views Beamont and the Fiscal, both of whom pursue her, as participants in a larger geopolitical competition: 'If my English lover Beamont, my Dutch Love the Fiscall, and my Spanish Husband, were Painted in a piece with me amongst 'em, they wou'd make a Pretty Emblem of the two Nations, that Cuckold his Catholick Majesty in his Indies' (2, i, 226–30).

Amboyna's staging of violence, of sacrifices made and battles fought, in the theatres of overseas trade reminds us that even propagandistic celebrations of the *rightness* of English activities overseas are implicated in the larger contemporary drama of European conquest and territorial control. In a study of late seventeenth- and eighteenth-century English poetry on public themes, I have argued that such writing, even at its most bellicose, always contains within itself some recognition of the human and cultural costs of European expansion, even if each text finds ways in which to sideline or repress such recognition (Kaul 2000; on Dryden see 75–84). Dryden's *Amboyna* is one such text, its characters, themes, and plot details registering not just Dutch greed and English civility, but the historical centrality of intrigue, treachery, and violence in mercantile and territorial ventures in places like the Spice Islands. After she is raped, Ysabinda asks Towerson to flee Amboyna, and her anguish is more than personal: '[F]or my sake, fly this detested Isle, where horrid Ills so black and fatal dwell, as Indians cou'd not guess, till Europe taught (IV, v, 15–17). At this moment, the play (like several other texts that this book will examine) articulates a consciousness of native despair at the ravages wrought by the European presence. It is another matter that, in the case of *Amboyna*, the ideological needs of an English nation readying for war with the Dutch supersede this insight; and Dryden joins the large number of his contemporary writers who found rhetorically convincing justifications for the growth of overseas English power.

The dynamism imparted by this growth was palpable at home: England's expanding military capabilities, on land and perhaps even more importantly, at sea, required an enormous apparatus that ranged from financiers to victuallers and suppliers to shipbuilders to the men who fought in the armies and manned the ships. Late seventeenth-century England saw unprecedented growth in the shipping trades and in warfare, and seamen and demobilized soldiers became a visible feature of urban and rural life. Their numbers were large enough, and the military codes and sea-fellowship that bound them individuated enough, for them to emerge as an identifiable social bloc, whose adventures overseas, style, and behavior at home, prompted playwrights into writing memorable characters along the lines of Manley, the hero of William Wycherley's *The Plain Dealer* (1676), or Colonel Fainwell in Susanna Centlivre's *A Bold Stroke for a Wife* (1718). Several comedies like Aphra Behn's *The Rover* (1677) were set outside England, but for the most part they were located at home.[9] If heroic plays often called attention to people and locales outside England, comedies satirized and celebrated local ways, and in doing so put on display the myriad characters whose interactions helped define English sociality. But the local and the domestic were always juxtaposed with – incidentally or in well worked-out detail – norms of behavior and social arrangements elsewhere. French fops minced on the stage, Irishmen staggered about, laughed at for their speech as for their drunkenness, bargain-hunting Dutch businessmen sought profits, and adventuring Englishmen brought home stories of faraway lands that captivated heroines as they did foolish antiquaries.[10]

Wycherley's *Plain Dealer* makes much of the fact that Manley's mode of plain dealing (excessive and impolitic as it is) is fashioned from his experiences as a veteran of the recent Anglo-Dutch war and a would-be colonist. That is, the play derives a behavioral and ethical characteristic (his manliness) that would, over the next century and more, come to be celebrated as one of the defining features of Englishness, from spaces and practices removed from English lives at home. Manley's self-definition is worth quoting because its terms are representative of the contradictions of colonial discourse in this period: rather than be part of social hypocrisies in England, he says he chooses 'to go where honest, downright barbarity is professed; where men devour one another like generous, hungry lions and tigers, not like crocodiles; where they think the devil white, of our complexion, and I am already so far an Indian' (I, i, 612–16). He is Indian enough to know that dissembling is a feature of the white devils who devour them like crocodiles, but colonialist enough to say to Fidelia, his future wife, to whom he has given a gift of jewels, that the gift 'was too small for you before, for you deserve the Indian world, and I would now go thither out of covetousness for your sake only' (V, iii, 145–6). As it turns out, Fidelia has an inheritance that allows them to stay home, but these lines make clear that the Manley (and covetous) way to endow his wife is to go prospecting in Indian lands. Colonial plain dealing, that is, allows Manley to recognize and bemoan the ethical and political divides between Indians and white devils even as he prepares, as a white man himself, to profit from them.

Aphra Behn, Colonial Self-making, and the Uncertain Consolations of Romance

The novelty of colonial lives, and their uncertain connections with England, provides the basis for Aphra Behn's *The Widdow Ranter, or, The History of Bacon in Virginia. A Tragi-comedy* (probably written in 1688, and first performed the next year). The play emphasizes the opportunities of self-making available to English colonists in Jamestown and the colony of Virginia more generally. Since people and information travel slowly across the Atlantic, it is easy for newcomers, or indeed long-time residents, to pretend to be other than they are. The newcomers are typified by Friendly, who comes to Virginia because he inherits a plantation, and his friend Hazard, who comes 'with a small Cargo to seek my fortune' (I, i, 45). They meet and quickly resolve on an imposture: Hazard is to pretend to be a kinsman of a rich and elderly merchant, Surelove, so that he can gain entry to Surelove's home and woo his wife while the merchant lies ill – and unlikely to regain his health – in England. Versions of such self-making characterize many of the Englishmen in the colony, including some members of the Ruling Council (Friendly says that some of them 'have been perhaps transported Criminals, who having Acquired great Estates are now become your Honour, and Right Worshipfull, and Possess all Places of Authority' (I, i, 107–10)). The point is not that the colony allows even criminals to make their fortunes and to repress their past, but that it encourages all manner of reinvention: the Parson Dunce was in fact a blacksmith in England, and Flirt, the inn-keeper, the daughter of a tailor, claims to be the daughter of a 'Barronet' ruined by the ascendancy of Cromwell.

Behn's play derives a great deal of its comic energies from the fluidity of identities and class boundaries in the colony. Characters remake themselves, reveal their true selves, cover up those revelations, and are opportunistic in their allegiances and friendships – these comic flip-flops all suggest the range of possibilities that are available to Englishmen in the colonies but are denied to them at home. But the play also takes seriously the political disorder that follows from the lack of established and enforceable forms of political authority, and in doing so, Behn addresses historical crises experienced both in Virginia and in England in the late seventeenth century. In 1676, Nathaniel Bacon, a substantial landowner in Virginia, became the leader of a group of colonists who wished to take forceful action against Native American tribes, rather than accept the more placatory policies of the governor, Sir William Berkeley. Bacon did seize Jamestown and depose Berkeley briefly, but Bacon died of fever shortly after and the rebellion did not last. In his proclamation justifying his rebellion, Bacon indicted Berkeley's councilors as ill-born and ill-bred men who acted in their own, rather than the Crown's interests, and he styled himself a royalist defending the King's colony.[11] For Behn, a life-long monarchist herself, Bacon's rebellion could not but evoke the specter of Cromwell, even though the Virginian claimed as motivation the King's interests.

Behn wrote *The Widdow Ranter* in the months in which the Stuart monarchy came to an end in England with the departure of James II. This political crisis is perhaps figured in the play as the absence of the governor of Virginia, and the play makes clear that much of the disorder, including Bacon's rebellion, is precipitated by the lack of legitimate authority. Behn of course rewrites history in suggesting that Governor Berkeley was absent (rather than deposed by Bacon), but in leaving out a direct confrontation between the two, the play does render Bacon's rebellion less politically suspect. Bacon is also legitimized by insisting on his aristocratic bearing and motivations: Friendly describes him as 'a Man indeed above the Common Rank, by Nature Generous; Brave, Resolv'd, and Daring; who studying the Lives of the Romans and Great Men, that have raised themselves to the most Elevated fortunes, fancies it easy for Ambitious men, to aim at any Pitch of Glory' (I, i, 113–17). Equally importantly, Friendly says that Bacon understands himself as a character in an aristocratic romance, who, 'fancying no *Hero* ought to be without his Princess,' falls in love with Semernia, the Indian Queen (I, i, 122–3). Semernia is married to Cavarnio, the Indian King, their names another indication of the romance conventions within which Behn re-imagines the bloody confrontation between colonists and Native Americans. As it turns out, when she was younger, Semernia was attracted to Bacon at her father's court, and now must balance between her renewed desire and her duty to her husband.

As in Davenant's *Siege of Rhodes*, the triangulated inter-racial romance helps soften intractable political oppositions as well as the dividing line that is racial difference in the colonies. Bacon first confesses his feelings to Semernia when she comes to plead with him for peace between her people and the colonists. Her trembling and distracted response sums up the power of romance conventions to dissolve colonial politics into the tremors of desire: 'I'le talk no more, our words exchange our Souls, and every look fades all my blooming honour, like Sun beams, on unguarded Roses. – take all our Kingdoms – make our People Slaves, and let me fall beneath your Conquering Sword. But never let me hear you talk again or gaze upon your Eyes – ' (II, ii, 145–9). At this moment Semernia becomes one in a long line of native women on the English stage whose love for colonizing white men becomes both alibi and apologia for colonial conquest. Nor does Behn exempt Cavarnio from the mystifications of romance: before he fights, and is killed, by Bacon, he says of his sword ''tis for *Semernia* that it draws, a prize more valu'd than my Kingdom' (IV, ii, 30–3). In so speaking, Cavarnio shifts into an idiom very different from the conversation with Bacon in which he regrets their 'fatal difference' that follows from a particular history: 'we were Monarchs once of all this spacious World; Till you an unknown People landing here, Distress'd and ruin'd by destructive storms, Abusing all our Charitable Hospitality, Usurp'd our Right, and made your friends your slaves' (II, i, 9–14).

In this fashion, *The Widdow Ranter* registers the dispossession and enslavement of Native Americans only to disavow this history by rewriting bloody colonial and racial antagonisms into the courtly adversarial relations of romantic rivalry. But not quite, for Bacon does kill Cavarnio (in battle) and also Semernia (unknowingly, but also in battle) before he poisons himself. As Orr suggests, these deaths may mark Behn's 'awareness that just as the Stuarts were passing into history, so too certain modes of heroic representation, in which the colonizer and colonized figured in equally "Romantick" terms, as similar and assimilable human subjects were becoming less and less viable, as vehicles for figuring the interaction of Europeans and Indians' (Orr 2001: 238). In any case Bacon, who earned his notoriety by leading raids against the Paumunkey Indians among others, is particularly difficult to refigure as a sympathetic character who loves not only Semernia, but, in ordinary circumstances, all her tribe. That Behn attempts this translation is a testimonial to heightened ideological need – she was aware that the circumstances of colonial life in Virginia (and elsewhere, as she demonstrates powerfully in *Oroonoko*) made impossible non-coercive relations between white Europeans and Native Americans, and that this was the case with interracial sexual relations too. Behn's Bacon might woo Semernia on the London stage, but Bacon's pursuit of Semernia's compatriots in Virginia was altogether more destructive.

Heroic romance – at its ideological limits – is here the theatrical form in which inter-racial desire is expressed and cauterized. However, the colonial location of this play also allows it to feature the relatively unfettered performance of female desire, and to do so in a comic mode that became possible only with the advent of actresses on the Restoration stage. This is the breeches part, in which the Widow Ranter dresses as a man to pursue one of Bacon's generals, Dareing. Ranter is rich and generous, and, as befits her name, garrulous and loud as she carouses and smokes. As a cross-dressed colonist, she is a figure for the unusual embodiments of sexuality and female agency possible in the more free-ranging (not to say free-booting) environs of Virginia. After Dareing agrees to marry her, she suggests waiting till the war is over, only to have him insist on quicker satisfaction: 'Nay, prithee, take me in the humour, while thy Breeches are on – for I never lik'd thee half so well in Petticoats.' Ranter's reply furthers the delicious inversions that mark their desire: 'Lead on General,' she says, 'you give me good incouragement to wear them' (IV, ii, 281–4). She is to wear the pants so that he might love her as a man – this brief moment suspends, and mocks, the relentless performance of male authority and heterosexuality that structures this drama of love and war in the colonies.

Colonial locations allowed the staging not only of crises of patriarchal sovereignty that commented obliquely on similar questions of law and disorder in England, but also, in the case of *The Widdow Ranter*, for comic inversions of the proper hierarchy between metropolis and colony. Dullman and Timerous, drunken butts of humor in the play, comment caustically on England ("tis nothing to 't'), reporting the dullness and sobriety that characterizes the London Court of Aldermen, the pretensions of those returned from the Grand Tour of Europe, the covetousness of the aged and wealthy, and the narrow-minded pursuit of business by merchants. Dullman declares that the solution to these problems is to send colonial Virginians to run all 'Offices, both Civill and Military,' in England, and also to dispatch 'young Gentry' from England to the colonies in order to 'learn the misteries of State' (II, ii, 71–103). This is not quite the world turned upside down, but it certainly allows for double-edged humor that laughs at drunken, vainglorious colonists as it does at legal, cultural, and commercial practices in England. Nor does the parody derail the historical insight offered here, that relations between England and its colonies would need constant re-adjustment as the latter developed their own administrative and economic structures.

In my description above, *The Widdow Ranter* is a play fully (and playfully!) receptive to postcolonial analyses of literary reworkings of colonial histories. It provides a very good instance of the overlap between literary form and ideological function, as we see how the political turmoil and sexual license, including miscegenation, associated with the colonies is translated into scenarios of disorder purged by tragedy or laughed away in comedy.[12] Its themes, characters, points of cultural and legal reference, as well as its focus on inter-racial desire and politics and warfare all emphasize the imaginative and erotic stimulus provided by colonial novelty, which could also provide spectacular, or at least exoticized, entertainment on the stage. Indians in the play 'dance Anticks' (II, i), Negro footmen and valets wait on their owners, a bagpiper plays for a 'Scots Dance' performed by a 'highland-Varlet' (II, ii), and Act IV begins with imagined Indian religious rituals, including 'ridiculous Postures,' incantations ('Agah Yerkin, Agah Boah, Sulen Tawarapah, Sulen Tawarapah'), 'confused Tunes,' and priests who 'Dance Antickly Singing between.' These animated tableaux of colonial fantasies are designed to delineate cultural difference, but also, as Joseph Roach has argued, to render imaginable (and thus *manageable*) faraway places and peoples (Roach 1996).[13] In plays like this one, the late seventeenth-century London stage also arrogates to itself the power to define – discursively, visually, ethnographically – those at the receiving end of English colonial power.

Not surprisingly, Behn's *The Widdow Ranter* has become part of what we might think of as the new 'postcolonial canon' of English literary history. Indeed, in the past three decades, Behn's entire corpus has been disinterred from critical oblivion by the efforts of feminist editors, and postcolonial critics have aided this project by taking seriously texts like *Oroonoko* and *The Widdow Ranter*. Behn's recent return to literary-historical and critical prominence is a reminder that the advent of postcolonial studies in the academy has necessitated a revision not only of critical aims and strategies of interpretation, but also a reconsideration of the texts central to the definition of English public culture in the age of empire. A generation ago, Restoration comedies of manners attracted the largest critical attention, as critics marveled at their linguistic ingenuity and cynical intelligence, and at their depiction of fiercely manipulative and caustic gender and class relations. Critics celebrated the energies that coursed through plays like Etherege's *The Comical Revenge, or Love in a Tub* (1664) or his *The Man of Mode or Sir Fopling Flutter* (1676), Wycherley's *The Country Wife* (1675), and Congreve's *The Way of the World* (1700), even though several found them amoral or distasteful. There was, finally, a controlling masculinity to these plays (even as they contained memorable portraits of manipulative, hypocritical, seductive, and powerful women) that made them attractive to male critics who saw in the libidinal pleasures of these plays the flowering (or the regrettable last gasp!) of aristocratic male privilege in England. While these plays have by no means disappeared from university syllabi or the pages of academic journals, they now share critical attention with other comedies from this period like Behn's *The Rover* or *The Widdow Ranter* which feature colonial locations, free-booting cavaliers or merchants and colonists abroad, and which define Englishness in juxtaposition with non-English peoples and places, rather than via the more insular, London-centric practices featured in the more domestic comedy of manners.

These shifts in institutional practice and canon formation are in part the result of postcolonial evaluations of the relations between the institutions of culture and the development of imperialist modes of representation. Increasingly, 'national identity' or 'nationalism' are crucial mediating terms in analyses of the links between the theatre and empire, as critics turn to those plays that self-consciously meditate upon crises and contradictions in models of English or British collectivity that result from the uneven and uncertain progress of commercial and colonial initiatives in different parts of the globe. However, most plays did not specifically address these themes, important as they were for the evolution of 'Great Britain' as an international political and cultural system. The stage in this period is populated by varieties of Englishmen and women, whose concerns seem quite local – love, sex, marriage, inheritance, fashion, intrigues and plots – even when they interact with visitors from Scotland or Ireland or from European nations or further overseas. Traditional literary critics took their cue from these 'local' concerns and distilled from them a sophisticated and heady cocktail of Englishness. Postcolonial critical emphases have since shown us that much that is self-consciously English, whether in matters of style or in the stage formulae of inter-generational conflict or cultural self-definition, is shaped by the burgeoning pressures of commercialism and colonialism. Even scholars who do not style themselves as postcolonial critics have recognized that the prospect of empire – the term understood as an amalgam of expansionist colonial and commercial activities – exerts an extraordinary power over the cultural imagination of late seventeenth- and eighteenth-century writers. Margaret Ann Doody, for instance, writes of the 'unconscious presence in poetry (and poetics) of the same qualities or mental dispositions that made, in the practical or historical sphere, for England's expansion and domination of trade,' and her comment can fruitfully be extended into a description of literary writing in general in this period (Doody 1985: 17).[14]

A representative instance of such theatrical energies is available in Susanna Centlivre's fast-paced comedy *A Bold Stroke for a Wife*

(1718), in which Colonel Fainwell has to win the hand of the heiress Ann Lovely by duping each of her four guardians into giving their assent. One is Modelove, an effeminate, Frenchified social dandy; the second is Periwinkle, a would-be scholar obsessed with antiquities from around the globe; the third is a greedy merchant, Tradelove; and the last a lecherous and puritanical Quaker called Prim. The action of the play does not leave London, but the cast of characters (and the city) embody competitive international trade (in fashions, collectible artifacts, commodities), traffic with the North American colonies, and military aggression. Fainwell fools guardian after guardian by acting (in turn) as a man conversant with French fashions, mythic and magical artifacts from faraway places, commercial practices (he pretends to be Jan van Timtamtirelereletta Heer van Fainwell, a rich Dutch merchant), and finally by impersonating a Quaker visitor from America. He is all these people and yet remains – crucially – a fervent nationalist who describes himself at the end of the play as a man who has 'had the honour to serve his Majesty and headed a regiment of the bravest fellows that ever pushed bayonet in the throat of a Frenchman; and notwithstanding the fortune this lady brings me [he has won Ann Lovely], whenever my country wants my aid, this sword and arm are at her service' (V, i, 547–55).

Civil Tragedy, Commercial Humanism, and Colonial Consciousness

A brief mention of a different kind of theatrical project must close this chapter: while military men and sea captains provide the Restoration and eighteenth-century stage with fine protagonists, even if their crusty ways occasionally need softening, the growth of colonies and overseas trade also brought into view a new public figure, the nationalist merchant. Or perhaps it is more accurate to say that the fortunes made in, and the management of, trade created a newly powerful cross-class network of financiers, merchants, wholesalers, and retailers that allowed even the middling amongst them to see themselves as crucial to the vitality of the nation. However, the merchant or stockjobber was conventionally portrayed as grasping, to be laughed at for his single-minded and ungentlemanly pursuit of wealth or condemned for his avarice. Thus, when George Lillo wrote *The London Merchant, or The History of George Barnwell* (1731), he did so against stage precedent and with a view to elevating the merchant (here named Thorowgood) to exemplary ethical, social, and national status.[15] (Lillo dedicated the play to Sir John Eyles, Baronet, Member of Parliament for and Alderman of the City of London, and Sub-governor of the South Sea Company.) In doing so, Lillo was part of a larger cultural effort to craft, as J. G. A. Pocock has termed it, a 'commercial humanism' that posited, in the supposedly refined manners and protocols of commerce, a substitute for the more austere virtues traditionally understood as necessary for civic leadership or indeed citizenship (Pocock 1985: 37–50).[16] But it is not only past (or even archaic) models of citizenship that commercial humanism sought to disavow – the contemporary practice of commerce was dangerously linked to the depredations and corruptions of colonialism, and proponents of *doux* commerce (commerce as a civilizing force) sought to distance such associations by creating idealized scenarios of the domestic behaviour of noble merchants.[17]

In these ways, playwrights made certain that the theatre continued to be a central social institution for modeling these complex relations of power and personhood. As Daniel O'Quinn has written recently of the London stage in the late eighteenth-century, on 'any given night, events in the transformation of British imperial society were brought to the stage, often mediated by the sexual and commercial relations that accompanied all class interactions in the metropole at this time.' 'In other words,' he suggests, 'the theatre tends to bridge the conceptual gap between realms understood to be explicitly political or economic and those understood to be specifically private and social' (O'Quinn 2005: 6). The immediacy of theatrical performances encouraged playwrights and impresarios to create characters and situations that render visible in performance the connections between events far away and those at home. In many cases, the stage, always agile in its sense of popular interests, enlivened the stories and scandals reported in newspapers and magazines. Scenic effects swept audiences away to locations in India or the South Sea Islands, and framed visitors (or returning Englishmen and women) from those spaces as they stumbled though, or were fêted in, English drawing rooms. Theater galvanized interest in worlds larger than those of England, and immersed its audiences in conversations about distinctions internal to the body politic as well as about national differences. Importantly, as this chapter has shown, plays enabled the idea, crucial to the formation of Great Britain, that the state of the nation was now contingent upon the state of the empire.

Notes

1. Janet Clare writes that Davenant's plays 'endorsed the imperial expansionist policy of the Protectorate' (Clare 2002: 2). This endorsement functioned as an important justification for the revival of theatre.

2. My discussion of *The Siege of Rhodes*, Parts 1 and 2, is based on the critical edition (Hedbäck 1973). Janet Clare suggests that the 'advertisement of the play as a "representation by the art of perspective in scenes" indicates the importance which Davenant attached to scenery as a medium for the drama.' Clare also reprints several of John Webb's set designs, which emphasize vast landscapes or opulent interior spaces (Clare 2002: 187, 188–90).

3. The Prologue to the Second Part of *The Siege of Rhodes* (which was performed at the Duke of York's Theatre in 1663) returns to this theme:

   > But many Trav'lers here as Judges come;
   > *From* Paris, Florence, Venice, *and from* Rome:
   > *Who will describe, when any Scene we draw,*
   > *By each of ours, all that they ever Saw.*
   > *Those praising, for extensive breadth and height,*
   > *And inward distance to deceive the sight.*
   > *When greater Objects, moving in broad Space,*
   > *You rank with lesser, in this narrow Place,*
   > *Then we like* Chess-men, *on a Chess-board are,*
   > *And seem to play like* Pawns *the* Rhodian *warr.*

   The Prologue concludes with an appeal for money to widen '*contracted Scenes*' and for '*greater Engines*' with which to stage the spectacle of fierce armies, raging seas, and fighting fleets.

4. Orr argues persuasively that the 'attractions of heroic plays arose from their spectacular satisfaction of curiosity about exotic cultures, as well as their ability to stage and perhaps exorcise anxieties about domestic and continental politics' (Orr 2001: 46). Orr's book is a wide-ranging elaboration of the relation between post-Restoration English socio-political history and empire. Ann-Marie Hedbäck, in her 'Introduction' to *The Siege of Rhodes*, points to the many earlier stage representations of Turkish and ancillary materials, going back to 1586 (Davenant 1973: xxviii–xxxi).

5. Janet Clare suggests that the first part of *The Siege of Rhodes* weaves a 'royalist fantasy narrative' which links Henrietta Maria and Charles I to Ianthe and Alphonso, and which rewrites 'history as romance' (Clare 2002: 184–5).

6. *The Siege of Rhodes* also suggests that the Ottoman armies are motivated by their expansionist faith, in contrast with the Christian kingdoms of Europe, which compete with each other for their own national empires and do not come to the aid of Rhodes (1, II, i, 17–26). Pirrhus, Solyman's Vizier, remarks that 'our valiant Prophet did/ In us not only loss forbid,/ But has enjoyn'd us still to get./ Empire must move apace,' he says, 'And apter is for wings, then feet' (1, III, i, 25–30).

7. Traders from the Dutch East India Company had been dominant there since 1609, and the ensuing competition led to the arrest, torture, and execution of ten Englishmen, including their leader, Gabriel Towerson. Accounts of this event, dubbed a 'massacre' in England, featured in the build-up to the First Anglo-Dutch war (1652–4), and the victorious Cromwell did exact some compensation for these deaths (and the stain on national honor) thirty-one years earlier. Amboyna was a patriotic point of reference during the Second Anglo-Dutch War (1665–7) too.

8. To that extent Dryden's dramatic methods recapitulate, but simplify, the romance between the island princess Quisara and her Christian Portuguese suitor Armusia in John Fletcher's *The Island Princess* (1647). Fletcher's play, set in Tidore (another of the Spice Islands), is populated by a variety of competing local elites in addition to Portuguese traders, but it too understands the union

of Armusia and Quisara (who converts to Christianity) to be a resolution of the political tensions and racial differences it explores (see Loomba 2002).

9. The Rover is set in Naples, then held by the Spanish. There, visiting English Cavaliers including the hero Wilmore, who are all impoverished by their exile from Cromwell's England, repair their fortunes (and reassert their masculinity) by successfully wooing Neapolitan heiresses away from their Spanish suitors.

10. Mita Chaudhuri's study of the give and take between English nationalism and the international themes, characters, and theatrical practices of eighteenth-century London theatre concludes that:

> the London theater (in comic, tragic, farcical and every other mood) through its curious, creative, recuperative, appropriative, myopic, violent, and resuscitative gazes becomes a volatile intercultural landscape even when the individual instances and examples of performance are seemingly contained within the parameters of traditional, customary, and very British theatrical practices. (Chaudhuri 2000: 174–5)

11. Details are available in Behn 1996: 287–9, Hutner 2001: 92–106, and Orr 2001: 234–8.

12. In his critical edition of *The Widow Ranter*, Aaron R. Walden reprints as appendices several contemporary public documents and proclamations concerning Bacon's revolt, including his *Manifesto Concerning the Present Troubles in Virginia* (1676); the state response issued by Whitehall, *A Proclamation for the Suppressing of a Rebellion lately raised within the Plantation of Virginia* (1676); and the 1677 report by the Royal Commissioners who enquired into these events. These documents testify to the volatile political matrix for Bacon's actions, and make clear to us the imaginative work required for Behn to fashion her play *against* this discursive milieu (Behn 1993).

13. Roach's account of eighteenth-century theatricality in London is motivated by two important questions: 'At issue for me is how freedom is created and then takes on a life and meaning of its own as one of the truth effects of English literature. At issue likewise is how the very concept of English Liberty rested on an edifice (and an artifice) of human difference, a difference propagated by representations of human bodies marked by race as either 'Free-born' or enslaved' (Roach 1996: 75).

14. Her observations on style are equally pertinent: 'the stylistic qualities of "Augustan" poetry are metaphorically and more than metaphorically related to the qualities and activities of that energetic and greedy time, and the qualities of appetite and expansiveness can be seen in the poetry of the period, along with the desire to mix, to import, to remake and remodel. The vices and virtues of Augustan poetry are the vices and virtues of buccaneering millionaires, intelligent, ingenious and insatiable' (Doody 1985: 18).

15. John Gay's *The Beggar's Opera* (1728) had been an extraordinary success in London, and audiences had thrilled to this ballad opera as it linked the criminal underworld to those responsible for policing and incarceration. 'Accounts' are constantly settled in this play in ways that make clear that such 'business practices' are more corrupt than the forthright thievery of highwaymen and burglars. (Characters in this play speak of being 'bubbled' or cheated (II. xiii. 60), a colloquialism whose urgency derives from the collapse of the South Sea Company.) The long shadow cast by Shakespeare's *The Merchant of Venice* also dulls any celebration of merchants on stage. (For a longer discussion of *The London Merchant*, see Kaul 2003.)

16. Pocock has argued influentially that in the eighteenth century, Anglophone political theory was no longer concerned with monarchical absolutism but with

the corruptive power of 'patronage, public debt, and professionalization of the armed forces,' that is, with the development of the political, financial, and military apparatuses of the modern state and commercial society. This is undoubtedly the case, but with an important proviso: the political field from which these issues were derived was international and colonial, and modern conceptions of virtue and corruption were defined by their effects on citizens and others in the empire as much as within the nation. Political theorists have been slow to take on board this larger frame for their analyses of political discourse, even while briefly acknowledging, as Pocock does, that theories of history in this period were quasi-anthropological and comparative in nature and involved models of uneven human progress that contributed to the legitimation of imperialism (Pocock 1985: 48–9).

17. The spectacular collapse in 1720 of the value of stocks issued by the South Sea Company (immortalized as the South Sea Bubble) was a reminder that such joint stock companies, including those trading in profitable slave markets, were open to manipulation by corrupt businessmen-speculators and politicians. Only a few months before the bursting of this bubble, Paris had seen the similar collapse of the Scotsman John Law's Compagnie Perpétuelle des Indes, which held a royal charter to trade with, and develop, French colonies in Louisiana and elsewhere.

Chapter 2

'The Expanding Frontiers of Prose'

> The Novel was produced in antiquity by people from non-Greek and non-Novel areas, by writers who came from the Near East and from Africa. The Novel, that is, is a 'foreign' import – or rather, it is the product of combination, of contact between Southern Europe, Western Asia, and Northern Africa. And behind these regions, the regions of Greece and Syria and Ethiopia and Egypt, there lie other areas, hinterlands not without influence. We can assume the possibility of story and style filtering in from the Balkans and the Celtic lands in the West, from Persia and India in the East, from the Sudan and Kush and Katanga in the South. The homeland of the Western Novel is the Mediterranean, and it is a multiracial, multilingual, mixed Mediterranean. (Doody 1998: 18)[1]

Most critics who sketch a history of the English novel or develop a reading of a single novel feel it necessary to detail the social and cultural history of places – London, say, or Bath – within England in order to understand better the world the novelist crafts from these locations. It is very possible, however, to discount such attentiveness when it comes to novels set overseas, particularly in colonial locations, because, as J. Paul Hunter puts it in his book on the cultural contexts of early English fiction, 'Everyone knows the lengthy story of England's growing interest in foreign (especially exotic) cultures, and there is no need to rehearse the history of audience fascination with even the most mundane and boring narratives of exploration and adventure' (Hunter 1990: 352.)[2] Myriad critics of novelistic practice continue to show us exactly why the social history of land, class, or gender relations within British society merits nuanced understanding, but most of them refuse to take on board representations of comparative racial and class and gender differences as they are imagined or experienced by English subjects engaged in trade or colonization overseas.[3] For postcolonial critics, the latter experiences play a constitutive role in any modeling of British social relations or subjectivity in the novel, particularly when we keep in mind that the very idea of Britishness or of the Briton (however variously defined or argued over in novels) was, in format and in tone, insistently comparative, internationalist, and increasingly imperialist. Especially when we factor in the presence of Irish or Scottish figures in these novels, we recognize that the representation of provincial differences are resonant too with the English tribalism and nationalism that derives from conquest and the uneven amalgamation of autonomous or semi-autonomous peoples within the islands that comprised Great Britain (the process that Michael Hechter has termed 'internal colonialism').

That the early history of the novel prominently features provincial and international difference is no surprise to those who take seriously literary and formal history, and recognize the English novel (or prose fiction more generally) as an innovation influenced by the epic (via its redaction in the romance), historical writing, and the presentist immediacy of 'news' and reportage. In the early modern period, the descriptive and ethnographic practices of travel writers added the excitement and mystifications of the little-known to this international historical matrix, within which writers of fiction (who were occasionally journalists or travelers themselves) crafted their prose novelties. Percy Adams details the mass of travel writing that flooded Europe: letters, diaries, travelers' guides (for overland journeys within nations as well as across contiguous territories in Europe and Asia), reports to their superiors from merchants and missionaries (particularly the Jesuits), ships' journals, the observations of doctors, botanists, or cartographers, or indeed the more formally edited narratives of journeys across the oceans and of settlement and trade. Adams argues that reports of travels were consequential to 'every realm of thought, to every significant business, political, religious, academic, or creative enterprise' undertaken during the seventeenth and eighteenth centuries (Adams 1983: 80).

Adams's is an important observation about the history of ideas and of cultural practices, one that postcolonial scholarship builds upon when it argues that this burgeoning, complicated sense of the world (faithfully observed, fabricated, or both) was crucial to the development of nationalist and – as overseas territories were conquered and trade monopolies established – imperialist notions of Englishness and Britishness. All this writing quickened the pace of exploration, trade, and colonization in the seventeenth century, and offered pictures of peoples and places either tribal and 'uncivilized' (in the trans-Atlantic context and in coastal Africa) or overly wealthy, corrupt, and tyrannical (the Ottomans, the Mughals, the ruling dynasties of China and Japan).[4] Not all these portrayals were without sympathy or wonderment, but most translated those they observed into peoples whose social and ethical values were inferior to practices and ideas in Europe. From such translation followed many of the comparatist truisms about national character and social development that enabled the growth of imperialist self-conception and self-confidence in British media.

Fiction played a popularizing role here, both in its themes and characters, but also in the prefatory materials that led readers into its world (prefaces of all kinds, like Prologues and Epilogues in the theater, were the privileged textual space for the elaboration of nationalist sentiments or panegyric). This is the case with Penelope Aubin's *The Noble Slaves: or, The Lives and Adventures of Two Lords and two Ladies, who were shipwreck'd and cast upon a desolate Island near the East-Indies, in the year 1710. The Manner of their Living there: The surprizing Discoveries they made, and strange Deliverance thence. How in their return to Europe they were taken by two Algerine Pirates near the Straits of Gibraltar. Of the Slavery they endured in Barbary; and of their meeting there with several Persons of Quality, who were likewise Slaves. Of their escaping thence, and safe Arrival in the respective counties, Venice, Spain, and France, in the year 1718. With many extraordinary Accidents that befell some of them afterwards. Being a History full of most remarkable Events* (London: 1722). Aubin's 'The Preface to the Reader' begins:

> *In our Nation, where the Subjects are born free, where Liberty and Property is so preserv'd to us by Laws, that no Prince can enslave us, the Notion of Slavery is a perfect Stranger. We cannot think without Horror, of the Miseries that attend those, who, in Countries where the Monarchs are absolute, and standing Armies awe the People, are made Slaves to others. The* Turks *and* Moors *have been ever famous for their Cruelties; and therefore when we Christians fall into the Hands of Infidels, or Mahometans, we must expect to be treated as those heroick Persons, who are the Subjects of the Book I here present to you. There the Monarch gives a loose to his Passions, and thinks it no Crime to keep as many Women for his Use, as his lustful Appetite excites him to like; and his Favourites, Ministers of State, and Governors, who always follow their Master's Example, imitate his way of living. This caused our beautiful Heroines to suffer such Trials: The Grand Signior knowing that Money is able to procure all earthly things, uses his Grandees like the Cat's Paw, to beggar his People, and then sacrifices them to appease the Populace's Fury, and fills his own coffers with their Wealth. This is* Turkish *Policy, which makes the Prince great, and the People wretched, a Condition we are secur'd from ever falling into; our excellent Constitution will always keep us rich and free, and it must be our own Faults if we are enslav'd, or impoverish'd.*

This passage is an impressive demonstration of Aubin's ability to efficiently marshal crucial tokens of cultural difference: political structures, religious beliefs, systems of property ownership, gender relations, sexual practices, and moral codes. All except racial difference is specified, but then the fearful focus on the special horror that is white slavery resonates so ironically with the British (and European) slave trade that it leaves little doubt about the contemporary difference between white and black. There are black slaves in the novel, of course, but there is no comment on their enslavement.[5]

Yariko and Inkle and the Staging of Polite Culture

Of the several long-ignored texts from the late seventeenth and eighteenth century that have been re-evaluated and restored to academic study in the past three decades, none has been more consequential than Aphra Behn's *Oroonoko* (1688). This restoration has a great deal to do with feminist literary historians who have revived Behn's fortunes, but also with the fact that postcolonial critics have found in this novella a foreshadowing of many of their analytical concerns. Behn's account of the travails of a royal African slave, Oroonoko, who is forced from his home in Coramantien to Surinam, where he leads an unsuccessful slave insurrection and is hanged and quartered for his efforts, is astonishing (almost *sui generis*) in featuring a range of issues important to the study of colonial discourse, from the construction of the cultural authority of the white observer, to the representation of colonized (or colonizable) spaces and peoples, to the delineation of desire, including miscegenous desire, as an ineluctable feature of life in the contact zones of the plantation or the colony.

In *Oroonoko* the narrator travels to bring home her tale; her claim to having been in Surinam reminds us that narratives of travel were often sources of prose fiction. Travelers who described the routes they took, the places they visited and the people they encountered, were not embarrassed about embellishing their experiences, and the combination of verifiable facts and more imaginative fiction that results defined the genre all throughout the early modern period. For our discussion here, I would like to point to an instance of the cultural power of travelogues exemplified by a little story included by Richard Ligon in his *A True and Exact History of the Island of Barbadoes* (London: 1673).[6] This story was to take on a life of its own over the next 100 years and more (versions are performed even today),[7] but here I want to suggest that these stories entered English culture not simply as oddities or novelties, but because they served a domestic purpose. That is, their mode of insertion into domestic cultural circulation will remind us of the importance of colonial themes in determining the cultural conversations, gender relations, and ethical and affective codes, of 'cultured' English women and men.

On 13 March 1711, Richard Steele retold in *The Spectator* (number 11) the story of Thomas Inkle and his lover, the '*Indian* maid' Yariko. Before I recount its details, we should note the drawing-room location in which it was first spoken, for this location, and the conversation Steele describes, is an important staging of the modes by which news and stories from plantations, colonies, or overseas spaces circulated into and recast the social dynamics of the most domestic of English spaces. The Spectator describes a visit he pays to Arietta (whose afternoon assembly welcomes all those 'who have any Pretence to Wit and Gallantry'), where he encounters 'a Common-Place Talker' who turns out to be neither witty nor gallant as he insists on repeating Petronius's 'celebrated Story of the *Ephesian* Matron' and thus railing against women's inconstancy and hypocrisy in love. Arietta is angered by what she hears and in response invokes two stories, the Fable of the Lion and the Man, and the History of Inkle and Yariko. The first is a fable in which a lion, shown a painting depicting a lion being slain by a man, retorts that lions are not painters, '*else we could shew a hundred Men killed by Lions, for one Lion killed by a Man.*' Arietta draws from this fable lessons about the history and modalities of misogynist storytelling: 'You Men are Writers,' Arietta says, 'and can represent us Women as Unbecoming as you please in your Works, while we are unable to return the Injury.' Male authors, she states, 'leave behind them Memorials of their Resentment against the Scorn of particular Women, in Invectives against the whole Sex' (Addison et al. 1945: 1. 34–7).

Arietta then speaks of reading '*Ligon*'s Account of Barbadoes' and repeats the Inkle and Yariko story she found there (on page 55, she is careful to say!).[8] (Ligon's text does not in fact contain precisely the story Arietta tells – Ligon mentions Yariko, an Indian house slave 'of excellent shape and colour' who 'would not be woo'd by any means to wear Cloaths.'[9] She already has a baby by 'a Christian servant' when she protects and falls in love with an English sailor who is attacked by Indians when he and others come ashore and wander deep into the island. She does go off on the sailor's ship with him, and he in turn sells her into slavery as soon as 'he came ashore in the *Barbadoes*.') Arietta embellishes this story: the twenty-year-old Thomas Inkle, in whom his father had instilled 'an early Love of Gain,' sails to the West Indies to 'improve his Fortune by Trade and Merchandize.' His ship anchors off the coast of America for provisions, but the sailors, including Inkle, who go ashore are 'intercepted by the Natives, who slew the greatest Number of them.' Inkle escapes into the deep forest, where Yariko stumbles upon him, and a mutual attraction ensues: 'If the *European* was highly Charmed with the Limbs, Features, and wild Graces of the Naked *American*; the *American* was no less taken with the Dress, Complexion, and Shape of an *European*, covered from Head to Foot.' This distinction, and the articulation of desire across it, is a rhetorical standard in early modern stories of trans-Atlantic inter-racial romance, and allows writers to both detail cultural difference and efface the violence that followed from it in colonial spaces. In keeping with such figuration – whose type is the Indian queen who gifts her white lover her riches in return for his love – Yariko turns out to be no ordinary maiden but a 'Person of Distinction, for she every Day came to him in a different Dress, of the most beautiful Shells, Bugles, and Bredes. She likewise brought him a great many Spoils.'

The lovers learn 'a Language of their own,' and Inkle tells Yariko 'how happy he should be to have her in his Country where she should be Cloathed in such Silks as his Wastecoat was made of, and be carried in Houses drawn by Horses.' Persuaded, Yariko keeps a lookout for a ship, and finds one that turns out to be bound for Barbadoes and its plantations, where, Arietta tells us, 'there is an immediate Market of the *Indians* and other Slaves, as with us of Horses and Oxen.' As Inkle nears '*English* Territories,' he begins to rethink his priorities, and given that he has lost 'many Days Interest of his Money' while with Yariko, he sells her 'to a *Barbadian* Merchant; notwithstanding that the poor Girl, to incline him to commiserate her Condition, told him that she was with Child by him: But he only made use of that Information, to rise in his Demands upon the Purchaser.' Arietta concludes her story about this colonial merchant's inconstancy in love and hypocrisy, and the Spectator, overcome by her tale, leaves her salon in tears. In Arietta's retelling, a brief story from Ligon's mid seventeenth-century travelogue becomes part of the polite cultural conversation that *The Spectator* performed for its readers. She counters Petronius's misogynist satire of the Ephesian lady via a fable and a colonial romance, and all three are forms of storytelling that originate in spaces and contact zones distant from – but now equally domesticated within – her London drawing room. As Latin classicism jostles for cultural authority with the fable of the Lion and the Man and the 'history' of Inkle and Yariko, the new polite world of English letters is brought into being, anchored in the social authority of Arietta, the sentimentality and good manners of the Spectator, and the narrative excitement and pathos generated by Yariko's love for, and suffering caused by, Inkle.

Another way to think about this is to note that, in Arietta's telling, an enslaved Indian woman teaches Steele's readers the proper ethical response not just to colonial exploitation but to gender inequities closer to home. The abject condition of slaves was often invoked by eighteenth-century writers as a parallel for the domestic condition of women in Britain, and however inappropriate and self-interested this parallel seems now, such comparisons did encourage the development of both anti-patriarchal and anti-slavery sentimentalism, as is the case in Steele's essay. Arietta has Yariko's fate stand in for the condition of women in Europe as well as in the Atlantic plantations – she is cognizant that it is Yariko's race that causes her enslavement, but her conclusion sets aside this knowledge in order to focus on man's cruelties to woman, and thus to best the vulgar misogyny of the salon 'Common-Place Talker.'[10]

Crusoe the Merchant-adventurer – and Friday

Steele's embellishment of Ligon's tale is one instance of the inter-animation of forms of storytelling encouraged by the remaking of domestic society by the powerful material and cultural energies of overseas trade and colonization. We now move to the most important fiction of adventuring and its travails and possibilities in the eighteenth century (and till Joseph Conrad, possibly in all of the English novel), Daniel Defoe's *Robinson Crusoe* (1719). As a magnificent instance of fearful contemporaneity, *Crusoe* features an English merchant and colonist, who is wrecked onto an uninhabited island, teaches himself how to live there (first in isolation and then with a black servant), and overcomes adversity and the occasional threatening native to achieve the plantation and the trading riches he had set out to find. I stress the contemporaneity of this novel in keeping with J. Paul Hunter's listing of this element as crucial to the perceived novelty of the form in the eighteenth century: 'Unlike literary forms that feature an appeal to the exotic and the far-away in place and time, novels are fundamentally stories of now, or stories about events in a relevant past, one that has culminated in a now, a moment poised in instability and change.' However, as this chapter argues, we might note that the specifics of the new in eighteenth-century English culture are provided precisely by the 'exotic and the faraway.' Behn and Defoe (or even Delariviere Manley or Penelope Aubin or Jonathan Swift in *Gulliver's Travels*) define their contemporary moment in stories of colonial plantations, 'discovered' islands, or via captivity narratives that arise from shipwreck or military setbacks. So even as we stress the strangeness and the innovation thematized in these early novels, and focus on their emphasis on 'Credibility and probability,' 'Individualism and subjectivity,' and their 'Self-consciousness about innovation and novelty,' we need also to acknowledge that the energy of these novelistic attributes often derives from the new worlds of mercantile exploration and colonization.[11]

Crusoe's narrative style, the stories it tells, and the protagonist's struggle to preserve himself (which is at once a novelistic struggle to cast a self adequate to the difficulties of colonial venturing) can best be understood by keeping in mind Srinivas Aravamudan's pithy characterization of the modern European colonist: no 'mere conqueror, the colonialist subject is the accompanying historian, trader, and missionary' (Aravamudan 1999b: 73).[12] Defoe's protagonist exemplifies this protean quality, but also, more compellingly, reveals the messy anxieties, uncertainties, and will to overcome required by a successful colonialist (or merchant-adventurer). Success might seem far removed from a protagonist marooned, for the most part of the novel, on an uninhabited island, but precisely the length of Crusoe's tribulations emphasizes his resourcefulness and ingenuity, and leads to an eventual (providential?) accounting in which he notes that he is now 'Master . . . of above 5000 *l.* Sterling in Money, and had an Estate, as I might well call it, in the *Brasils*, of above a thousand Pounds a Year, as sure as an Estate of Lands in *England*.' He is astonished at the turn his fortunes have taken, and says he scarcely knows how to 'compose my self, for the Enjoyment of it' (Defoe 1972: 285). Crusoe's need to compose himself at this moment might in fact be taken as a figure for the novel as a whole – the narrative features the dis-composed self that follows from loss, isolation, doubt (both existential and theological), and fear, as well as the recasting of self made possible by his domination over Friday and his victories over other natives of Caribbean lands near the '*Mouth of the Great River of* OROONOQUE.'

Robinson Crusoe's narrative begins with an extended account of his merchant father's advice to him not to venture abroad: 'He told me it was for Men of desperate Fortunes on one Hand, or of aspiring, superior Fortunes on the other, who went abroad upon Adventures, to raise by Enterprize, and make themselves famous in Undertakings of a Nature out of the common Road.' He believes that they belong to the 'middle State, or of what might be called the upper Station of *Low Life*' (1972: 4) and that this 'middle Station of Life was calculated for all kind of Vertues and all kinds of Enjoyments' (1972: 5). Having lost a son on a military campaign overseas, and having no desire to lose another, Crusoe's father offers to settle his son into an appropriately sedate life in York. In this opening, it is easy to differentiate the mid seventeenth-century English merchant-traveler (Crusoe was born in 1632) vis-à-vis those so poor or so persecuted at home that they were forced to seek their living abroad. It is harder, however, to maintain the distinction (which the father wishes to make) between the adventurism required now of the middling merchant who would make his fortune and the buccaneer whose aspirations to vast overseas fortunes were exemplified in the Elizabethan exploits of Sir Francis Drake. Unlike the poor who go overseas to sell their labor, Crusoe's venture is based on the same exchange fantasy that drove early European adventuring across the Atlantic, that 'Toys and Trifles' (on which he spends £40) can be exchanged for gold. He does in fact return from his first voyage (appropriately enough, to Guinea) confirmed as 'both a Sailor and a Merchant, for I brought Home L. 5. 9. *Ounces* of Gold Dust for my Adventure, which yielded me in *London* at my Return, almost 300 *l.* and this fill'd me with those aspiring Thoughts which have since so completed my Ruin' (1972: 17).

This success, which represents a painless 700 per cent return on his initial investment, reminds us of the kinds of returns that motivated English merchants and joint-stock companies (not all ventures were successful, of course, but many were spectacularly so).[13] This sizeable profit is important because it must over-ride Crusoe's recurrent fears, precipitated by the storms that wreck his first ship even before he reaches London from Hull, that filial disobedience and impiety will doom him (a fear confirmed by the Captain of the foundered ship, who tells him that the storms are '*a Taste Heaven has given you of what you are to expect if you persist*' (1972: 15). This is the framework within which Crusoe's self-understanding develops uneasily, as Puritan providentialism and his recurrent need to reconcile terrestrial events with spiritual or scriptural sanction runs up against his equally insistent desire to wrest handsome returns, as others have done before him, from well-trafficked Caribbean trading routes and colonial practices. Crusoe's narrative, with its initial focus on his naiveté and its long account of isolated survival, invites us to see his life and concerns as unique and personal; this is ironic, for, as Peter Hulme points out, Crusoe 'claims novelty at each stage of his life and gun-prowess in the Caribbean . . . in spaces that had been criss-crossed by Portuguese, Spanish, French, Dutch and English ships and scarred by their violent engagements with natives and with each other' (Hulme 1986: 185–6).

The concerns and location of the novel are those of the myriad artisans, merchants, and colonists who sailed the Mediterranean and the Atlantic, and the opening sections of the novel make that clear. After he sets up as 'a *Guiney* Trader,' his ship is taken captive and he is enslaved for two years by a Moorish captain.[14] He escapes, taking along Xury, a young Muslim boy who was with him on the boat. He sails along the coast of West Africa hoping to make contact with a European ship, and while he does so, he awes first Xury, and then some friendly Africans they come across, by using his guns to kill a lion and other large animals. They do in fact meet a Portuguese ship bound for the 'Brasils' and the kind Captain agrees to take them there without charge. Crusoe sells the boat he had escaped on and most of its contents, including the skins of the lion and leopard he had shot, and uses this capital to invest in a plantation. But he also sells Xury – who has endeared himself to Crusoe, at one stage offering to go ashore in dangerous territory just to test its safety – into indentured labor to the Captain, on the assurance that he will be freed ten years later, after converting to Christianity. Crusoe's matter-of-fact ease with all these transactions reminds us that they are the standard practices that define seventeenth-century trans-Atlantic commerce, planting, and the slave trade, and are precisely the skills that any enterprising young adventurer would learn.[15]

Two details in the opening section are important for their anticipation of major themes in the novel: Crusoe's Moorish enslavement is a reminder that slavery is not an exclusively European practice, and to that extent this episode functions as a historical alibi for the specifically European provenance and control of trans-Atlantic slavery. This form of exculpation is paralleled when Xury introduces the cannibal theme that is so central to the narrative – when he offers to test the safety of the shore, he says, '*If wild Mans come, they eat me, you go wey*' (1972: 25). That is, Crusoe's paranoia about cannibalism that defines his relation to the Caribs (and to the island on which he is shipwrecked) begins as a fear articulated by someone native to the lands he traverses. But Crusoe sets aside these reminders of vulnerability once he is in Brazil, and plants food crops, tobacco and sugar cane, and three years later is productive enough to take on two indentured servants and buy a 'Negro Slave' (1972: 37). Crusoe's success in planting is not enough, for he is still troubled by 'a rash and immoderate Desire of rising faster than the Nature of the Thing [planting] admitted' (1972: 38), a desire sharpened by his memories of 'how easy it was to purchase upon the Coast [of *Guinea*], for trifles, such as Beads, Toys, Knives, Scissars, Hatchets, bits of Glas, and the like; not only Gold Dust, *Guinea* Grains, Elephants Teeth, &c. but *Negroes* for the Service of the *Brasils*, in great Numbers' (1972: 39). His fellow planters invite him to lead a private and illegal expedition to Guinea to bring back slaves (whose traffic was controlled by rights granted by the King of Spain), and Crusoe agrees, leaving on 1 September 1659, eight years to the day after he had first left Hull (this is one of several coincidences that Crusoe notes in order to lend a tenuous structure to his adventures). All he takes with him to trade are the 'odd Trifles' listed above (1972: 41).

The ship, battered by storms and forced towards the mouth of the River Oroonoque, founders on the sandbank off an island, and Crusoe is the only one cast ashore. What follows is his story of survival for almost three decades, composed equally of logistical challenges and of existential and theological struggles to make sense of his life as it unfolds on the island. His salvation initially is the ship itself, which, while aground, has not broken up, and contains supplies that he salvages in eleven trips before a storm destroys it. This food, and even more importantly, carpenter's tools and supplies, rope and canvas, some cables and ironwork, arms and ammunition, compasses and navigational charts and instruments, printed matter and pen and ink, allow him to establish himself on the island, and to thus bring to bear on his new surroundings technology, skills, and attitudes derived from his experience as a colonial planter, slave trader, and merchant. (Here too, when Crusoe kills a bird, the clamor of other birds allows him to think his 'the first Gun that had been fir'd there since the Creation of the World' (1972: 53).) He also finds some money and bullion, which causes him to meditate upon its uselessness there.

Materials from the ship allow him to survive, but they are also an important source of spiritual reassurance, for when he plunges into gloom about the 'determination of Heaven' to cast him into a 'desolate Place,' he remembers that he must thank 'Providence' for making him the sole survivor and for enabling him to gather the 'Necessaries of Life, or Necessaries to supply and procure them' from the ship (1972: 62–3). Even as Crusoe is convinced that his is now a 'silent Life, such perhaps as was never heard of in the World before' (1972: 63), it by no means recapitulates a pre-technological existence – as his narrative makes clear, his survival within, and then his mastery over, nature derive from his experience and knowledge as an English participant in trans-Atlantic trade and plantation. (Crusoe does imagine being shipwrecked without anything from the ship, and fears that 'I should have liv'd, if I had not perish'd, like a meer Savage' (1972: 131).) His consciousness, in turmoil as it is every now and then, is calmed by his focus on details – he enumerates reasons for acting as he does, and explains (for instance) his choice of techniques, materials, and innovations, as he builds a camouflaged redoubt for himself and his supplies. This process of reasoning shores up Crusoe's sense of self (even as it enables Defoe to provide his readers with a credible account of survival). It becomes an accounting whose purposive rationality is, particularly in contrast with Friday and the other Indians Crusoe comes across, a demonstration of cultural and racial specificity, and to that extent an explanation of his dominance over his circumstances (he embeds his building of a table and chair in precisely such a discussion 68–9). Writing and record keeping are for Crusoe, as they were for New World colonists since Columbus, technologies of the European self, markers of cultural and racial difference.[16]

Friday comes late into Crusoe's life on the island; before that, Crusoe must demonstrate skills across a wide variety of otherwise specialized occupations: construction, agriculture, hunting, clothes-making, bread-making, basket-weaving, goat rearing, dairy farming, book-keeping. His successes are all designed, within the cultural politics of the novel, to show that he has nothing to learn from anyone native to those islands. Past knowledge and present ingenuity allow Crusoe to play out the fantasy of European self-sufficiency that was the historical correlative to their encounters with peoples native to the Caribbean and the Americas – the more the local knowledge they shared in, the greater the desire to discount acknowledgement of the sources of such knowledge. Thus, Friday, a Carib native to the islands at the mouth of the 'Oroonoque,' seems to know nothing about island life in comparison to Crusoe, who by then has shown that he quite literally knows it all. As Peter Hulme trenchantly puts it, the '"ignorance" of the savage Caribs is *produced* by the text of *Robinson Crusoe*, which enacts a denial of those very aspects of Carib culture from which Europe had learned.[17]

Self-sufficiency is not the only colonial fantasy Crusoe indulges in – more directly, he knows 'a secret Kind of Pleasure . . . that I was King and Lord of all this Country indefeasibly, and had a Right of Possession; and if I could convey it, I might have it in Inheritance, as completely as any Lord of a Mannor in *England*' (1972: 100; this is a repeated sentiment: see 128, 148). Crusoe's ambition here oscillates precisely between the twin poles of colonial expropriation, the exculpatory legal and ethical illusion of a 'Right of Possession,' and the hope of conveying those overseas properties into the propriety of a manorial estate in England. These visions of engrossing the land are complemented by recurrent fears about being consumed himself, for he has heard 'that the People of the *Carribean* Coast were Canibals, or Man-eaters' (1972: 124). His fears are brought to a peak when, after fifteen years on the island, he comes upon 'the Print of a Man's naked Foot on the Shore' (1972: 153). Crusoe has often feared meeting the Caribs, and now is forced into a frenzy of defensive preparations. Two years pass, and then, while traversing the island, he realizes that one aspect of it might well provide shelter for '*Canoes* from the Main,' and also be an area where enemy Caribs might fight each other, take prisoners, and 'kill and eat them' (1972: 164). His fears anticipate (or perhaps precipitate!) his reality, and he finds that shore 'spread with Skulls, Hands, Feet, and other Bones of humane Bodies,' and a fire-pit where he presumes 'the Savage Wretches had sat down to their inhumane Feastings upon the Bodies of their Fellow-Creatures' (1972: 165). His fears for himself pale beside his nausea at what he imagines, and when he is calmer, he gives 'God Thanks' for causing him to be born in that 'Part of the World, where I was distinguish'd from such dreadful Creatures as these' (1972: 165).[18]

This moment of divinely enabled ethnographic self-distinction is an iconic summation of much of what is at stake in *Robinson Crusoe*, the pay-off, as it were, for all the labor Crusoe, and his narrative, perform. He has now mastered his domain, and his mastery is confirmed as righteous by the 'Degeneracy of Humane Nature' (1972: 165) that defines the Caribs who live on the mainland and in neighboring islands. Two further years pass, and he finds himself secure enough again to imagine intervening if he sees the Caribs preparing a victim, and he readies himself militarily for that possibility. As he does so, however, he has qualms about his right to judge and slaughter Caribs, on the grounds that their practices are as local to them as the actions of Christians who 'put to Death the Prisoners taken in Battle.' Worse, he imagines that his entry into unprovoked combat might 'justify the Conduct of the *Spaniards* in all their Barbarities practis'd in *America* . . . where they destroy'd Millions of these People' (1972: 171), and earned a bloody reputation (which is later confirmed by Friday (1972: 215)). After twenty years in isolation, Crusoe's thinking still reiterates forcefully the ideological rivalries articulated by Protestant England as it sought to replace Catholic Spain as the dominant European power in the Caribbean.[19] At issue is an ethical subjectivity, one that disavows the violence of colonial conquest and bases its claims to territories on rightful hard work.

Crusoe's near-hallucinatory fears of the Caribs, developed over many years, now lead to an astonishing dream, one in which he rescues a 'Savage' from others who are preparing to kill and eat him. In gratitude he becomes Crusoe's 'Servant,' and a likely pilot who will navigate as Crusoe sails to the mainland (1972: 198–9). This dream is itself a compelling reminder that even as Crusoe is alone on the island for decades, he is never removed from the political unconscious crafted by two centuries of European trans-Atlantic colonialism and slave trading. As a young merchant, once enslaved himself, he presumed Xury was his to sell into slavery; now, even after two decades of isolation, his dreams model for him the only relation that he can conceive between himself, the white lord of the island, and a young 'savage.' Crusoe might be a castaway and a survivor, but his dreams of, and his presumption of, colonial authority never fade. (In moving Crusoe from the Mediterranean and North Africa to the Caribbean and South America, Defoe engages two crucial theaters of early modern English adventuring; Crusoe's journeys to Asia and the Spice Islands are told in the sequels to this novel).

Crusoe's dream – a fantasy that melds castaway survival with colonial mastery – is realized some eighteen months later when a young Carib breaks away from the larger party who are about to kill him and is pursued by only three of them. Crusoe rescues him and the captive kneels, kisses the ground, and sets Crusoe's foot upon his head, which Crusoe takes as a 'token of swearing to be my Slave for ever' (1972: 204). A colonial and homosocial idyll follows, and Crusoe's description of his companion is worth quoting at length:

> He was a comely handsome Fellow, perfectly well made; with straight strong Limbs, not too large; tall and well shap'd, and as I reckon, about twenty six Years of Age. He had a very good Countenance, not a fierce and surly Aspect; but seem'd to have something very manly in his Face, and yet he had all the Sweetness and Softness of an *European* in his Countenance too, especially when he smil'd. His Hair was long and black, not curl'd like Wool; his Forehead very high, and large, and a great Vivacity and sparkling Sharpness in his Eyes. The Colour of his Skin was not quite black, but very tawny; and yet not of an ugly yellow nauseous tawny, as the *Brasilians*, and *Virginians*, and other Natives of *America* are; but of a bright kind of dun olive Colour, that had in it something very agreeable; tho's not very easy to describe. His Face was round, and plump; his Nose small, not flat like the Negroes, a very good Mouth, thin Lips, and his fine Teeth well set, and white as Ivory. (1972: 205–6)

His looks, suitably developed against a checklist of offending non-European facial and epidermal features, endear him to Crusoe, as does his demeanor. He once more sets Crusoe's foot upon his head, and Crusoe is thrilled into alliterative pleasure: 'he made all the Signs to me of Subjection, Servitude, and Submission imaginable' (1972: 206).

Crusoe names him Friday (in keeping with the practice of giving slaves new names, as when Oroonoko is renamed Caesar in Surinam), and teaches him to 'say *Master*, and then let him know, that was to be my Name' (1972: 206). Two names are bestowed here, each a confirmation of differential status and subjecthood. In their repetition, 'Friday' functions as a temporal marker of Crusoe's power to grant life, and 'Master' allows, in this society of two, the enunciation of Crusoe's visions of manorial authority. Crusoe now proceeds to remake Friday in his own image, teaching him English, dressing him, but, most importantly, warning him away from cannibalism (initially by threatening to kill him, later by feeding him other kinds of cooked meat). Friday is a quick and willing learner: Crusoe believes 'never Man had a more faithful, loving, sincere Servant, than *Friday* was to me . . . his very Affections were ty'd to me, like those of a Child to a Father; and I dare say, he would have sacrific'd his Life for the saving mine' (1972: 209).[20] Indeed, Crusoe is so struck by Friday's abilities that he is moved to a meditation on the ways of 'Providence,' which grants people like Friday great qualities of humanity and intelligence but denies them the 'saving Knowledge' that they 'would make a much better use of . . . than we did' (1972: 210). These are the moments (and there are others, though they alter little) in which Crusoe's sense of the Caribbean world is re-shaped by his experiences, and he is led to brief questions about the cultural assumptions of European colonialism.

More than anything else Crusoe looks to Friday for a confirmation of a particular version of himself, so long imagined but only now put into practice. As Friday learns English, Crusoe recovers his own speech, and indeed his own capacity for feeling: 'I began really to love the Creature; and on his Side, I believe he lov'd me more than it was possible for him ever to love any Thing before' (1972: 213). Crusoe's last claim embodies the ignorant hyperbole of colonial assumptions about native subjectivity, for it claims not only knowledge of Friday's present affection, which is feasible, but also presumes to know the capacity of Friday's emotions before his contact with Crusoe. In any case, Crusoe is so committed to his certainties that he cannot recognize those moments when Friday's responses to his instruction unwittingly parody them, as when Friday says Crusoe's Christian god must be greater than his own '*Benamuckee*' because the former could hear his believers even though he lived in the sky beyond the sun, while the latter required priestly intervention even though he lived just beyond the great mountains (1972: 217). Thus, when Friday tells Crusoe of seventeen white men who had been shipwrecked but saved from drowning by his people, Crusoe can only fear that they were killed and eaten. He reacts little to Friday's assurance that these men had been living for four years as brothers amongst his people (1972: 223). Despite his self-satisfied protestations, Crusoe's faith in Friday is tenuous and easily shattered – when Friday is excited, on a clear day, to see the distant outline of his own country, Crusoe instantly fears that Friday will find his way home and return with a war party to 'Feast upon me' (1972: 224). Crusoe regrets his own jealousy, but that does not prevent him from probing Friday further about his loyalties.

Friday, alert to Crusoe's mood, realizes he is being tested and refuses to countenance sailing home without Crusoe. His refusal heals not only Crusoe's wounded *amour propre*, but it is couched in terms that vindicate his civilizational mission, in so far as Crusoe the merchant-planter embodies one. Friday says that Crusoe must '*teach wild Mans be good sober tame Mans; you tell them know God, pray God, and live new Life . . . you teachee me Good, you teachee them Good*' (1972: 226). This declaration leads Crusoe to begin crafting a large sailing canoe with Friday (which becomes another occasion for Crusoe to teach him better building techniques) and they await favorable winds to sail to the mainland. At this point, a Carib war party brings to their island three victims, one of whom turns out to be white, and that enormity is enough to overcome any scruples (or fears) Crusoe has about attacking people who have not done him any harm. A carnage follows, as Crusoe and Friday and their weapons kill almost twenty Caribs and rout the others. Their killing spree is halted only by the fact that they discover another captive, who turns out to be Friday's father. Crusoe, haunted for the last twenty-seven years by his own act of filial disobedience, marvels at Friday's loving care of his father, and indeed of the Spaniard who they rescue. Their return home becomes an occasion for Crusoe to indulge in his colonial fantasies again, as he believes his 'Island was now Peopled' and that he has an 'undoubted Right of Dominion' over 'the whole Country.' Secondly, he argues to himself, 'My People were perfectly subjected: I was absolute Lord and Law-giver; they owed all their Lives to me.' In a further flight of fancy, he allows 'Liberty of Conscience throughout my Dominions,' as evidenced by the fact that Friday is a Protestant, his father a 'Pagan and a Cannibal,' and the Spaniard 'a Papist' (1972: 241). Once again, as at crucial moments in the narrative, we are reminded that Crusoe contextualizes his adventures with reference to colonial or mercantile ambitions (both personal and national).[21]

I will pass over the extended episode in which an English ship captured by mutineers anchors off the island and the mutineers bring their prisoners, including the captain, on shore, allowing Crusoe to intervene, and in stages, win back the ship. Of interest for our purposes are the quasi-legalization of Crusoe's authority, as the ship's captain announces him to the sailors as the English governor of a colonized island (1972: 268), and Crusoe's discovery, once he is offered English clothes, that they are 'unpleasant, awkward, and uneasy' (1972: 274). In the matter of his clothing, if nothing else, he has gone native. Thus outfitted, Crusoe leaves the island after twenty-eight years, and a six-month voyage returns him to England. What follows is remarkable in its brevity and its particular lack of affect: Crusoe lists his dead father and mother, meets two surviving sisters and the children of a brother, and moves rapidly back to an accounting of his fortune, which is at this point slim. He goes to Lisbon to see if he can get news of his plantation in Brazil and, in due course, is rewarded by his partners there with goods and money that add up to the fortune described earlier. Crusoe and Friday travel back to England overland via France, a journey marked by their encounters with man-eaters of another kind, wolves. Upon his return, he sells his estates in Brazil to his partners there. Now a very rich man, he marries, has three children, loses his wife, and, after seven years at home, decides to travel again (these events take all of two paragraphs to narrate!). His destination is 'my new Collony in the Island,' where he, while reserving 'to my self the Property of the whole,' apportions parts amongst the Spaniards and English living there (1972: 305–6). The narrative closes with the promise of 'new Adventures' but also with Crusoe confirmed in his status as a wealthy merchant and owner-settler of an island plantation colony.

Robinson Crusoe is an exemplary text for discussions of English colonial land settlement, but its lessons were of consequence for the management and ownership of land within Britain too. Crusoe's planted and constructed fortifications indicate his fears and also parallel land-development practices in the colonies and in Britain: hedges and fences enforce ownership as well as signify 'improvement.' The extension of the regime of land ownership within Britain was intimately connected with the expropriation of colonial lands, and there was an underlying appropriative logic that underlay both processes, which is the supposed conversion of 'waste' or 'underused' lands (in Britain via various forms of enclosure; in overseas contexts, via warfare) into worked and properly owned property.[22] Both in Brazil (where the local population is not visible) and on the uninhabited island, Crusoe converts land, via work, husbandry, and demarcation, into improved and alienable private property. Thus, early in the century in which property rights in Britain were modernized in law, *Robinson Crusoe* enacts a signal instance of the translation of un-owned land into property. The novel thus not only features the dreamscapes of mercantilist and colonialist desires, but landscapes which obey the logic of property relations that were negotiated in English legal practice over the course of the century.

Crusoe's embodiment of commercial energy, which is restive, roving, adventuring, and profit-taking, with the principles of land ownership, which is more stable, and defined by rights of possession confirmed in husbandry, allows Defoe to finesse (though not entirely, for Crusoe remains a merchant-adventurer at heart) the contemporary tension between the commercial and landed interest in England, a tension that defined not only different forms of wealth, but also different models of personhood. The transitions Crusoe makes between trading (including in slaves), plantation farming, and settling the island, suggest larger circuits of economic exchange important to British prosperity. His fantasies of a manorial estate in England link the volatile prospects of trade with the older, domestic form of social status and power, and even as he does not finally retire to an estate (as many successful traders did), his career suggests that these worlds are not incompatible. To that extent, Defoe's novel can be read as working in tandem with the efforts made in Whig periodicals to suggest that the dichotomy between the landed and the moneyed was, as Lawrence Klein puts it, 'a source of value in the civil order, not of disruption' (Klein 1995: 223–4).

This reading of *Crusoe*, and this chapter more generally, has focused on stories of colonial encounters and their rendition of race and slavery in the extended Caribbean. The anxieties, fantasies, and desires generated in the intra-European struggles over plantation colonies and favorable trading practices swirl into and around definitions of the would-be imperial subject, whether merchant or planter, slave trader or slave owner. In these tales, English subjectivity in the Caribbean is defined against not only Dutch competitors or Spanish Catholics but also, crucially, in their transactions with natives of the islands or of the Americas and with African slaves. Their experiences are novel enough to challenge existent political protocols and ethical values but also to force shifts in modes of seeing and telling the world. We touched upon innovations in literary technique like Behn's ethnographic observations and first-person narrative, before analysing at length Steele's socio-cultural domestication of tales of interracial romance and exploitation and Defoe's exploration of providential and material concerns precipitated within the high-risk worlds of Atlantic plantation and slavery. Crusoe's triumphs, or rather, his tribulations leading to and punctuating his successes, become a template for the history to be made by adventuring Englishmen or Britons.[23] Indeed, as Martin Green argues, after *Crusoe* 'adventure tales' become 'the energising myth of English imperialism (Green 1980: 3).[24] But they are also, in terms of literary prestige, somewhat sidelined, as a different kind of novel, more insular, more concerned with the nuances of class and gender relations within England, more precise in its delineation of psychological interiority and 'character,' is elevated to the status of the novel proper.[25]

Major mid-century novels like Samuel Richardson's *Pamela* (1740) and *Clarissa* (1748) and Henry Fielding's *Joseph Andrews* (1742) and *Tom Jones* (1749) turn away from the direct exploration of racial difference in overseas contexts and towards a more minute dissection of cultural, regional, and familial patterns of behavior at home. The other more expansive, more exploratory tradition – both thematically and formally – continues as the 'oriental tale' or the 'gothic' or 'spy fiction,' which Aravamudan prefers to call the 'surveillance chronicle,' but we are only now recovering those histories, or rather, we are only now reading them as repositories of an international, inter-cultural, inter-racial, colonial imagination that is the free-wheeling counterweight to the provincial specificities of the domestic novel in Britain (Aravamudan 2005: 50).[26] However, it is worth remembering that even if the contrast between black and white, or Briton and non-Briton, becomes less central to novelistic consideration, novels continue to play a crucial role in defining race, that is, in defining whiteness in Britain. As Roxanne Wheeler argues in her examination of the 'racial work of the character sketch in novels,' the British novel racializes

> Britons as surely as natural history did. In its overall effects, the novel tends to advertise and ossify a desirable set of androgynous European features, which are, however, attached to moral variety . . . Overall, the novel's plots and characters tend to illustrate a variety of ranks and behaviors that were the very definition of a liberal, commercial society. (Wheeler 2005: 437)

Wheeler's observations are pertinent reminders of the nationalist cultural and racial work of the novel as it defines 'a variety of ranks and behaviors' within the borders of the nation. To these tasks we might add the work also of regionalist specification, as is pointed out by an earlier critic and novelist of provincial variety, Walter Scott, whose words on Fielding, who he describes as a 'painter of national manners' (by which Scott means English manners), will close this chapter:

> Of all the works of imagination to which English genius has given origin the novels of the celebrated Henry Fielding are, perhaps, most decidedly and exclusively her own. They are not only altogether beyond the reach of translation, in the proper sense and spirit of the word, but we even question whether they can be fully understood, or relished to the highest extent, by such natives of Scotland and Ireland as are not habitually acquainted with the characters and manners of Old England. Parson Adams, Towwouse, Partridge, above all, Squire Western, are personages as peculiar to England as they are unknown to other countries. Nay, the actors whose character is of a more general cast, as Allworthy, Mrs Miller, Tom Jones himself, and almost all the subordinate agents in the narrative, have the same cast of nationality, which adds not a little to the verisimilitude of the tale. The persons of the story live in England, travel in England, quarrel and fight in England; and scarce an incident occurs without its being marked by something which could not well have happened in any other country. (Scott 1825: 1. 1–2)[27]

Notes

1. Margaret Anne Doody's is a welcome reminder of the vast swathes of cultural history and geography at play in the formal and thematic inheritance of the modern novel, including the novel in English. Doody suggests that this trans-national, poly-cultural, history was, in late seventeenth- and eighteenth-century France and England, 'bound to cause unease in members of a newly emerging structure of power that was developing a social and intellectual culture sympa-thetic to the aims not only of a new capitalism but also of a new domination of the world through science and conquest' (Doody 1998: 262). As a result, the (realist) novel is 'localized, whether in the capital or the provinces, it is nation-ally in-turned. It does not take kindly to foreignness, either for excursion or for importation' (292).

2. Hunter does, however, state that 'Travel literature provides a . . . kind of macrocontext, and some of the novels' outreach to larger issues – especially those involving far-off places, anthropological data, sea lore, and the accrual of knowledge through the experience of physical movement though space – was eased by the broad cultural consciousness of travel books of many kinds' (Hunter 1990: 352).

3. The broader eighteenth-century intellectual context within which the novel functions is stated pithily in the 'Introduction' to *The Enlightenment and its Shadows*:

   > Enlightenment writers themselves were not great travellers . . . But they were voracious readers. Their footnotes are packed with references to the travel writers of the day . . . They also sent their fictional heroes around the world, some – like Robinson Crusoe and Candide – travelling within the realms of the known world, others – like Gulliver – exploring the edges of that world as a way of dramatizing the crucial questions of the age concerning the nature of human nature. (Hulme and Jordanova 1990: 8)

4. The geographical spread and historiographical ambition of contemporary historical narrative is enacted in the title page of Penelope Aubin's translation of Pétis de la Croix's *The History of Genghizcan the Great, First Emperor of the Antient Moguls and Tartars; in Four Books: Containing His Life, Advancement and Conquests; with a short History of his Successors to the present Time; the Manners, Customs and Laws of the Antient Moguls and Tartars; and the Geography of the vast Countries of Mongolistan, Turquestan, Capschac, Yugurestan, and the Eastern and Western Tartary. Collected from several Oriental Authors, and European Travellers; whose Names, with an Abridgement of their Lives, are added to this Book* (London: 1722). Perhaps even more interesting than the account of Genghis Khan and his successors is the 'scholarly apparatus' at the end, which lists earlier texts in Turkish, Arabic, Hebrew, Persian, and Greek, Latin, Portuguese, French, Italian, but under two separate headings: 'An Abridgement of the Lives of the Authors, out of whose Works the History of *Genghizcan* has been collected' and 'The Names of the *European* Authors and Travellers, who are made use of to prove the Truth of the Facts related in the History of *Genghizcan*.' Non-European texts provide the archive whose truth-claims are vetted by European enquiry – this juxtaposition looks forward to the power, and the limits, of colonial scholarship and historical enquiry.

5. Aubin's captivity narratives are fictional elaborations on a well-known theme; see the stories collected in Vitkus 2003. Joe Snader shows that the British cap-tivity tradition (both by captives and in fiction) 'worked to define non-Western

peoples as by nature given to despotism and slavery, while the captive's struggle to escape often defined an inborn liberty within the British people.' This genre also became an important source of (often titillating) ethnographic lore (Snader 2000: 5). Snader's systematic analysis of captivity narratives (including those by Aubin) is well worth consulting.

6. Another instance of inter-genre overlaps – between Ned Ward's popular travelogue *Trip to Jamaica* (1698) and W[illiam]. P[itts].'s novel, *The Jamaica Lady or The Life of Bavia* (1720) – is traced in MacBurney 1963: xx.

7. For subsequent versions, see Felsenstein 1999. For a powerful reading of these tales vis-à-vis Caribbean colonial politics and the extirpation of Carib populations, see Hulme 1986: 224–63.

8. Smith points out that Steele's 'interest in Barbados was more than literary, for he had inherited, in 1706 . . . a plantation there, worth £850 per annum' (Addison et al. 1945: 1. 523).

9. Ligon's description of Yariko's nakedness focuses on her skin colour, breasts and nipples and reminds us of the voyeuristic delight of such narratives (the unclothed white female body exposed to the male gaze is of course a staple of early modern European art, but colonial locations yield only non-white women's bodies, most often as an embodiment of the vulnerability and desirability of the land itself) (Ligon 1673: 54–5). Steele's use of Ligon's tale is one more instance of the myriad ways in which travel narratives informed English creativity and debates about socio-cultural and moral issues.

10. On a more speculative note, we might ask why Arietta tells Yariko's story, rather than the far more common stories of English women wronged by men? One answer might be that Yariko's colonial location does not matter, and her foreignness is an incidental counterpart to that of the Latin satirist Petronius, whose cultural power Arietta rebuts. A more convincing answer might be that Yariko's tragedy condenses dual contemporary burdens, those of racist exploitation and misogyny, and thus provides a greater affective counterweight than a simpler story of gender exploitation.

11. The quoted phrases are analytical rubrics that Hunter believes useful for the study of early English novels (Hunter 1990: 23–4).

12. Robert Mayer argues that Defoe's narratives were, for contemporary readers, 'situated within the discourse of history.' Accounts of voyages by William Dampier (1697), Edward Cooke (1712) and Woodes Rogers (1712) were precursory instances of the adventures of mariners and *Crusoe*, Mayer writes, was 'assimilated to this type of historical writing' (Mayer 1997: 182–4).

13. To take two well known examples that were of national significance: Elizabeth I retired England's foreign debt with the money from Francis Drake's privateering and invested £42,000 in the Levant Company, whose profits allowed her to help fund the East India Company. As John Maynard Keynes puts it, 'the booty brought back by Drake in the *Golden Hind* may fairly be considered the fountain and origin of British Foreign Investment' (Keynes 1950: 1. 156–7). In 1687, William Phips salvaged treasure from the sunken Spanish ship *Concepción* off Hispaniola; his backers saw returns of 10,000 per cent on their investment. Defoe characterized Phip's voyage as quixotic and 'a Lottery,' but one whose success exemplified the money to be made from such projects (Defoe 1697: 16–18).

14. Nabil Matar reminds us that in the sixteenth and seventeenth centuries 'thousands of English, Scottish, Welsh, and Irish men and women interacted directly with the North Africans of the Barbary States as sailors, traders, soldiers, craftsmen, and artisans who either went to North Africa in search of work and opportunity or were seized by privateers and subsequently settled there,' often

after converting to Islam. Some were ransomed from captivity, and others (like Crusoe) escaped. Money for ransoms was occasionally raised in churches and public houses, and sermons and petitions circulated captivity tales across Britain (Vitkus 2003: 1–6).

15. Defoe draws upon a large number of narratives of Barbary captivity and of island castaways in his account of Crusoe (Adams 1983: 124–31). It is notable, however, that Defoe offers few details about Crusoe's captivity or his captors and thus sidesteps the content typical of recent narratives such as Joseph Pitts's *A True and Faithful Account of the Religion and Manners of the Mohammetans, with an Account of the Author's Being Taken Captive* (1704).

16. Ian Watt notes 'Crusoe's book-keeping conscience' as an 'embodiment of economic individualism,' but does not trace any connections between this historic individualism and early modern colonial and mercantile traffic. Similarly, Watt's compelling argument that 'Crusoe's "original sin" is really the dynamic tendency of capitalism itself, whose aim is never merely to maintain the *status quo*, but to transform it incessantly' (Watt 1957: 63, 65) fails to recognize that the most egregious instances of such transformative energies were manifested in European actions in the contact zones of trans-Atlantic colonialism and trade. In this, Watt is a signal instance of brilliant historicist and materialist literary criticism that pays little attention to the enabling overlaps between European colonialism and early modern capitalism.

17. Hulme points out that both 'barbecue' and 'canoe' are 'Carib (or strictly speaking, Island Arawak) words' and technologies (Hulme 1986: 210–11). When Crusoe makes a mortar and pestle, he fashions the former 'as the *Indians* in *Brasil* make their *Canoes*' (Defoe 1972: 122). When he builds a sailing canoe with Friday he consults him about the best wood to use (1972: 227). He does not acknowledge any other transfer of non-European techniques or knowledge.

18. Lest Crusoe's forensics be thought of as inaccurate, some years later he sees a group of naked Caribs sitting around a fire and then dancing (another trope of Indian-ness in early modern accounts of the Americas). After they paddle away, he finds human remains from their 'Merriment and Sport' (1972: 183). Critics have noted that accusations of cannibalism in early modern European accounts of non-European peoples are often the basis of racist religio-cultural distinctions, particularly those used to justify colonial domination (Barker, Hulme, and Iversen 1998).

19. Some years later, Crusoe makes his way to the wreck of a Spanish ship off his island and observes evidence of 'a great Treasure' that he is not able to recover. This ship functions as a reminder, once again, of the perils, but also of the potential profits, of the traffic between the Americas, the Caribbean, and Europe (1972: 192). Also worth noting is Crusoe's belief that Peruvian Indians had little use for gold before the Spanish arrived (1972: 195).

20. Crusoe's formulation is of course the daydream of the patriarchal colonialist, in which the perfect native subject exudes cheerful servitude, filial piety, and absolute loyalty. And yet Friday's devotion is more fearful than Crusoe suggests, for a short while later, when Crusoe discharges his gun at a kid goat, Friday misunderstands, falls to his knees in terror and begs Crusoe not to kill him (1972: 211). Without any trace of irony, Crusoe tells us that Friday 'would have worshipp'd me and my Gun' and that Friday spent days refusing to touch the gun, but spoke to it at length, asking it not to kill him. Friday's fear of, and apotheosis of, the gun turns out to be the necessary obverse of Crusoe's lordly benevolence.

21. Indeed national rivalries weigh heavy in Crusoe's calculations as he discusses the future with the Spaniard, since he fears that if he helps the Spaniards and Portuguese amongst Friday's people build a ship and sail away, they might, once

in Spanish territories in the Caribbean, imprison him and hand him over to the Inquisition.

22. In 1803, Sir John Sinclair, President of the Board of Agriculture, wrote, 'let us not be satisfied with the liberation of Egypt, or the subjugation of Malta, but let us subdue Finchley Common; let us conquer Hounslow Heath, let us compel Epping Forest to submit to the yoke of improvement' (quoted in Turner 1980: 88). Sinclair's rhapsody is one more instance of the process in which, in the eighteenth century, terms and conceptions derived from colonial practices came to inform discussions of domestic policies.

   McLeod shows how Defoe's prescription for land development in Scotland in Defoe's *A Tour Through the Whole Island of Great Britain* (1724–6) 'neatly summarizes the policy and ideologies of mercantilism and conquest' (McLeod 1999: 212; see 206–15).

23. Robert Markley argues that the two sequels to Crusoe's adventures, *The Farther Adventures of Robinson Crusoe* (1719) and the *Serious Reflections* (1720), repudiate the model of European colonialism signified by the settling of Crusoe's fictional island. Instead, they hope for trading success in the Far East and the South Seas, but turn increasingly xenophobic as they recognize that Chinese and Japanese trading networks and cultures are not as penetrable as other networks in the Spice Islands (or the Atlantic). Worse, Crusoe discovers the 'irrelevance of western conceptions of identity and theology in a sinocentric world,' which leads him to 'fervid, nearly hysterical assertions of European – specifically British and Protestant – superiority to Asian cultures' (Markley 2005: 26–9). For Bruce McLeod, however, the 'sequels do not represent a progression in Defoe's thinking, from supporting colonialism in *Crusoe* to a commercial policy. Rather the sum of the three books is a realistic portrayal of Britain's spheres of action in the world as well as a marketing ploy to cover those worlds' (McLeod 1999: 259, n. 15). Hans Turley argues that the *Crusoe* trilogy should be read as 'a complex meditation on early eighteenth-century attitudes towards ethnocentrism and ethnocide and their relation toward imperialism' that draw upon 'a belief in the superiority of Christianity' as a 'justification for the subjugation and colonization of non-western societies' (Turley 2004: 182).

24. Green believes that students in post-imperial Britain need to study these stories in order to understand the cultures of colonialism and empire that shape their inheritance (or indeed the cultural histories of English-speaking peoples elsewhere).

25. For a suggestive discussion of the critical process in which the multinational origins of the novel are rewritten as 'an English story,' as part of a 'national literary history – where the people, the race, and the national culture become subject and object, heroic agent and telos of their own autoproduction;' see Warner 1998: 26–44.

26. Aravamudan suggests that 'even though there are certainly national realist strains that claim pre-eminence by mid-century and after, these are deified at the expense of counter-currents that still pull away from the dominant 'posited essence' of realism – whether these be the later oriental satire, adventure tale, or gothic romance' (Aravamudan 2005: 66).

27. Robert Crawford also notes the Englishness of novels like *Tom Jones*, *Clarissa*, and *Tristram Shandy*, and remarks that the new Britain or Britishness was 'not a subject that . . . particularly impinged on English authors' (Crawford 1992: 46). As we will see in the next chapter, a Scottish novelist like Tobias Smollett took these concerns to heart.

Chapter 3

'Imaginative Writing, Intellectual History, and the Horizons of British Literary Culture'

My discussion here begins with a summary of the role played by writing and publishing in the making of several features of eighteenth-century British society: the public sphere, consumer society, scientific and technological development, and the military, bureaucratic, and financial infrastructure of the modernizing state and of civil society. My analysis will suggest that imaginative writing, from the *Spectator* papers to a novel like Smollett's *Roderick Random* (1748), made available to readers a sense of the *international* commercial and cultural dynamism of London as well as the new circuits of travel and adventure that link Scotland to London to the Caribbean to Europe. Addison and Steele's essays and Smollett's novel (while in most ways not companion pieces) contain a vital sense of the *novelty* of the world enabled by overseas trade and colonization, and the cast of characters and experiences they put on display bring home to Britain the larger international circuit which increasingly defines both its domestic and its overseas priorities.

My choice of Smollett allows me to include a discussion of the philosophical and conceptual models of human social organization and historical development advanced by eighteenth-century English philosophers and the Scottish Enlightenment theorists of human collectivities and civilizational hierarchies. This discussion, as that of Adam Smith writing on the making of a global 'free trade' economy, will emphasize the overlaps between travel narratives, ethnography, and philosophy in the making of imperialist (and indeed anti-imperialist) conceptions of human difference, conceptions that are both developed in, and contested by, literary texts. While this novel is set overseas, my discussion of Addison's and Steele's *Spectator* papers (1711–14) charts, in a more 'domestic' vein, the perceptible impact of overseas activity on daily life in Britain. Rather than see the Spectator as a Londoner concerned only with the fabric of social difference in London, or Britain, I will follow the work of recent critics to show that key ideas and energies that motivate the Spectator derive from social transformations attendant upon the rise of British colonial and commercial power.

Of the many social and cultural changes that were much debated in the eighteenth century, perhaps the most fervid condemnation was reserved for the consumption of newly visible (and increasingly more affordable) consumer goods. Writers attacked not only the conspicuous consumption and vanity of the rich, who sported on their bodies and arranged in their homes sumptuous – and more often than not, imported – luxuries, but they also worried that the taste for consumables like sugar, tobacco, and linen had infected the lower classes.[1] As goods hitherto considered luxuries were converted into seeming necessities, critics feared the unhealthy demand made on the nation's balance of payments, since most of these consumables were produced elsewhere. Thus, critiques of consumption were not simply exercises in Christian morality, a condemnation of personal choices and ethics, but also featured a more secular, politico-economic vocabulary, which linked patterns of consumption to changes in domestic relations and national mercantile and foreign policies. Attitudes to the consumer society emerging in London and more generally in urban England, as well as in urban Ireland and Scotland, could thus express enthusiasm for, or anger about, broader historical change. Several terms that derived their force from the contemporary expansion of commodity culture – consumption, circulation, luxury – became important to debates about the progress of Britain as a nation and an empire.[2] Printed books, pamphlets, and papers played an important role here, for their content as for their form. They were both the medium for such debates, and also spectacular instances of commodities made more affordable by improvements in production techniques. When 'moralists' attacked the pernicious effects of reading, especially of novels, on women and servants, they spoke as one with their compatriots who bemoaned the decline in moral standards and social proprieties that resulted from the circulation of fashionable commodities more generally.

Much more than fashion was at stake – historians today are clear that this 'commercialization of society' went beyond 'the world of advertising and selling, beyond the world of fashion and credit.' It can be traced in 'the political world of eighteenth-century England, into the commercialization of leisure, and of childhood, and into the world of invention and creation, where unabashed by any sense of the plenitude of Nature men deliberately sought to create new and improved species and exciting novelties with which to delight the eye, to exhibit one's taste and to assert one's wealth' (McKendrick, Brewer, and Plumb 1983: 2). The creative thirst for novelty was sharpened by the quickened stream of chinoiserie, textiles, spices, dried fruits, sugar, tobacco, rum, and other goods that flowed into Britain in the seventeenth century and after, the bulk brought home by British merchants on British shipping.[3] English merchandizing benefited, of course, as did the shipbuilding and outfitting industries, as an armed navy expanded. The enlargement of trade also resulted in the creation of a domestic network of wholesalers and retailers, linked now to the great world beyond the oceans by the consumer economy they enabled. Of particular interest to us is the fact that news, communicated regularly in newspapers and periodicals, became a consequential habit for rural shopkeepers, who understood that wars and foreign policy had a bearing on imports and exports, and on 'business confidence and credit' in general (Brewer 1983: 215–16).

A focus on the consumption of imported goods, and the social changes that were seen to follow from their increased circulation, allows us to think about the ways in which people experienced the over-lapping energies of capitalist and colonialist expansion. The finance, manufacturing, and marketing infrastructure of pre-industrial British capitalism was virtually the same as that of colonial and overseas com-merce. Certainly the rapid socio-economic transformation of Britain that economists have labeled capitalism was sparked off and intensified by trade to the Spice Islands, Asia, and in the Mediterranean, and even more so by colonial and plantation settlements in the Caribbean and North America, including the trade in slaves, sugar and rum, tobacco, and manufactured goods across the Atlantic. 'Traditional' agriculture and animal husbandry continued to be the largest share of the national economy, but agricultural, and particularly horticultural, practices themselves had been greatly altered by imports (as Addison will tell us below). Also, significant rural industries like sheep rearing and the wool trade came under pressure from imports of cotton cloth or were tied increasingly to export markets in North America and elsewhere. Further, men who made large fortunes in the colonies or in colonial trade often bought estates once they returned, and these landowners were envied, ridiculed, and blamed for a series of ills from a lack of social graces, to an ignorance about age-old relations between lords of the manor and their tenants, to the dispossession of landless rural labor consequent to the enclosure of waste and commons land (as in Oliver Goldsmith's poem *The Deserted Village*). Accompanying these develop-ments was the steady movement of bodies, both forced and voluntary – from the provinces to the colonies and to London, from the countryside to the towns and cities (and into the navy and the military), and back from the theaters of war and conquest to villages and cities. For the many who did not leave home, this traffic was a continual reminder of the extraordinary compulsions of overseas trade and settlement, and of military action, in the making of Great Britain.

The Spectator, Print Culture, and the Circulation of International Value

The Spectator, and eighteenth-century periodicals more generally, are vital sources for any understanding of the transformation of daily life in Britain, particularly of the urban middle and upper classes. These papers commented not only upon topical issues ranging from fashion to consumer behavior (a staple of the popular press then as now), but also on all manner of geopolitical and ethnographic issues, as well as on the philosophical and aesthetic discussions that accompanied the rise of Britain to commercial and colonial power. The periodical press was itself energized by these developments, and its modes of production and circulation are models of the innovative entrepreneurial spirit that was seen – for good and for bad – as central to the manufacturing and merchandizing of other commodities. The press created its own markets and readership, and it did so by entertaining and educating, and by generating the sense that trading and colonization had so accelerated changes in English and British self-conception and behavior that trustworthy guides were needed to arbitrate class and gender relations (including ideas of sexuality); to define more supple and accommodating links between country and city living; and to allow the Briton to become a citizen of the world being trafficked by its merchants, settled by its colonists, and catalogued by its travelers and naturalists.[4]

Periodicals were also quick to recognize that, as Kathryn Shevelow, puts it, 'women were, to a degree unprecedented in Western Europe, becoming visible as readers and writers,' though this extension did not lead to more egalitarian conceptions of gender difference.[5] Indeed, this visibility resulted from the examination, in many of these papers, of consumer behavior, which featured women as the agents – and exemplary victims – of conspicuous consumption. Such moral condemnation came easily to those commentators regretful about the expansion of the national economy by colonization and trade, for they feared the net loss of material wealth from Britain, gold and silver sailing away in order to finance the appetite for imported commodities. Land ownership, the traditional basis of patriarchal standing and authority, also seemed threatened as a social norm by spectacular competitive fortunes made by city merchants and financiers.[6] Nowhere were these shifts more visible than in London, for it took the lead in developing 'consumer-oriented industries that relied . . . heavily on wealth derived ultimately from overseas trade and government expenditure, and no other town evolved such refined gradations of status as were found among London's service class' (Cain and Hopkins 2002: 69).[7] The periodical press played an enormous role in delineating and attempting to regulate these 'refined gradations of status.' Codes of gentlemanliness and femininity, of good husbandry and conservation, of civic being and kinship relations, were redefined; as was their obverse, most instrumentally in the figure of the uncaring, vain, avaricious woman (a second best was the effete, parasitic, non-productive fop), and more generally in benign and avuncular addresses to 'the Woman of Quality' or 'the fair Sex.'[8]

Periodical literature also performed much other cultural work: since the modern forms of intellectual and cultural specialization, each with its own media and modes of publicity, were not in place, generalist discussions were the order of the day. Discussions ranged from politics and ethics to philosophy and aesthetics, and took as their subject civic being in all its manifestations; as Jonathan Kramnik has argued, 'Criticism then was still a public affair, one not yet confined to the seminar room or the learned essay. Whether the subject was *Paradise Lost* or the waters at Bath, critics imagined themselves in dialogue with the whole of the reading public, and the public imagined itself in a struggle with political power' (Kramnik 1998: 238).[9] This last observation is important, because periodicals were seen as civic institutions within which the rights and obligations of citizenship could be articulated in a manner different from, and supposedly less partisan and self-serving than, those legislated by functionaries of the state or demanded by self-interested financial or political bodies.[10] Some historians have traced in this development the making of the 'public sphere,' an ideal of participative democracy functioning outside of the British parliamentary process (Habermas 1989). In this public sphere, the older aristocratic credentials of leadership were interrogated and supplanted by bourgeois codes of productivity and conduct more suited to contemporary overseas enterprise.

In the discussion of *The Spectator* that follows, we will see how its world is shaped by English expansionism, and we will connect the gentlemanly ideals and style it espouses to both commercial culture and empire. In *Spectator* no. 2 (2 March 1711), Sir Andrew Freeport, a 'Merchant of great Eminence in the City of *London*,' (and as close to a hero as there can be in this periodical) is dissociated from armed colonization:

His Notions of Trade are noble and generous, and . . . he calls the Sea the *British Common*. He is acquainted with Commerce in all its Parts, and will tell you that it is a stupid and barbarous Way to extend Dominion by Arms; for true Power is to be got by Arts and Industry . . . He has made his fortunes himself. . . . [and] there is not a Point in the Compass but blows home a Ship in which he is an Owner.

Addison's essay on the Royal Exchange (no. 69, 19 May 1711) continues in this vein: commerce, the Spectator says, makes 'this Metropolis a kind of *Emporium* for the whole Earth.' The Spectator is moved to tears by the efforts of merchants, their enhancing of their 'own private Fortunes, and at the same time promoting the Publick Stock; or in other Words, raising Estates for their own Families, by bringing into their Country whatever is wanting, and carrying out of it whatever is superfluous.' The Spectator states a mercantilist commonplace when he suggests that Nature (others thanked divine power) had so arranged the globe that no country had a monopoly on necessities or luxury goods, which meant that the circulation of commodities is natural and divinely ordained. Thus, he says, there

> are not more useful Members in a Commonwealth than Merchants. They knit Mankind together in a mutual Intercourse of good Offices, distribute the Gifts of Nature, find Work for the Poor, add Wealth to the Rich, and Magnificence to the Great. Our *English* Merchant converts the Tin of his own Country into Gold, and exchanges his Wooll for Rubies.

This vision of *doux commerce* must be contextualized; armed conflict was always an important business strategy for English joint-stock merchant companies like the East India Company (EIC). C. A. Bayly has shown that the EIC had, from the mid-seventeenth century, 'the capacity, will and legal right to wage war and had an intermittent interest in territorial power and revenue.' A 'flexible structure of military conquest – and a set of arguments to support it – was already in place early in its history, even if the juggernaut was not loosed at full tilt until the mid-eighteenth century' (Bayly 1994: 325). After being granted a royal charter in 1660, the Royal African Company (then known as the 'Company of Royal Adventurers Trading to Africa') established its trade in slaves on the west coast of Africa and across the Atlantic via its military power. The South Sea Company's armed ships ensured its share of the slave trade. Virtually no English ocean-going merchantmen were unarmed; from Drake and Raleigh onwards, overseas adventuring required skills in warfare as well as in accounting and bargaining. European rivalries continually intensified into skirmishes and long drawn-out ocean engagements, and, as we have noted earlier, adventuring merchants secured profits by raiding each other's goods as well as from trading. It is safe to say then that the non-bellicose forms of trade that Freeport stands for did not exist. He may prefer that English energies swell trade and not colonies ('Dominium'), but the former was as much a product of 'barbarous . . . Arms' as it was of 'Arts and Industry.' Indeed, the Spectator's account of peaceful British commerce linking the trading regions of the globe is an ideological fiction that denies the record of overseas violence and expropriation.

The Spectator's and Sir Andrew Freeport's gentlemanly disregard for the violent realities of overseas trade are crucial both to their discussions of the beneficial effects of imports (and re-exports) on the English economy and to their pride in the development of civic and social institutions in London. Their subject matter is often personal and collective codes of behavior, and *politesse* in every sense forbids the acknowledgement of brutality. Thus, the conduct and indeed the motivations of business overseas have to be refigured in order to make feasible the gentlemanly good sense and benign cosmopolitanism for which *The Spectator* is celebrated. Other tropes do parallel ideological work in enabling the characteristic rhetoric of disinterested authority: in a well-known instance (also in no. 69), the Spectator condenses the power of global traffic into this arresting image of a fashionable woman:

> The single Dress of a Woman of Quality is often the Product of an hundred Climates. The Muff and the Fan come together from the different Ends of the Earth. The Scarf is sent from the Torrid Zone, and the Tippet from beneath the Pole. The Brocade Petticoat rises out of the Mines of *Peru*, and the Diamond Necklace out of the Bowels of *Indostan*.

Feminist critics have pointed to myriad similar eighteenth-century representations of women consumers as the motivation behind the expansion of trade – accounts of their changeable desires slip easily into a condemnation of their vanity, even as their supposed avarice deflects attention from the ethics and actions of men in search of profits overseas (Brown 1993: 116).[11] What remains sacrosanct is the principle of benign English commerce, which enhances Arts and Industry, whether embodied in the personal philosophy and ethics of Sir Andrew Freeport or the Spectator's judicious meditations on English cultural values.

The Spectator's systematic concern with ethics, aesthetics, as well as with style (how to carry oneself in the world in a way appropriate to station and gender) should not be understood as trivial. Rather, as Paul Langford has argued, 'politeness' was understood to be 'a logical

consequence of commerce,' which encouraged those new to money
to spend it on acquiring status. Particular forms of consumption thus
became crucial to civic improvement. Langford is emphatic about all
that was at stake in English celebrations of the civilizing power of commerce: 'Commerce did not simply signify trade . . . [but] suggested a
definitive stage in the progress of mankind, as evidenced in the leadership
of western Europe, and the manifold social and cultural consequences
thereof' (Langford 1989: 2–4).[12] Commerce as the enabler of global
control is also commerce as the initiator and guarantor of civic proprieties; this is the continuum within which city and country ways are
discussed in *The Spectator*. In no. 69 the Spectator also details his historical sense of the transformation of British horticulture and everyday life
enabled by overseas traffic:

> If we consider our own Country in its natural Prospect, without any of
> the Benefits and Advantages of Commerce, what a barren uncomfortable
> Spot of Earth falls to our Share! Natural Historians tell us, that no Fruit
> grown originally among us, besides Hips and Haws, Acorns and Pig-Nutts,
> with other Delicacies of the like Nature; That our Climate of it self, and
> without the Assistances of Art, can make no further Advances towards a
> Plumb than to a Sloe, and carries an Apple to no greater a Perfection than
> a Crab: That our Melons, or Peaches, our Figs, our Apricots, and Cherries
> are Strangers among us, imported in different Ages, and naturalized in our
> *English* Gardens . . . Nor has Traffick more enriched our Vegetable World,
> than it has improved the whole Face of Nature among us. Our Ships are
> laden with the Harvest of every Climate: Our Tables are stored with Spices,
> and Oils, and Wines: Our Rooms are filled with Pyramids of *China*, and
> adorned with the Workmanship of *Japan*: Our Morning's-Draught comes
> to us from the remotest Corners of the Earth: We repair our Bodies by the
> Drugs of *America*, and repose ourselves under *Indian* Canopies. My Friend
> Sir ANDREW calls the Vineyards of *France* our Gardens; the Spice-Islands
> our Hot-Beds; the *Persians* our Silk-Weavers, and the *Chinese* our Potters.
> Nature indeed furnishes us with the bare Necessaries of Life, but Traffick
> gives us a great Variety of what is Useful, and at the same time supplies us
> with every thing that is Convenient and Ornamental.

'Trade,' the Spectator concludes, 'without enlarging the British Territories,
has given us a kind of additional Empire.'

Here, the Spectator muses over changes wrought by imports over a
long period, but there is no suppressing the excited contemporaneity
of his vision of the 'additional Empire.' The architecture of the Royal
Exchange, rebuilt after its destruction in the 1666 Great Fire, was
purposive and grand enough to indicate that it was a center of more
than commerce, and that is in fact how the Spectator sees it when he

describes it as the home of 'a great Council, in which all considerable Nations have their Representatives. Factors in the Trading World are what Ambassadors are in the Politick World.' He glories in its internationalism and the languages spoken there, and marvels that merchants negotiate 'like Princes for greater Sums of Mony than were formerly to be met with in the Royal Treasury!' The Spectator's Whiggish support for commercial projects is partly defensive in that his celebration of the cosmopolitanism and national importance of merchants rebuts reams of older and indeed contemporary denunciations of the self-centered cupidity of commercial men (particularly in stage caricatures). There is another reason, however, for the cultural confidence on display here: this periodical enacts not the ascendancy of merchants (Sir Andrew Freeport) and the decline of the prestige of landowners (Sir Roger de Coverley), but demonstrates their interdependence as leaders of the national economy and as exemplars of morality and polite behavior.[13]

For Addison and Steele, men as different as Sir Roger and Sir Andrew could meet in clubs and make common cause, and do so precisely by sharing information, debating ideas, and formulating policies. Clubs in the eighteenth century were often also business partnerships or associations. Booksellers for instance met in the Chapter Coffee House to finance their 'more ambitious publishing enterprises' (Brewer 1983: 223). Even when men gathered in coffee houses in more informal circumstances, they became participants in a modern clearing-house of ideas and information.[14] An idealized view of public assemblies like these embodies the Spectator's certainty about the socio-economic, ethical, and *cultural* value of the world enabled by international trade. Almost fifty coffee houses are named in these essays, and the opening essay lists several which support the Spectator's social and cultural aims: these are places 'of general Resort,' coffee houses such as *Will's*, *Child's*, *St James's*, the *Grecian*, the *Cocoa-Tree*, and *Jonathan's*. Each of these London coffee houses was patronized by different and often overlapping constituencies – politicians, authors and booksellers, the *beau monde*, professionals like lawyers and physicians, stockbrokers, clergymen. In the Spectator's celebratory view, their occasional partisan differences are of less consequence than the fact that they encourage the ideas and information – the public *conversation* – that improves collective and individual behavior.

Erin Mackie has emphasized the mutual reinforcement provided by coffee houses and the periodical press in helping to constitute a loosely-defined public sphere of upper-class and bourgeois ideas, fashion, and culture in this period (Mackie 1998: 14–32; and also Mackie 1997). The Spectator tells us that he goes to coffee houses (and elsewhere) to participate in various debates, and he calls attention to the periodicals and newspapers that also circulate through and enable these conversations. That was, after all, the role played by *The Spectator* itself as it remarked on various modes of class and gender being, while listing the socio-economic, cultural, intellectual, and ethical values specific to them. Without exaggerating the role played by the periodical in making a 'consensual' understanding of culture feasible (practitioners of print often have an inflated sense of their centrality), there is no question that printed texts, and the conversations they spawned in both public and domestic spaces, allowed increasing numbers of Britons to better realize their world and its many provincial, national and international determinants. Thus, even as we read *The Spectator* for its rich evocation of London and English life, we need to note the foundational importance, for Addison and Steele, of the international matrix of consumerism, trade and colonization that enabled the politeness and cultural advances that they celebrated (and indeed the abominations that they castigated) in their periodicals.[15]

These are not inferences we need to make; Addison and Steele spell them out for us, particularly in the remarkable *Spectator* no. 367 (1 May 1712). Here, the Spectator defines '*Material*' reasons why periodicals are beneficial to the nation: 'they consume a considerable quantity of our Paper Manufacture, employ our Artisans in Printing, and find Business for great Numbers of Indigent Persons.' People are employed in collecting waste materials for the manufacture of paper, in merchandizing waste materials, in the paper mills themselves, in the renting of lands on which the mills are located, all of which strengthens the nation, which was otherwise obliged to import paper from elsewhere. Once the paper reaches the presses, another circuit of work and employment is initiated; 'innumerable Artists' produce and others distribute papers, such that each time he writes 'a *Spectator*, I fancy my self providing Bread for a Multitude.' After the paper has been read, it is useful as kindling, for spice-wrapping, and for lining baking pans! The gentle irony that runs through these lists of producers and consumers does not muddy the understanding that prowess in fine printing is a national achievement: the 'politest Nations of *Europe*,' the Spectator comments, 'have endeavored to vie with one another for the Reputation of the finest Printing.' Further, printing and publishing add luster to and confirm the greatness of empire: 'The several Presses which are now in *England*, and the great Encouragement which has been given to Learning for some Years last past, has made our own Nation as glorious upon this Account, as for its late Triumphs and Conquests.' The proper comparative frame within which the expansion of print culture is to be celebrated is, not surprisingly, that of Britain's international 'Triumphs and Conquests.'

The Spectator's occasional reminders of the foundational importance of trade and conquest to British lives are in some ways not as rhetorically and ideologically consequential as the more throwaway remarks that flood these papers about places, peoples, and practices elsewhere. On occasion, the Englishness (or in some cases the 'whiteness') of physiological, psychological, political, and cultural characteristics is established via rapid comparisons with characteristics observed in, or imputed to, other people. Instances can be mounted, as when the Spectator discusses Cleanliness, which he recommends as a 'Mark of Politeness,' and exemplifies by remarking: 'The different Nations of the World are as much distinguished by their Cleanliness, as by their Arts and Sciences. The more any Country is Civilized, the more they consult this part of Politeness. We need but compare our Ideas of a Female *Hottentot* and an *English* Beauty, to be satisfied of the Truth of what hath been advanced' (no. 631, 10 December 1711). Such remarks that obviate the necessity for, rather than further, discussion are made in spite of the Spectator's disclaimer that he does not offer generalizations 'in derogation of a whole People, having more than once found fault with those general Reflections which strike at Kingdoms or Common-Wealths in the Gross' (no. 435, 19 July 1712). In any case, the derogation of other cultures is hardly the Spectator's ambition (though it is occasionally the price of his celebrations of national achievement). His ambition is to be traced in the extraordinary web of historical and cultural references that is woven in *The Spectator*, with filaments that run backwards into Greek, Roman, early Christian, and Islamic texts and events and others that connect to contemporary travelogues, accounts of Indians in Atlantic contexts, of Asians and of Africans, of western European social mores and thought. The Spectator's assurance in his world, and the cultural reassurance he offered his readers and correspondents, comes from this conversational confidence in being able to credibly knit together the history and geography of known and little-known worlds, the whole centered around the English mores he recommends. In doing so he creates the 'common-sense' of educated Englishmen and women, and achieves a lasting cultural centrality.[16]

And not only for the English, because Addison's essays become staples of formal and informal education in language, writing, and good sense in Britain (and the colonies) more generally. Hugh Blair taught them as models of English style to his Scottish students at the University of Edinburgh in the 1760s and 1770s. [17] Adam Smith had already recommended such emulation in his Edinburgh Lectures on Rhetoric and Belles Lettres, given between 1748 and 1751. It is notable that Smith and Blair both proceed by *correcting* Addisonian style when necessary, that is, their pedagogy enacts the self-confidence of educated Scotsmen whose lessons will enable their students to learn from English writers in order to best mold *British* culture and life. Here too more is at stake than style alone (this is a set of ideas I will turn to later in this chapter). As Carey McIntosh argues, the search for linguistic politeness and refinement was central to the historical self-conception that underlay the Scottish development of the four-stage model of human or civilizational development (McIntosh 1998: 163–68). Smith and his brethren understood commercial society (which, it is worth reiterating, in England as in urban Scotland, was colonial in its origins and its contemporary orientation) to be the highest state of human development, and the Spectator's carriage and assurance exemplifies that certainty.[18] The Spectator is not a man who works for a living nor a traditional landlord; he is a friend of trade whose wonders he celebrates while he satirizes the vanity of foolish consumers; he follows with interest the Iroquois men who visit London and empathizes with the victims of the slave trade (while holding that slaves are in fact better off in English hands); he is no scholar, but his conversation is enlivened by his knowledge of classical Greek and Latin texts and history; he casts an ironic eye on English foibles while certain that English ways and character are superior to those of Europeans – in short, as the definitive gentleman of his time and place, he occupies the cultural center of Great Britain, and demands emulation.

The Languages of National Difference: Becoming Roderick Random

'a scholarly man, though a Scot'

Samuel Johnson on Tobias Smollett

In the wake of Culloden, as they walked in London with their swords drawn, Smollett (1721–71) cautioned Alexander Carlyle to silence, for fear that their accents would betray their Scottish origins and expose them to the anger of the mob (Carlyle 1860: 190–1). Smollett's fears, exacerbated on this occasion by the Jacobite rebellion of 1745, are part of a longer, if less immediately threatening, history of contentious Anglo-Scottish relations. After the Union of 1707, a steadily increasing number of Scotsmen moved south, and overseas, in the service of Great Britain. Economic and political compulsions at home worked hand-in-hand with the promise of opportunities elsewhere, and a steady movement of people resulted. Not all of this movement of people was one-way, and the commercial centers of the Lowlands, particularly the university towns of Edinburgh, Glasgow, and Aberdeen, benefited greatly from the circulation of personnel, ideas, and cultural practices. London gained even more as educated Scotsmen moved there to make livings as writers, surgeons, and teachers. As these professionals and the mercantile Lowland elites sought for themselves a constitutive role in the new imperial nation, they enabled profound shifts in ideas of Britishness. Of course, in doing so, they entered contentious cultural and ideological territory, for any more inclusive definition of Britishness demanded a re-figuring of both what it meant to be English, and what it might mean to be Scottish (or indeed to be provincial) in this new dispensation. As commentators have noted, Scottish philosophers, natural scientists, publishers, novelists, poets, and periodical writers played a disproportionate role in the intellectual life of eighteenth-century Great Britain. They formulated the terms of national debates about the relations between archaic and modernizing societies, offered innovative solutions to historiographical and sociological problems, and, while occasionally questioning the terms of commercial and imperial expansion, helped confirm the intellectual grounds for Britain's dominance in the world. But they always did so from an ex-centric point of view, even when their power in the world of print suggested far greater authority.

Thus, when Smollett, a twenty-four-year-old aspirant man of letters in London, walked its streets and spoke its language, he knew always his own difference, and guarded against its consequences. In this section, I will pay attention to Smollett's first novel, *Roderick Random* (1748), in order to underline some of these larger cultural paradoxes, in which the crafting of a new Scoto-British subject, a landed gentleman enthusiastically knowledgeable about commercial and civil society, involves a renegotiation of those English mores that both confirm gentility and corrupt its public and private manifestations.[19] The path to Great Britain lies via England here, and more particularly, via an English demi-monde ripe to corruption with fashion, opportunism, and hypocrisy. Their lives in London and Bath, but also on estates in the countryside, glitter with imported fashions, luxuries, and profits from the colonies, but are wilfully ignorant of the human costs – at home, on its fleets, in its plantations – of such consumption. As Roderick is tossed about in the oceans, and on land, his life and observations enable Smollett to provide a forceful, and in large sections, raw and unvarnished, view of all that is required *internationally* in the making of English commercial and colonial culture. No wonder then that his sense of urban luxury is of unmitigated social and moral corruption, of men whose only living is to be made from posturing and gaming, of women reduced to false pretences or prostitution, all living on the threshold of debtors' prison or worse. The margins between gentility and criminality are very narrow here, and those margins often hinge on profits to be made abroad, in warfare on the open seas, the capture of foreign treasures, or, finally, in the relatively secure 'adventure' that is the slave trade.[20]

The circumstances of Roderick's birth and his grandfather's vindictiveness do not allow him to stay in Scotland to achieve his destiny as a gentleman-landowner. The only path available is to travel into England, and via England, into the byways of Britain's European and trans-Atlantic engagements, in order to seek his fortune. In his travels, his most potent weapon is what Janet Sorensen calls his 'mastery of the linguistic standard,' which turns out to be far more important that any professional skill he might have as a surgeon (Sorensen 2000: 107).[21] Roderick is proud of his early competence in *belles lettres*, and this literary and linguistic training grants access to a higher echelon of English society than is enabled by his surgical training. The paths he takes, or is forced to take, are frequently taxing, and in detailing them Smollett paints a vivid picture of the human costs of naval service, warfare, overseas plantations and trade, before going on to show the ways in which this same violent infrastructure enables great profits. As Roderick claws his way back to gentility, or rather, waits for its inevitable (though constantly deferred) reassertion, he traverses an extraordinary range of English and British society and encounters what seems to be the entire gamut of professions precipitated by the growth of a diversified international commercial economy.[22] His many occupations, from ship's surgeon's mate to domestic servant on a country estate to mercenary soldier in Europe to urban fortune hunter to slave trader similarly expose him to the surface glitter and the miserable, bloody underbelly of an unforgiving imperial and mercantile society. At these moments, Smollett's novel insists that its readers recognize the price of the civil society of culture and refinement to which Roderick aspires.

In its mapping of regional and class differences in Britain, *Roderick Random* makes visible the individuation, and the tug of war, of specialist vocabularies and provincial idioms.[23] The ebullience of different regional and professional languages are contrasted with, and contained within, 'the imperial dialect of English' (to use Ian Duncan's phase), here performed by the narrator and by a few genteel others like Narcissa (Duncan 2004: 41). That is, while Roderick's own accent is Scottish, the narrative he produces is 'unaccented,' and standardized. The novel is very sensitive to the different class and gender affiliations and exclusions at work in the construction of English norms, but also makes clear that there is no 'authentic' and ethical Englishness already in place and available for Roderick's learning, or indeed for expansion into the hegemonic culture of Britain. In fact English ways are precisely suspect, and Roderick must learn to distance their corruptions and venery before he can return to his proper status in Scotland. He takes home an English wife who is untainted by the fashionable vices of the parasitical, non-working class, and their union indicates the promise of a properly British future. What sees him through his tribulations is not only his school-fellow Hugh Strap's fealty and his own luck in repeatedly finding kind sponsors, but also his bel-letristic education, which comprises a training in classical languages, a knowledge of the cultural import of classical literature, and an ability to perform the florid flourishes of sentimental expression. Most importantly perhaps, such knowledge is for Roderick (and others in their welcoming or skeptical response to him) a confirmation of class-being, and a cultural and psychological guarantee of his birth and education as a 'gentleman' even when he is reduced over and over again to dependency or servitude.

In the three years that Roderick spends at university in Scotland (where he is settled by his uncle Mr Bowling), he learns Greek, mathematics, 'moral and natural philosophy,' but, he tells us 'above all things, I valued myself on my taste in the *Belle Lettre*, and a talent for poetry, which had already produced some morceaus, that brought me a great deal of repu-tation' (Smollett 1999: 21).[24] He learns some practical skills when he is forced to take a position as apprentice to Mr Crab the apothecary, but this course of action is not one that suggests great future advantage. In general, for Roderick, as for other young Scotsmen (and indeed Britons) in his circumstances, advancement lies overseas, and it is entirely appro-priate that Crab encourages him to leave this position after two years in terms that link Roderick's fortunes to those of colonial competition:

> before I was of your age, I was broiling on the coast of Guinea. – Damme! what's to hinder you from profiting by the war, which will certainly be declared in a short time against Spain? – You may easily get on board of a king's ship in quality of a surgeon's mate, where you will certainly see a great deal of practice, and stand a good chance of getting prize money. (1999: 30)[25]

This war, the so-called War of Jenkins's Ear (1739–44), was designed to wrest Caribbean possessions from the Spanish and to consolidate British control of the trans-Atlantic triangular trade; it offers Roderick employ-ment but, more importantly, the possibility of a share in any treasures taken from the Spanish. While Roderick's itinerary is far more complicated and troubled than the course of action envisaged here, by the end of the novel his greatest success does in fact come from slave trading and trans-Atlantic merchant-adventuring (which, along with a plantation, is also the source of his long-lost father's great wealth).

Roderick leaves for Newcastle on the way to London, and enters the intersecting worlds of the English and of expatriate Scotsmen, one of whom, the barber Hugh Strap (once Roderick's schoolfellow), attaches himself to Roderick as a companion. Over time Strap becomes crucial to Roderick's economic well-being and self-approbation. Strap rescues Roderick from debt and shame, and his unselfish devotion confirms Roderick's sense of his own worth, even when there is no reason to believe that he possesses the personal traits and material wherewithal to be the gentleman he understands himself to be. In fact, Roderick's client-relation with the English aristocrats and gentlemen from whom he begs favors is reversed in the lachrymose and somewhat sadistically exploitative relation he has with Strap.[26] Thus, Roderick's seeming naiveté, which gets him into all kinds of trouble, is in fact the convenient innocence of someone who presumes that his destiny as a gentleman cannot be denied, and that it is acceptable for that reason alone to be condescending about, and to take advantage of, Strap's loyalty and earnings. That Roderick relies upon (while being ironic about) Strap's essentially feudal feelings for him makes his exploitative ways worse, not better. Roderick is, after all, a Scottish landlord in the making, and he assumes that the Scottish underclasses know their place. As he says of the tenants and peasants who welcome him and his father when they return to his grandfather's estate, which they have now purchased: 'As there is no part in the world, in which the peasants are more attached to their Lords, than in Scotland, we were almost devoured with affection.' The 'whole scene, though rude,' he says, 'was so affecting' (1999: 434). Roderick's travels teach him lessons germane not only to his place in English society, but also to his position in Scotland, and both are important to allow Roderick to overcome his provinciality and claim a rightful place in the *British* social hierarchies explored in the novel.

Roderick's Scottish triumph at the end of the novel, as well as his victory over the crude English squire Orson Topehall (Narcissa's bibulous brother), could not be predicted early in the novel. When Roderick and Strap enter London, they are the butt of anti-Scottish mockery, and their many humiliations are detailed in Chapter XIII. Their accent and clothes are laughed at, a coachman bespatters them with mud, a street wit calls Strap 'Sawney' and asks if he has 'oat-meal or brimstone' in his knapsack (a double hit at Scottish food and Presbyterian religiosity), they are given incorrect directions, and are finally rescued only when they meet a shopkeeper who is their countryman (1999: 63–4).[27] He is the first of the many Scotsmen they meet (a Naval examiner complains that 'you Scotchmen have overspread us of late as the locusts did Egypt' (1999: 86)). The Scottishness of these expatriates is constantly remarked upon, as in the case of the teacher of 'the Latin, French and Italian languages,' whose primary work though is the 'pronunciation of the English tongue,' in which he is so unsuccessful, Roderick tells us, that he was as unintelligible 'as if he had spoke in Arabick or Irish.' Roderick's comments notwithstanding, he himself needs to learn 'the pronunciation of the English-tongue,' without which, he is told, 'you will be unfit for business in this country' (1999: 96). This teacher in turn tells Roderick that his clothes might be acceptable in Scotland but in London is a 'masquerade' which makes him 'look like a cousin-german of Ouran Outang.' He also advises Roderick to crop off his red hair, another sign of his origins, and to wear a wig (1999: 66–8). After forty-eight hours in London, Strap moans about being 'jeered, reproached, buffeted, pissed upon, and at last stript of our money [Roderick has been cheated by a cardsharp]; and I suppose by and by we shall be stript of our skins.' Roderick, far from being contrite about his gullibility, rounds on Strap, only to have the latter, in distress, give him his purse, saying 'There's all I have in the world, take it, and I'll perhaps get more for you before that be done – if not, I'll beg for you, steal for you, go through the wide world with you, and starve with you.' Roderick tries to refuse, but finally accepts when Strap tells him that 'it was more reasonable and decent that he should depend upon me who was a gentleman, than that I should be controuled by him' (1999: 72–3).[28] A pattern is set here, and repeated throughout the narrative.

In what follows, Roderick's attempts to procure a position as mate to a ship's surgeon make him intimate with corrupt systems of patronage, but also bring him into contact with other men, who like him, have no prospects and are living off their wits, that is, by borrowing from or cheating others. The medical examiners who grant him his license at Surgeons' Hall are opinionated and argumentative, and their bookish ignorance is starkly contrasted with Roderick's later experience with the horrors of illness and injuries abroad ship. All he meets seem to be on the make, and his encounters become a satiric lens that reveals the uncaring bankruptcy at the heart of British naval institutions. Since Roderick's funds are limited, he gets nowhere, and is saved from distress by Strap, one of whose relatives finds him a job as an apothecary's assistant. Roderick's encounters with women too reveal rampant social and sexual hypocrisy (from which he is not immune, but which, as a man, he is happy to exploit).[29] He sleeps, under false pretences, with the apothecary's daughter, forges scandalous letters as if from the apothecary's wife to her lover, and, by degrees, begins to style himself 'a gentleman in reality.' He tires of Strap's acquaintance (becoming ashamed of his friendship with a journeyman barber), learns to dance, frequents plays, discourses at an alehouse, and courts an heiress who turns out to be a prostitute. In short, even as an apothecary's apprentice, he plays the gentleman; equally predictably perhaps, he finds himself in trouble: 'my good name was lost, my money gone, my friends were alienated, my body infected by a distemper contracted in the course of an amour' (1999: 114).

The ebbs and flows of Roderick's fortunes, indeed the sheer speed of his transitions from one 'profession' or location to another, is a testimonial to the energy that characterizes English society, and London in particular. Sections of the novel explore this world, and in particular the relations between people and things, people and commodities. In this world personhood is defined by possessions, or rather, if we keep in mind Strap's refusal of this world even when he has the money to cut a figure in it, *gentility* is the function of possessions. The novel emphasizes, often feelingly, hypocrisies of class and gender, and is one of many such contemporary critiques of commercial society (and thus bears affinities with Addison's portrayal of this world, as my earlier discussion might suggest). However, Smollett's lasting contribution, in this his first novel, lies elsewhere: Roderick and his like live in a world of fashion and showy consumption, whose glitter – whether at soirees, the theater, gaming halls, taverns, and coffee houses – reveals no trace of the labor, or the international economy, that enables these riches. Smollett connects these lives with those of sailors and merchants and planters, and shows in the difficulties of the latter the human price being paid at the margins of British commercial and colonial society (this exposé includes the reiteration of Strap's labor as the basis of Roderick's occasional gentlemanliness). The slave trade and slave plantations are taken for granted here, and while there is no extended account of them, their profitability fuels the dreams of aspiring Britons.[30] Along these lines, the central section of *Roderick Random* is an extended circuit away from England that stages the frenzied competitiveness and violence of trade and military relations between Britain, different European imperial states, and their possessions in the Caribbean and elsewhere. The ships, and the terrain that Roderick traverses, are littered with broken, wasted, and ill-treated bodies, and Roderick discovers that the class distinctions that separate him from them are, partly because of his provincial origins, shadowy.[31]

Roderick is pressganged into this world, which is a precipitous refusal of his gentility and presages the inhumanity of social relations on board ship. In one of the many coincidences in this novel, Roderick is rescued from his confinement by a sailor who is an acquaintance of Mr Bowling, and then by his surgeon friend Thomson, both of whom happen to be on board the *Thunder*. Thomson's intercession leads to Roderick's appointment as third mate to the surgeon, and Roderick begins his discovery of the hellish life on board. His visit to the chandler's shop takes him into the 'dismal gulph' below the deck, rank with the smell of putrid cheese and rancid butter, which is a foretaste of sights and smells to come (1999: 144). As Roderick views the ship's hospital, he is astonished that any sailor recovers there:

> Here I saw about fifty miserable distempered wretches, suspended in rows, so huddled upon one another, that no more than fourteen inches of space was allotted for each with his bed and bedding; and deprived of the light of the day, as well as of fresh air; breathing nothing but a noisome atmosphere of the morbid streams exhaling from the own excrements and diseased bodies, devoured with vermin hatched in the filth that surrounded them, and destitute of every convenience necessary for people in that helpless condition. (1999: 149)

The chapters that follow extend this nightmarish scenario by describing the impossible conditions under which the surgeon's mates treat the sailors. Roderick's attempt to maneuver between the sailors' hammocks causes him to overturn a container of the excrement that lies under them, and he, and they, are overwhelmed by the smell. (The ship's first mate Morgan, disgusted by Roderick's stink, links it to the putrid cheese served on board.) Roderick finds himself covered in maggots too, and shaves his head to protect against them. Thus ends his first day as a surgeon's mate.

The horrific conditions on board ship are enabled by a strict hierarchy of control. Thomson's description of the chain of command he deals with emphasizes distinctions: he tells Roderick that he knows the surgeon to be good natured, Mr Morgan somewhat choleric, 'the lieutenants I have no concern with; and, as for the captain, he is too much of a gentleman to know a surgeon's mate, even by sight' (1999: 144–5). By this token, Roderick too is invisible to the 'gentleman' in command of the ship, but his 'birth and talents,' in Thomson's recounting of them, allow Morgan to treat him kindly, as befits a 'shentleman in distress.' Morgan's Welshness is emphasized in his speech and in his temper, but also in his account of his descent from the 'famous Caractacus king of the Britons,' a genealogical claim that insists upon a historic authority and independence long marginalized by English political and cultural power (1999: 147). Provincial distinctions, prejudice and violence are close at hand in the little Britain that is the ship, and life on board is rife with aggression and insults. The midshipman Crampley slights Scotland to needle Roderick, which leads to a fight (Morgan expresses solidarity with Roderick on the grounds that 'in all likelihood, the ancient Scots and Britons were the same people' (1999: 156)). But above all, power is arbitrary and vindictively enforced, with the result that a change in the ship's surgeon leads to the overturning of all forms of medical protocol and practice, and, when Morgan protests, to a threat by the new Irish surgeon Mr Mackshane to have Morgan 'pinioned to the deck.'[32]

Oakhum has, quite literally, the power of life and death over the sailors, and in collaboration with Mackshane, has all the sixty-odd patients brought to the quarter-deck for examination, since he believes that they are not sick. He declares them to be malingerers, and condemns them to cures ranging from whipping to exposure. Many die in short order, reducing their numbers to 'less than a dozen; and the authors of this reduction,' Roderick tells us, 'were applauding themselves for the service they had done to their king and country' rather than recognizing the 'inhumanity and ignorance' with which they 'so wantonly sacrificed the lives of their fellow-creatures' (1999: 159). The grotesque features of this scene are magnified in others to come, in which the numbers of the ill and the wounded multiply during the voyage to the West Indies and the expedition to Carthagena.[33] Roderick sees naval battle for the first time when Captain Oakhum's nationalist preening is mirrored by that of the commander of a French man-of-war they encounter and a sea fight results for no reason other than injured vanity. Ironically, Roderick is in shackles on the deck of the *Thunder* (Mackshane has accused him of being a spy), a vantage point that encourages his helpless sense of the destructive absurdity of such inter-national aggression. I will not go into the details of the violence that unfolds around Roderick, but his descriptions of blood and gore, of mangled bodies and spilled brains, make no bones about the forms or intensity of suffering. Roderick, Morgan, and Thomson are all subject to the caprices of the Captain's authority to a point where Thomson, 'foreseeing that the whole slavery of attending the sick and the wounded' will now fall to him (since Roderick and Morgan are both in chains), chooses to disappear (1999: 169).

Roderick's account of the planning and execution of the attack on Carthagena records official malfeasance and a bankrupt, self-serving leadership who care little for their sailors and ill-trained soldiers, 'most of [the latter] having been taken from the plough-tail a few months before' (1999: 179). Death, injury, and disease reduce a force of 8,000 men to 1500 fit for service, and large numbers of sick and wounded are assembled on poorly equipped 'hospital ships,' where, the patients being neglected, their 'wounds and stumps' contracted 'filth and putrefaction, and millions of maggots were hatched amid the corruption of their sores' (1999: 187). In a short while, the expedition founders in a situation so disastrous that Roderick tells us that

> Such was the oeconomy in some ships, that, rather than be at the trouble of interring the dead, their commanders ordered their men to throw the bodies overboard, many without either ballast or winding-sheet; so that numbers of human carcasses floated in the harbour, until they were devoured by sharks and carrion crows; which afforded no agreeable spectacle to those who survived. (1999: 189)

The coming of the rainy season brings an epidemic of fever, which kills three-quarters of those it infects. Roderick is also infected, but survives, perhaps because he refuses to use the treatment prescribed!

When Roderick is offered the option of sailing home, he declines, believing that the 'success' he had originally desired from his voyaging would only be available in the West Indies (1999: 199). Now a surgeon's mate on the sloop *Lizzard*, Roderick is almost immediately rewarded when they capture a Spanish ship, and he is given a silver-hilted sword and two silver-mounted pistols taken as plunder (1999: 201). They stop at Morant to care for their sick, and there Roderick stumbles upon Thomson, who is now the surgeon and overseer of a slave plantation in Kingston. Thomson has, in this colony, come into the fortune that Roderick too seeks (we should note how simple it is for Smollett to reverse Thomson's fortunes by causing him to surface in Jamaica). He loads Roderick with money and presents, and Roderick responds predictably: 'Being thus provided with money, and all necessaries for the comfort of life, I began to look upon myself as a gentleman of some consequence, and felt my pride dilate apace' (1999: 206). Equally predictably (our story is only half told here!), Roderick's arrival in England is ruined by his being knocked-out and robbed penniless in a duel with Crampley. Roderick is now in Sussex, and forced to take a job as a valet to an eccentric lady in the country, which allows him to experience close up the lives of the landed gentry. Here, in his new livery, and in the company of his mistress and her niece Narcissa, both of whom care for literature and languages, he returns to self-confidence, and reveals to them his education in these subjects. He also falls in love with Narcissa, but then must flee one of her suitors. As he does so, he is captured near the coast by a gang of smugglers, who take him with them to France.

In Boulogne, Roderick runs into his uncle Mr Bowling, who has survived by serving in the French navy. Not long after, Bowling returns to England, and Roderick's poverty leads him to sign up with a French regiment. Neither Bowling's French service nor Roderick's is commented upon, reminding us that mercenaries were a feature of European militaries, but also, within the terms of this novel, indicating a different trajectory available to Scottish men. In any case, Roderick's French stint provides the occasion for Smollett to examine the European theater of war in which the British are also embroiled. Roderick is led to compelling insights into the illusions of aggressive nationalism when he speaks to a loyalist French soldier who rejoices that he fights for the glory of Louis XIV. Roderick is amazed at the Frenchman's 'infatuation,' which allows him to think 'himself highly honoured in being permitted to encounter abject poverty, oppression, famine, disease, mutilation, and evident death, merely to gratify the vicious ambition of a prince, by whom his sufferings were disregarded, and his name utterly unknown.' However, Roderick's subversive understanding does not extend to English nationalism and subaltern loyalty to the British monarch, because he argues that the English have always acted – to the point of rebellion – to preserve the reciprocity between king and people (1999: 245–6). Coming from a Scotsman in a French military uniform, this is a powerful ratification of the idea of British liberty (and an important lesson to be imbibed by any would-be British subject).

Roderick's account of the battle at Dettingen, in which the British and their allies defeat the French, confirms French pusillanimity and English valor (1999: 248–9). The campaign moves on, his French regiment is sent to winter quarters, and Roderick finds himself in dire need again, only to be miraculously rescued by Strap, who appears as Monsieur d'Estrapes, now enriched by his service to a French marquis. Roderick is taken aback by Strap's class elevation – to which 'he had not even the ambition to aspire' (1999: 251) – and equally gratified when Strap, reverting to proper form, offers him all his possessions. Indeed, Strap offers his services as valet too, and plans for life in England: Roderick, once he appears 'in the character of a gentleman,' must secure his future by wooing 'some lady of fortune' (1999: 255). What follows is an extended account of Roderick's life as a fortune hunter amongst the beaux and belles of London and Bath (in two wonderful passages, Roderick first lists all his wardrobe, and then describes his 'thousand ridiculous coquetries' as he attempts to 'put on the gentleman of figure' in a London playhouse,

(1999: 256–8)). Glitter and show reign, and are enabled most often by trickery, borrowing, or gambling. Roderick also frequents a coffee house where French-speakers gather, though he makes clear that, unlike the bulk of the company, he never speaks 'in the French interest' (1999: 260). He and another Englishman espouse British constitutional protections against French absolutist monarchy, and this and other debates about politics, culture, and learning turn into occasions for the satiric unmasking of the pretensions of others present. Roderick begins to carouse with other 'gay figures' (1999: 269), and initiates his attempts to woo an heiress. He gambles away his money, fights a duel, plots revenge once a proposal of marriage is turned down – in short, he does all that a man of his supposed status is meant to do (all the while living off Strap's generosity). When Roderick is reduced to his last guinea, he has Strap pawn his sword (Strap is loath to do so, Roderick tells us, because 'he still retained notions of oeconomy and expence suitable to the narrowness of his education' (1999: 315)).

Roderick gambles with this money, and surprisingly, wins 150 guineas. This capital enables him to try his luck at Bath. Social forms at Bath repeat London hypocrisies, and the only difference is that it is here that Roderick meets Narcissa again, declares his feelings, and learns that she reciprocates them. He is too prudent to do anything that will jeopardize her inheritance, which she will gain only if she marries with her brother's permission (1999: 360). In fact her brother removes her to the country. Roderick, unsurprisingly, runs out of money and is arrested and sent to debtor's prison.[34] Equally unsurprisingly, he is rescued by Mr Bowling, now enriched by his success as a privateer. Bowling offers Roderick the position of Surgeon on board his ship, takes on Strap as his steward, and grants both loans that will allow them to buy shares in the ship's commercial 'adventure.' That adventure, as we learn, is to buy slaves and gold dust from the Guinea coast and to sell them in Buenos Ayres in New-Spain, with silver bullion to be brought back to England (1999: 407). Fever breaks out amongst the slaves on the voyage to South America, which means that Roderick, as ship's doctor and as investor, is doubly glad to be rid of 'the disagreeable lading of Negroes, to whom,' he complains without any irony, 'I had been a miserable slave' (1999: 410). His profits from this voyage alone lead him to dreams of purchasing a 'handsome sine-cure upon my arrival in England' and marriage to Narcissa (1999: 410). As it turns out, his discovery of his father, now styled Don Rodriguez and a very rich man in colonial Spain, means that he has resources enough to achieve the status he believes he merits and to marry Narcissa.

This entails purchasing Roderick's grandfather's estate in Scotland, and their return is a triumph. His English bride is so pleased with the 'civilities' she receives that she exclaims 'that she would never desire to live in any other part of the world' (1999: 432), and over time, continues to enjoy her stay, which is a strong vote of English confidence in the polite society of the Lowlands. Narcissa is pregnant at the end of the novel, and Roderick's future seems assured. His travels in England, and his immersion in English upper-class society, alongside his incarceration amidst debtors and sailors, teaches him about civility and its corruptions. His final success brings to fruition the promise that the British slave trade and plantations held out to entrepreneurial Scotsmen, and affirms that no matter how much anti-Scots prejudice might operate in London and Bath, the trans-Atlantic traffic between European colonies will allow for advancement, or, as in his case, a consolidation of lost status at home in Scotland. For Roderick the Scotsman then, the high road to London is only the first step towards fortune, for riches are to be made in the colonial theater, in the slave trade and in the triangulated commerce it enables. If Roderick, and of course his child, born of an English mother, are to be proper British subjects, they must learn the ways of proper British colonialists. *The Adventures of Roderick Random* thus follow upon the 'adventuring' featured in *Robinson Crusoe*, with the added benefit that difficult cultural and linguistic relations between Scotland and England can be both represented and resolved satisfactorily within the larger narrative of Roderick's colonial success.[35]

This reading of *Roderick Random* foregrounds the webbed connections the novel weaves between provincial ambition and British colonialism and trade; between the price paid by the underclasses who serve, or are pressganged into, naval service (as a reminder, we are told that thirty sailors on board Bowling's merchant ship were 'pressed on board a man of war' as soon as they return to England (1999: 420)) and the riches brought home on these ships; between the immorality and social hypocrisy of urban English society and the (unremarked upon) immorality and hypocrisy of the slave trade and slave plantations. Smollett's account of the British world – as it extends militarily into Europe and in colonies, trading, and privateering across the Atlantic – is of a violent, exploitative system designed to enrich a few while putting a great many into harm's way. The novel's satire is directed – unevenly – at urban consumption and pretension, at the tyranny of those in authority on board ship or in ancillary naval and military institutions, and on the anti-Scots prejudice that defined the cultural hierarchy of the British nation-in-the-making. Because he is a well-educated and poor Scotsman, Roderick's England

(London, Bath and the Sussex country estate), is necessarily connected to, but crucially at odds with, the public culture Addison celebrated (and, to be sure, gently satirized) as the world of the Spectator. Reading these texts in conjunction allows us to see larger patterns of circulation – of bodies, commodities, experiences, texts and ideas – both within Britain and in across its overseas possessions and trade routes. We are also provided with vivid evidence of the internal hierarchies of class and region that characterized British lives in the eighteenth century. Further, we are made aware of the cultural and ideological frames within which Britons understood their civic, military, and social institutions, whether these take the form of studied comparisons with French monarchical authority to throwaway references to Ottoman or Mughal absolutism. Addison's metropolitan view is qualified, and added to, by Smollett's provincial lens, and the world that is revealed ranges from the polished silver on a British dandy's cane to the mines in South America where it is mined and sold in exchange for slaves from Africa. Consumption in Britain, particularly of luxury goods, but also of 'necessities' like sugar and tobacco, is granted its historical context here.

Luxury, Commercial Society, Enlightenment Historiography

In the eighteenth century, to detail these circuits of the production and consumption of commodities is to outline Britain's colonial interests. This is not to claim that writers like Addison and Steele and Smollett were deliberately anti-colonial or even systematically against the unequal consumption patterns that they saw being confirmed by British successes in overseas trade and colonization, but it is to note that it was impossible for close observers of British society to avoid engagement with its colonial engagements. By this century, the very dynamic of historical change in Britain was perceptibly derived from energies and processes originating across the Atlantic and from Asian trade routes; to have your finger on the national pulse was to feel a domestic diastole as well as an international systole. The rise of a commercial society at home was inextricable from the growth of a colonial system overseas, which meant, as John Sekora has pointed out, that critiques of consumption – of 'luxury' – were at once debates about colonial trade.[36] The historical critique of luxury was tied into models of the decline of empires; this too was the case with the contemporary celebration and the critique of consumption. 'Luxury,' Sekora writes, 'embraces a network of fluctuating social, philosophical, and theological presuppositions,' and this plasticity made it crucial to topical debates about society and nation (1977: 4).

Sekora suggests that the debate about luxury became urgent in this period for several reasons: first, the visible growth of consumer society and the expansion of the social circles that consumed imported commodities from tea and sugar to china and cloth led some social theorists to celebrate vital economic growth (as well as the making of a more 'polite' society) while others of a more conservative bent castigated over-consumption and the blurring of class boundaries when servants and laborers consumed goods once beyond their station. Second, as Britain laid claim to overseas territories and trading dominance, both those commentators who feared domestic corruptions that followed from this expansion, as well as some who supported such power but wondered how to perpetuate it, focused their anxieties via accounts of the rise and fall of the Roman Empire, and the role played by luxury in refining as well as, over time, in corrupting Roman society.[37] Third, the debate about the waxing and waning of luxury – variously defined, according to political temper – could be recast into theories of social and historical development and decline from the ancient world to modern nations. Sekora suggests that in the 1730s, the 'generalized theory of history' encoded in discussions about ancient luxury became a '*specialized* theory of contemporary English history' (1977: 81), in which partisans of Old England attacked those who had, post 1688, benefited most from commercial, financial, and colonial ventures. Fourth, luxury became central to the articulation of class tensions: spokesmen for the landed interest who feared a dilution of patrician power by the fortunes made in trade pointed to this *nouveau* wealth as inappropriate luxury; Whiggish partisans of trade had a more benign view of its effects, or spoke of more generalized social excesses that morality could curtail.[38]

There is another important reason why luxury became an idea that focused debates about the ethics, politics, social forms, and consumption patterns of commercial society, which is that the idea of commercial society itself became, particularly in the second half of the eighteenth century, and especially in the work of several Scottish philosophers and political economists, a crucial crux in a larger historiographical argument about the evolution of human societies. In this four-stage model of development, human communities evolved from hunting and gathering to pastoralism and animal husbandry to settled agriculture to trading and commercial exchange, with the present form of European commercial society being seen as the natural telos of global social development. A complex but orderly world-picture is generated here, one whose ways of explaining the movements of human history are deeply informed by the recent experience of European colonialism in the New World and in coastal Africa, and of commercial and colonial settlement on routes to and in Asia.[39] The tribal peoples of the world, as indeed pastoralists or agriculturalists are seen as at an earlier stage of development, and in need of the impetus provided by European commerce as well as of the colonial settlements that facilitate the circulation of goods. Those parts of the world that seem oddly self-sufficient and impenetrable (China in particular, Japan, even the powerful Ottoman states or those of Mughal India) can be understood as outside any kind of modernizing historical dynamic, as rendered static by political absolutism, religious prescription, ossified social hierarchies, or cultural and moral degeneration. In any case, their functioning, and their resistance to European ways of doing business, is contrasted with the development of polite society and civic institutions in parts of Europe, and in Britain.

Thus David Hume in his discourse 'Of Commerce' writes that once 'men quit their savage state' they become either 'husbandmen' or 'manufacturers,' and that while agriculture might, at an earlier stage, employ larger numbers, it is the 'finer arts, which are commonly denominated the arts of *luxury*,' that will 'add to the happiness of the state' (Hume 1752: 4–5). Foreign trade is crucial to national power, and 'a kingdom, that has a large import and export, must abound more with labour, and that upon delicacies and luxuries, than a kingdom, which rests contented with its native commodities. It is, therefore, more powerful, as well as richer and happier' (1752: 15). His picture of commercial society might be an idealized description of contemporary London or Glasgow:

> The more these refin'd arts advance, the more sociable do men become; nor is it possible, that, when enrich'd with science, and possest of a fund of conversation, they should be contented to remain in solitude, or live with their fellow citizens in that distant manner, which Is peculiar to ignorant and barbarous nations. They flock into cities; love to receive and communicate knowledge; to show their wit or their breeding; their taste in conversation or living, in cloathes or furniture . . . Particular clubs and societies are every where form'd: Both sexes meet in an easy and sociable manner, and mens tempers, as well as behaviour, refine a-pace. So that beside the improvements they receive from knowledge and the liberal arts, 'tis impossible but they must feel an increase of humanity, from the very habit of conversing together, and from contributing to each other's pleasure and entertainment.' ('Of Luxury,' 1752: 27)[40]

At the root of this evolution is the prosperity enabled by 'commerce and industry,' which creates 'that middling rank of men; who are the firmest basis of public liberty' (1752: 35). In England the House of Commons (which came about because of the 'encrease of commerce' and the growth of non-aristocratic power (1752: 36)), is the expression of political liberties and property-ownership: 'every man would think his life or fortune much less secure in the hands of a *Moor* or *Tartar*, than in those of a *French* or *English* gentleman, the rank of men the most civiliz'd, in the most civiliz'd nations' (1752: 37).

Hume's vocabulary and historical understanding is representative of Enlightenment thinking in all its inclusions – a stress on property rights, on middle-class probity and commitment to the nation, on an urban culture of conversation and refinement putatively open to both men and women – and in equally characteristic exclusions. In his essay 'Of National Characters,' he provides this telling footnote:

> I am apt to suspect the negroes to be naturally inferior to the whites. There scarcely ever was a civilized nation of that complexion, nor even any individual eminent either in action or in speculation. No ingenious manufactures amongst them, no arts, no sciences. On the other hand, the most rude and barbarous of the whites, such as the ancient GERMANS, the present TARTARS, have still something eminent about them, in their valour, form of government, or some other particular. Such a uniform and constant difference could not happen, in so many countries and ages, if nature had not made an original distinction between these breeds of men. Not to mention our colonies, there are NEGROE slaves dispersed all over EUROPE, of whom none ever discovered any symptoms of ingenuity; though low people, without education, will start up amongst us, and distinguish themselves in every profession. (Hume 1987: 208)[41]

There is also, in this welter of cultural and national comparison, a socio-sexual element swilling about. In a statement resonant with the compulsions of the slave trade and plantation slavery, Hume asserts: 'You may obtain any thing of the NEGROES by offering them strong drink; and may easily prevail with them to sell, not only their children, but their wives and mistresses, for a cask of brandy' (1987: 214). That this is not an incidental slur but part of a more complex explanation of the hierarchical evolution of society is made clear when Hume writes that the 'politeness of a nation will commonly much depend' on 'free intercourse between the sexes.' Thus, he holds that 'the people, in very temperate climates, are the most likely to attain all sorts of improvement; their blood not being so inflamed as to render them jealous, and yet being warm enough to make them set a due value on the charms and endowments of the fair sex' (1987: 215).

To note these sorts of comparative references in Hume is not to trace in them a betrayal of Enlightenment sympathies; on the contrary, it is moments like this that reveal to us the colonialist underpinnings of Enlightenment sociology and historiography per se. These are not moments to be excused away or condemned in historical retrospect; they in fact illustrate the historicity of any Enlightenment conception of human societies and their interaction and evolution. The large questions formulated by British political philosophers, and their varied answers, are shaped by the classical and medieval intellectual conventions they were trained in, but perhaps even more consequentially, by the patchy and motivated observations made available by merchant-travelers and naturalists, and Hume is no exception. He read widely, and it is precisely this varied archive that underwrites his view of the world and its peoples.[42] Enlightenment cosmopolitanism is, after all, as pointedly the intellectual viewpoint of European colonialism as it is of more egalitarian forms of contact and understanding. The information and knowledge flows produced by European expansion in the seventeenth and eighteenth centuries shaped Scottish Enlightenment thought too, encouraging a significant body of work that offered intellectual cogency to the idea of a hierarchy of social formations across the globe, with an accompanying debate about the climatic, cultural, and racial explanations of such difference.[43] Not incidentally, such work also explored 'developed' and 'backward' or archaic formations within Scotland, and contrasted the feudal relations of the Highlands with the commercial society of the Lowland urban centers (while establishing an equivalence between contemporary Scottish urbanity and English civility).[44]

As our final instance of the global framework, and the comparative ethnographic, political, and socio-economic references that informed commentaries about the evolution of human societies, we will turn briefly to Adam Ferguson's *An Essay on the History of Civil Society* (1767). Ferguson wished to trace the differences between 'polished' and 'rude' or 'savage' societies, and to ask how contemporary civil society might stave off the ills that history suggested beset both empires and successful commercial societies. Ferguson's ideas, which combine reasoned discussion with bursts of observation and assertion, are full of what we might think of as the received wisdom or the matter-of-fact knowledge of his age; that is, of the world-picture inherited from classical and medieval accounts of the peoples of Asia and of coastal Africa as it was modified by the descriptions of social formations in those areas and in southeast Asia and the Americas provided by early modern travelers.[45] Ferguson's historiography seems to enjoy paradox, as when he writes in his section 'Of the Influences of Climate and Situation,' that men 'have raised the fabric of despotic empire to its greatest height, where they had best understood the foundations of freedom' or says that 'the torrid zone, every where round the globe . . . has furnished few materials for history' but then writes that it is in India (which is in that zone) 'that the arts of manufacture, and the practice of commerce, are of the greatest antiquity (Ferguson 1966: 110–11).' Since climatological explanation of historical change and social development does not allow for any consistency, Ferguson's comments on the nations and peoples of the world that he knows of do not add up to a coherent argument, but they do allow him to range the globe for examples to set against the unstated norm that is contemporary commercial society in Britain. The purpose of this survey, he concludes, is to make clear that any history of 'civil society' must 'bid farewell to those regions of the earth, on which our species, by the effects of situation or climate, appear to be restrained in their national pursuits, or inferior in the powers of the mind' (1966: 121), and take as its proper subject matter the histories of classical Athens and Rome, and contemporary London and Paris.

Which is to say that when Ferguson writes 'On the History of Literature' (Literature being an important index of refinement) or 'Of the Manners of Polished and Commercial Nations,' his field of reference and his expertise are (unsurprisingly) limited to this European cultural and political genealogy. He understands well the power of writers to shape historical meaning: Greece and Rome continue to be celebrated, he writes, because of the imaginative powers of their historians and other writers who celebrate valor and heroism and thus draw attention away from the fact that the political and social histories of these nations were as vindictive, cruel and remorseless as those of their 'barbarous neighbours' (1966: 194). He is confident that even as examples of patriotism, stoicism, and independence of mind and spirit can be found aplenty in Graeco-Roman history, the modern nations of Europe have advanced beyond them in their emphasis on social compassion, on less brutal forms of warfare, and on the 'employing of force, only for the obtaining of justice, and for the preservation of national rights' (1966: 199–200). Whether in terms of 'degrees of politeness and civilization' or 'the advancement of commercial arts,' he states, 'we shall be found to have greatly excelled any of the celebrated nations of antiquity' (1966: 203). Ironically, though Ferguson's discussion of Greek city-states and of the Roman empire counterpoints their cultural and moral values against their military actions and imperial power, no parallel insight is brought to bear on the colonial violence or international wars that underwrite contemporary British commercial society.[46]

Notes

1. M. L. Bush writes that indentured service offered poor whites in the New World the hope of eventually changing their status, but it also supplied them and 'the poor in the Old World with a taste for luxury, since slavery, indentured service and debt bondage were very much involved in producing non-essential goods such as sugar, tobacco, coffee, chocolate and tea. Through the democratization of luxury, servitude was involved in the early development of consumerism' (Bush 2000: 240).

2. These terms also feature in Bernard Mandeville's enquiry into human nature and sociability, *The Fable of the Bees* (1714), and in the furious critiques that followed the 1723 edition (see Mandeville 1970: 7–46). Mandeville's argument that trade benefited the nation precisely by stimulating individual consumer demand, which in turn acted as a collective stimulus to the economy (and hence to the public good), was attacked repeatedly as encouraging corrupt behavior.

3. Various Navigation Acts from 1651 onwards made it mandatory for all goods coming into or exported from England, Scotland, Ireland, and the colonies to be carried on English ships, and in some cases, to be reprocessed and taxed in England before they could be re-exported. The restrictions helped cause the Anglo-Dutch wars of 1652–4 and 1665–7.

4. James Raven writes that publishers, particularly in the second half of the century, achieved more 'attractive design and faster, higher quality production,' and 'adopted innovatory commercial techniques to supply and stimulate market demand . . . Several leading London booksellers declared themselves to be arbiters of taste and propriety' (Raven 1992: 13).

5. Shevelow argues that the 'literary representation of women' including in periodicals, produced 'an increasingly narrow and restrictive model of femininity' (Shevelow 1989: 1–3).

6. It may well be the case that this opposition between landed and mercantile and financial interests has a more hyperbolic presence in eighteenth-century cultural media (and manifests itself particularly in discussions about style) than in business practice. As some historians argue, 'the fate of the City was entwined with that of the aristocracy in Britain after 1688 – with all the expected consequences in terms of wealth, prestige and incorporation into the body politic' (Cain and Hopkins 2002: 41).

7. Neil McKendrick calculates that 'one in six of the total adult population' of the nation were directly exposed to 'the influence of London's shops, London's lifestyle and the prevailing London fashions' (McKendrick 1983: 21).

8. In *The Spectator* no. 4 (5 March 1711), Richard Steele announces of his women readers,

> As these compose half the World, and are by the just Complaisance and Gallantry of our Nation the more powerful Part of our People, I shall dedicate a considerable Share of these my Speculations to their Service, and shall lead the Young through all the becoming duties of Virginity, Marriage, and Widowhood. When it is a Woman's Day, in my Works, I shall endeavour at a Stile and Air suitable to their Understanding. When I say this, I must be understood to mean, that I shall not lower but exalt the Subjects I treat upon.

Addison adds a less gallant comment on the 'State of ordinary Women' (which he plans to reform) in no. 10 (12 March 1711). The definitive edition of *The Spectator* is Bond 1965. Since the essays are short and available in many editions, I refer to them by number and date of publication only.

9. Addison famously wrote in *Spectator* no. 10 (12 March 1711): 'I shall be ambitious to have it said of me, that I have brought Philosophy out of Closets and Libraries, Schools and Colleges, to dwell in Clubs and Assemblies, at Tea-Tables and in Coffee-Houses.'

10. Kathleen Wilson argues that newspapers and pamphlets also disseminated the vocabulary with which to understand state power: they 'familiarized their readers with a discourse that diagnosed the structure, location, or distribution of power in the state as the source of many imperial, political and social discontents and grievances' (Wilson 1994: 133). In facilitating the public critique of state governance and functioning, periodicals embodied the culture of dissent, debate, and self-correction that became crucial to British imperial identity.

11. Shawn Lisa Maurer argues that periodicals also traced configurations of masculinity within the family and in public (Maurer 1998).

12. Langford also writes that every 'war in during this period was in essence a commercial war, and to a marked extent a colonial war, whether the enemy was a rival power or one's own subordinate colonists. Every peace was the continuation of war by economic means' (Langford 1989: 3).

13. *The Spectator* no. 174 (19 September 1711) stages a debate between Sir Roger de Coverley and Sir Andrew Freeport on the virtues of the merchant. Steele's essay calls attention to the tensions between the 'landed and trading Interest of Great Britain,' in order to suggest (by allowing Freeport the last word), that they are unnecessary. One measure of the paper's success might be viewed in the list of subscribers to the collected octavo edition of *The Spectator* (1712), which, as Douglas Bond shows, contains aristocratic supporters as well as a large number of London merchants and financiers, civil servants, military bureaucrats, judicial officers, and gentlewomen (Bond 1965: 1. lxxxviii–xciii).

14. J. H. Plumb estimates that there were 2,000 coffee houses in London in the reign of Queen Anne (Plumb 1983: 269). Merchants also conducted business in coffee houses; further, as Markman Ellis writes, 'coffee-houses, which had of course long been associated with the provision of news and newspapers, began in the 1690s to develop specialist news services for financial information' (Ellis 2005: 173). Ellis reminds us that the first coffee house (actually, a market stall) in London was opened, probably in 1652, by two merchants, Daniel Edwards and Thomas Hodges, who, as members of the Levant Company, traded with Turkey and the Ottoman states. Over the next thirty years, this Turkish public practice was central to London sociability and to a more limited extent, English commercial practices. (See also Hattox 1985 and Ellis 2006.) Several Restoration satires invoke the Turkish origins and dark color of the beans and the brew to register their corrosive effects on religion and culture, as in this example from *A Cup of Coffee: or, Coffee in its Colours* (quoted in Ellis 2006: 1. 57):

   > For Men and Christians to turn Turks, and think
   > T'excuse the Crime because 'tis in their drink,
   > Is more then Magick, and does plainly tell
   > Coffee's extraction has its heat from Hell.

15. *The Spectator* is like many periodicals and newspapers in making comparative references to the lives of masters and slaves in British and European colonies. For instance, no. 215 (6 November 1711) exemplifies its examination of the 'Human Soul without Education' with reference to plantation slaves in St Christopher's, and no. 287 (29 January 1712) argues that 'European Slavery is indeed a State of Liberty, if compared with what prevails in the other three divisions of the World.' *The Spectator* also celebrates British society (and that of

parts of Christian Europe) by comparing them to the political and civic systems of non-European monarchies, particularly those of Islamic empires.

16. John Barrell's discussion of the 'qualifications, character and viewpoint of the gentleman' is illuminating, particularly his argument that this ideal of the 'dis-interested' gentlemanly observer of society (to whom the system of social order is visible) becomes increasingly untenable over the course of the century (Barrell 1983: 31–40).

17. Blair's lectures were systematized in *Lectures on Rhetoric and Belles Lettres* (1783), of which Lectures XIX–XXIII focus on Addison's prose. In a further irony, Scottish university curricula, including Blair's rhetoric, influenced Robert Dale, the first professor of English in England (at University College, London), and were used in working men's and mechanics' institutes in nineteenth-century Britain (Blair 2005: xv–xxxvi).

18. Ronald Meek argues that the marked Scottish contribution to four-stages theory is 'a function, first, of the rapidity of contemporary economic advance, and, second, of the facility with which a contrast can be observed between areas which are economically advancing and areas which are still in 'lower' stages of development.' That is, changes in 'economic techniques and basic socio-economic relationships' in Glasgow that followed from commercial expansion contrasted starkly with 'older forms of organization' in the Scottish Highlands (or indeed with reports of Indian tribes in America) and encouraged Adam Smith, John Dalrymple, and Lord Kames to develop their 'progressive' theories (Meek 1976: 127–8). Meek correctly ascribes such social theory to the 'bour-geois optimism' of the eighteenth century (1976: 130), which received powerful impetus from accounts of the world then being re-arranged by colonial systems of knowledge into Eurocentric social and political hierarchies.

19. Smollett's last novel, *The Expedition of Humphrey Clinker* (1771), is usually favored by Smollett scholars who wish to outline his mature understanding of Scottish and English societies, particularly as it contains a developed account of unequal social relations internal to Scotland too. I focus on *Roderick Random* not as an anticipation of these later ideas but because it forcefully indicts the intersections between commercial culture, the hypocrisies of domestic civil society, and violence overseas.

20. Louis M. Knapp reminds us that from '1739 to 1743 Smollett came into contact with three new types of experience . . . the melee of London, the roaring life of the Navy, and romantic love in the West Indies' (Knapp 1949: 27). When Smollett married Anne Lassells, her family's estates and investments in Jamaica provided them income for years to come. In 1769, Smollett willed his wife 'all my Estate personal & real . . . in and about the Town of Kingston in Jamaica and elsewhere; as also Slaves, Mortgages, Bonds, Sums of money, Rents, arrearages, claims &c; and all my Possessions & Effects whatsoever moveable & immove-able' (quoted by Knapp 1949: 285).

21. Sorensen thinks of Smollett as the 'the eighteenth-century novelist most inter-ested in representing non-standard English alongside his measured English prose . . . Sensitive to its ability to indicate a wide range of social strata, as well as its slippery relationship to the world it would name, Smollett's writings frequently represent linguistic multiplicity.' Sorensen also argues that language 'was one of the most important sites of Scottish negotiations of Anglo-British identity' (Sorensen 2000: 104–5).

22. Barrell says that 'even more remarkable than the number of languages imitated or referred to' in the novel is 'the number of occupations followed' by its char-acters. He lists over 100, and points out that as many as eighty characters are named after their professions (Portion the apothecary, Rifle the highwayman,

Syntax the schoolmaster) (Barrell 1983: 180–3). Barrell argues that Roderick's experience of this professional and socio-linguistic variety prepares him most fully for his triumph at the end of the novel; his trials authorize his knowledge of the extended economic interests and social formations of the imperial nation (1983: 187–200).

23. Smollett's novelistic ear for deviations from the spoken 'standard' is a more playful variant of his trained eye, as an editor, for errors in English usage. He was vigilant in ridding his prose of Scotticisms, and, as an editor and reviewer in the *Critical Review* and the *The Briton*, in pointing them out in other writing (see Basker 1991: 86–90).

24. The dissociation of classical learning from the world at large is most starkly shown when Mackshane, a ship's surgeon who loathes Roderick, speaks Irish while pretending to speak Greek, and thereby convinces the ship's captain that Roderick does not know the language (1999: 175–6).

25. There are several instances of such success embedded within the novel's accounts of naval disasters; a crucial example is Mr Bowling's slave trading voyage off Guinea, his subsequent taking (as a licensed Admiralty privateer) of a 'merchant ship from Martinico, laden with sugar, indigo, and some silver,' which wins him 'a pretty sum of money' and also the command of a large ship with which to embark 'upon a very advantageous voyage' (1999: 398).

26. Strap the artisan sums up his relation to Roderick the would-be gentleman when he says at a moment when they are both penniless: 'On my own account . . . I am quite unconcerned; for while God spares me health and these ten fingers, I can earn a comfortable subsistence any where; but what must become of you, who have less humility to stoop, and more appetites to gratify' (1999: 370).

27. Moments like these, as well as the larger themes of the novel, lead Robert Crawford to comment that the 'British novel, as pioneered by Tobias Smollett, is a novel about prejudice, a subject which, as an ambitious eighteenth-century Scot with his eye on the British capital, Smollett was quite familiar' (Crawford 1992: 55).

28. Strap was a school fellow of Roderick's, and defines himself as 'a poor journeyman barber, tolerably well made, and understand some Latin, and have a smattering of Greek – but what of that?' Strap knows Roderick to be 'born a gentleman, and have a great deal of learning – and indeed look like a gentleman' (1999: 95). The markers of class difference Strap identifies here – birth, education, comportment and looks – do not in practice underwrite Roderick's gentility, and are only stabilized in the end when he comes into money via his merchant-adventuring and his father's generosity.

29. For instance, once Roderick learns the details of Miss Williams's life, and recognizes in them the double standards that condemn seduced and abandoned gentlewomen to prostitution, he compares his situation to hers and realizes that, unlike her, he can move from one 'scheme of life' to another, 'according to the emergencies of my fate, without forfeiting the dignity of my character, beyond a power of retrieving it, or subjecting myself wholly to the caprice and barbarity of the world' (1999: 136–7). Chapters XXII and XXIII are an extended meditation on the tribulations of women.

30. Thomson, another Scottish surgeon, prepares to work on a slave ship before he is employed by the Naval Office (1999: 144), and the 'Guinea' trade is referred to repeatedly.

31. Later in the novel, the sailors on Mr Bowling's merchant ship petition him not to fire upon an enemy vessel, because they say that there 'was no provision made by the merchants for those poor souls who are maimed in their service' (1999: 408). Bowling convinces them otherwise, but such fears were a feature of a sailor's life.

32. Mackshane is described as a 'Bashaw' to suggest his power (1999: 157), just as the ship's captain Oakhum is later compared to 'the Grand Mogul' (1999: 172) for much the same reason. When Crampley becomes equally tyrannical as commander of the Lizzard, he too is called a 'bashaw' (1999: 208). Absolute authority on board is dictated by Admiralty law, but Smollett, like many eighteenth-century British writers who call attention to structures of tyranny at home, finds it rhetorically opportune to deflect attention onto absolutisms elsewhere. These metaphors of Islamic absolutism work to suggest that British institutions are not in themselves authoritarian, but are only rendered so by individuals who pervert their benign purposes.

33. For a full discussion of these naval and military engagements (and Roderick's service in the French army), see McNeil 1990: 84–112.

34. At Marshalsea, Roderick meets Melopoyn the poet, who is a long-term resident. Melopoyn's career sums up the practical possibilities available to those who would make a living of their skills at belles letters (critics have suggested that he is based on Smollett's own disappointments in London).

35. This is not to suggest that Roderick's success is to be taken as Smollett's last word on the subject of Anglo-Scottish relations or on the development of commercial society. If anything, both as a novelist and as a journalist, he remained critical of the human price Scotland paid within the union and repeatedly castigated the mercantile interest that drove national policies.

36. John Sekora argues that the idea of luxury is one of the oldest 'and most pervasive negative principles for organizing society Western history as known' (Sekora 1977: 2). His particular interest is in the ways in which this concept changes its meanings, via debates about ethical forms of consumption, and he discusses the large number of writers (and especially Smollett) engaged in this conversation. My discussion (though not my critical emphases) follows Sekora's elaboration of this debate.

37. In Sekora's felicitious observation: 'To most literate Englishmen . . . the continual reminders of the fall of Rome appear to have been like the annual feasts of the Jewish and Christian calendars, regular commemorations of the most important event in European history' (Sekora 1977: 9).

38. Both aristocrats and middle-class writers, on the other hand, were united in their attack on the new demands of the poor; as Sekora argues, those who 'came to fear the discontented mass of the London poor . . . [who] seemed always on the brink of collective insurrection' found, in the critique of luxury, useful rhetorical weapons that 'could be brought to bear, at the height of England's quest for empire, upon the poorest of the poor' (Sekora 1977: 62).

39. Roxanne Wheeler provides a good discussion of these issues, particularly those germane to literary studies (Wheeler 2000: 33–8, 181–90). Wheeler shows that the graduated 'sense of difference' that four-stages theories developed applied not only to Africans or Indians (West and East) but also 'included Britain's national subjects, particularly the Irish and the Scots' (2000: 188).

40. As a Scotsman, Hume too was very concerned about his language and style, and for the same reasons as Smollett. In a letter to John Wilkes, on sending him a 'Copy of my History' (16 October 1754), Hume wrote: 'I beg of you to remark, as you go along, such Words or Phrases, as appear to you wrong or suspicious; and to inform me of them. You cou'd not do me a better Office: Notwithstanding all the Pains, which I have taken in the Study of the English Language, I am still jealous of my Pen. As to my Tongue, you have seen, that I regard it as totally desperate and irreclaimable' (Hume 1932: 1. 205).

41. Hume's editors never fail to point out that in his essay 'Of the Populousness of Ancient Nations,' Hume attacked domestic slavery in classical societies.

However, Hume's critique shows only that it was feasible to express anti-slavery feelings while believing entirely in the natural inferiority of Africans.

42. Commentators on Hume have described his fears that British power might decline rather than expand because of the government's [the elder Pitt's] full-blown commitment to militarism and imperialism. The prototypical rise and fall of the Roman empire (or the idea that empires are cyclical, and that imperial overreach and an enfeebling spread of luxury precipitate decline) echoes in these fears, which were shared by (Tory) writers like Samuel Johnson and Edward Gibbon. Their intellectual resistance to the spread of the British empire combined a general humanitarianism with a particular sense that the achievements of British society were fragile and needed preserving from the inevitability of imperial corruptions. They held that a combination of mercantilist protections (in which the state closed profitable trades to all but a few joint-stock companies) and imperialist ambition was already threatening traditional British economic and social strengths.

43. Key texts here are Adam Ferguson, *An Essay on the History of Civil Society* (1767), James Burnett (Lord Monboddo), *Origin and Progress of Language* (1773), Henry Home (Lord Kames), *Origin of the Distinction of Ranks* (1771), and James Dunbar, *Essay on the History of Mankind in Rude and Civilized Ages* (1780). As literary historians have shown, the Ossian controversy too is fully informed by the contemporary need to re-animate a folk-ish past, as is manifest in Hugh Blair's *A Critical Dissertation on the Poems of Ossian, the Son of Fingal* (1763). The Ossian debates are summarized in Moore 2003.

44. Karen O'Brien's *Narratives of Enlightenment: Cosmopolitan History from Voltaire to Gibbon* (1997) examines 'the internal dialogue between Scottish and English forms of historical self-understanding during the years immediately following the last Jacobite uprising of 1745,' and rightly interprets 'the cosmopolitanism of [David] Hume, [William] Robertson and Gibbon . . . in the context of the forms of national historical consciousness available in mid-eighteenth-century England and Scotland' (1997: 13). She argues that the intellectual world shared by Robertson, Hume, Adam Smith, and Hugh Blair was 'at once unionist, cosmopolitan and intensely proud of post-Union Scotland,' and represented 'a bid for respectability and prestige in Britain as a whole, particularly after the 1745 Jacobite Rebellion had rendered Scotland suspect in English eyes' (1997: 94). However, O'Brien's otherwise historical understanding of 'cosmopolitanism' does not take on board the comparative focus on the globe that follows from European colonial and commercial expansion.

45. For instance, Adam Ferguson tells us that he learns from a *Collection of Dutch Voyages* that in Formosa, men are prohibited from marriage before the age of forty and that any woman who gets pregnant before she is thirty-six must have an abortion (Ferguson 1966: 139).

46. However, Ferguson is clear-sighted about the 'remarkable' age in which, 'having found means to cross the Atlantic, and to double the cape of Good Hope, the inhabitants of one half of the world were let loose on the other, and parties from every quarter, wading in blood, and at the expence of every crime, and of every danger, traversed the earth in search of gold' (Ferguson 1966: 212). He is equally forthright about the domestic effects of mercantile expansion: 'In every commercial state, notwithstanding any pretension to equal rights, the exaltation of a few must depress the many' (1966: 186).

Chapter 4

'Perspectives from Elsewhere'

As this book has argued so far, literary texts are an invaluable archive of the desires and fears that accompanied the making – with all its stumbles and internal contestation – of an imperial nation. Equally, such texts (and the debates surrounding them) are wonderful resources for disaggregating national culture, for understanding how different constituencies or individuals experienced the costs and benefits of these large-scale processes. As we have seen, even as a large number of writers helped craft the nationalist self-conception that energized British efforts overseas, others catalogued the costs or objected to particular elements of the process. And yet others turned a bemused or angry eye on the national or provincial cultures of Britain as they were subjected to the demands of international traffic and power.

This chapter will follow a trail that will link disparate writers and books. Each example will feature the work of a writer dislocated – physically or imaginatively – from British culture or self-conception, even as their practice makes clear that they write within or to lay claim to this culture and literary tradition. The writers considered were each 'dislocated' differently: one wrote from Istanbul, another wrote in London, but imagined an Abyssinian kingdom and protagonists who traveled in Egypt and elsewhere. The lives, and writing, of two others were defined by the trans-Atlantic circuits of slavery. In each case their distance or their disaffection encouraged them to produce writing that was formally innovative and ideologically challenging. Lady Mary Wortley Montagu's *Turkish Embassy Letters* extended the familiar letter into unusual geographies and arenas of experience, and used her letters to revise misconceptions about the lives of Ottoman women that she had read in the works of earlier travelers and historians.[1] Samuel Johnson's *Rasselas* endows the oriental tale, and his Abyssinian protagonists, with a seriousness of purpose not usual to either the form or non-European characters.

The second half of this chapter will discuss two contributions, by Phillis Wheatley and Ukawsaw Gronniosaw, to a corpus of writing that is of particular importance to postcolonial criticism and pedagogy, which is the writing of Africans who were enslaved and literate, and who produced both eloquent arguments for freedom and systematic rebuttals of the racist canards that justified the enslavement of black people.[2]

While all writing functions as an intervention into social processes, the publication in the late eighteenth century of poems and prose by African slaves (some recently manumitted) had particular force. Books by Wheatley and Gronniosaw helped alter the material predicament of their fellow slaves, in part by demonstrating that black Africans could master the language and cultural idiom of those who had enslaved them and thus were their intellectual equals. Their writing expressed the creativity that had sustained them in the most adverse of human circumstances, and also claimed a share in the supposedly universal consolations and promises of Christianity. In doing so, they helped demolish several myths that sustained imperial arrogance, and reminded all those in Britain or British America who read them, or read of them, of the inhumanity of slavery. However, like many British (and even some American) anti-slavery writers, these writers were not necessarily anti-colonial in their attitudes, though some like Phillis Wheatley identified politically with the break-away American colonies. Their efforts were to that extent part of the British anti-slavery argument that the abolition of the slave trade would confirm the moral legitimacy of the empire and allow those enslaved full participation in its civic life and Christian mission.

The discussion that follows will focus on the reasons why these texts are, for very different reasons, of interest to students of colonialism. I will make no attempt to sum up or explore all the features of each text, but will point to the particular challenge each writer offers to cultural and ideological assumptions that inform contemporary British attitudes. These challenges do not always add up to a spirited anti-colonialism, but they do ensure that readers today recognize that even as the mass of British writers in this period had few qualms about the *rightness* of Britain's trading and territorial empires (even if they quarreled about some of its features), there were those whose writing suggested less belligerent modes of apprehending human community across social and cultural differences. With Wheatley and Gronniosaw we will also pay attention to the nature of the language and idiom utilized by each author, in order to probe key issues of language-acquisition and education important to postcolonial criticism. That is, members of each of the language communities that came under the sway of colonialism (this includes the African slaves brought to the Americas) learned (however partially) English, and a few were educated into biblical and literary conventions. In the case of African slaves, to speak and write correctly or in a literary fashion (not an ability possessed by the majority of British or American speakers of English at this moment) was to lay claim to the humanity and civility denied to them by the racist proponents of slavery. It was also to re-mold the resources of English language and literature to accommodate new subjectivities, experiences, desires, and a politicized point of view necessarily at odds with many of the cultural assumptions articulated in this language. The tensions between traditional usage (the culture of the masters, in this case) and these new agendas make for fascinating analysis, through which we can trace many of the historical contradictions – the strains between form and theme – that enliven the writing of those who, because of their race, were denied full membership in the culture of the colonizer.[3]

There is another literary-critical crux that this chapter will explore, which is the vexed question of how to read texts which contain instances of anti-colonial or anti-racist sentiment while being composed within a cultural idiom (and utilizing literary conventions) that more usually delineate ideological positions precipitated by colonialism. One way to think about this question is to note the power of discursive systems to mould the assumptions and writing styles of even those who would question or reject culturally dominant values. Lady Mary Wortley Montagu insists that her descriptions of Turkish seraglios revise the mendacity of travel writers who came before her, but her prose – and perhaps her entire way of seeing – is colored by the twin legacies of such historical writing and the even more fanciful portraits painted in 'oriental' tales. Samuel Johnson too derives important elements of his philosophical fable *Rasselas* from oriental tales, and even as some readers have found his text profoundly anti-colonial in its cultural and moral universalism, other critics are not convinced that *Rasselas* jettisons the cultural baggage of empire. Phillis Wheatley's poems have been condemned for their lack of outrage at the condition of her fellow-slaves, and her Christian – and apolitical – focus on redemption in the afterlife, both of which are seen to be develop from her education as the favored domestic slave of a family of Boston slave owners. Gronniosaw's autobiographical tale was composed for publication by an amanuensis, which might be an apt model for the way in which discursive systems – conventions of literary production and style – enable and mold narratives of individual experience.

Lady Mary Wortley Montagu and her Turkish Embassy Letters

In a letter Montagu wrote to her younger sister Frances Pierrepont, now Lady Mar, from Adrianople, she describes herself as in 'Turkish Habit,' which she sees as sumptuous and 'admirably becoming.' The pleasure she takes in her local clothes becomes a prelude to her commentary on the clothing, cosmetics, and beauty of the aristocratic Turkish women she meets. She is fully cognizant that her description functions within the form and vocabulary defined by travel writers before her, but her conclusions – based upon her access to women's lives – are at odds with their accounts, which she thinks devised either with an 'exemplary discretion or extreme Stupidity.' Turkish women's 'Morality' and 'good Conduct' are not different from those of Englishwomen, Montagu observes wittily, for they 'don't commit one Sin the less for not being Christians.' Indeed, since they are required to be veiled from head to toe when in public, their anonymity grants them an ironic freedom to follow their 'Inclinations without danger of Discovery.' 'Thus you see, dear Sister,' Montagu writes, 'the manners of Mankind doe not differ so widely as our voyage Writers would make us beleive [*sic*].'[4]

Montagu's letters, written between 1716 and 1718, but published in London only in 1763 as *Letters of the Right Honourable Lady M – y W – y M – e, Written, during her Travels in Europe, Asia and Africa, To Persons of Distinction*, are remarkable in their ability to jettison the straitjacket of conventional values and to enjoy – even luxuriate in – the lives of women who were usually invoked either as victims of the sensuality and depravity of Turkish patriarchs or as the equally licentious and manipulative denizens of seraglios and harems. In the short time Montagu spent in Adrianople and Constantinople, she used her position as wife of the Ambassador Extraordinary to the Court of Turkey to learn Arabic and to read Turkish poetry, and to gain access to noblewomen's lives as they were lived in private and in communal spaces (Wortley Montagu's appointment as Ambassador was confirmed by the Levant Company, which is a nice reminder of the overlap of trading and political interests in this period). She wrote about them with empathy and excitement, and always within a comparative view, just as she had done when she described women at the Austrian court at Vienna ('Letter to Lady Mar, September 14, 1716' and 'Letter to Lady Rich, September 20, 1716,' among several others). Herself a bon vivant and creature of fashion, Montagu was constantly alert to the convoluted forms of gender relations and women's lives in elite

European society, and is quick to comment on ironies and contradictions in the codes that govern women's behavior in all the societies in
which she travels. In doing so, she provides an exceptional comment on
ideologies of gender central to the definition of peoples and nations, and
a refutation of the discursive tradition that saw in the Ottoman court
the negation of all the social and political values of Christian kingdoms
like Britain or France.[5]

In her commentary on Turkish homes and social practices, Montagu
reminds her correspondents that she has first-hand knowledge because
she has, as a woman, gained access not available to Christian men: 'You
will perhaps be surpriz'd at an Account so different from what you
have been entertaind with by the common Voyage-writers who are very
fond of speaking of what they don't know.'[6] In 'Letter to Lady – ,' June
17, 1717,' she writes at greater length to correct the misconceptions
of her correspondent, who has asked her to buy a Greek house-slave
for service in England: 'Your whole Letter is full of mistakes from one
end to "tother" because it is based on "Ideas of Turkey" taken from
travel writers.' Montagu writes that these accounts are 'so far remov'd
from Truth and so full of Absurditys I am well diverted with 'em. They
never fail giving you an Account of the Women, which 'tis certain they
never saw, and talking very wisely of the Genius of the Men, into whose
Company they were never admitted, and very often describe Mosques,
which they dare not peep into.' In a less serious vein, Montagu debunks
a cosmetic (the 'Balm of Mecha'), news of whose wondrous properties
has reached her correspondent, and ridicules beliefs strenuously held by
Turkish women she knows that there 'are certain Compositions to inspire
Love,' and that a knowledge of 'Enchantments' allows some women
the upper hand over men (Montagu 1965: 1. 367–70). Montagu takes
an ironic view of credulity, superstition, and hypocrisy on either side
of the cultural and religious divide, and in doing so sets herself at odds
with many of the representational modes of contemporary ethnographic
observation.

Thus, in her observations on Turks, with its comparative asides
on equivalent social mores in England, Montagu's letters provide an
instance of cultural and ideological horizons widened, rather than
contracted, by knowledge of an Islamic empire with which Britain and
other Christian nations were often in competition in European and
Mediterranean theaters. In 'Letter to Lady Mar, April 18, 1717,' she
calls attention to the myopia induced by such confrontation, as when she
describes a Turkish noblewoman as so beautiful and poised that 'nobody
would think her other than born and bred to be a Queen, thô educated

in a Country we call barbarous.' In this letter, she is fully aware of the occasional extravagance of her descriptions of the personal beauty and opulent homes of the noblewomen that she encountered, but such rhetorical self-consciousness only enhances her desire to describe scenes of female pleasure that had been the subject of censorious fantasy in male travel writers. Her description of the music and dance (probably belly-dancing) performed for her in this home registers female homoeroticism, but without discomfort or condemnation, and as no more remarkable than other elements of her entertainment:

> This Dance was very different from what I had seen before. Nothing could be more artfull or more proper to raise certain Ideas, the Tunes so soft, the motions so Languishing, accompany'd with pauses and dying Eyes, halfe falling back and then recovering themselves is so artfull a Manner that I am very positive the coldest and most rigid Prude on Earth could not have look'd upon them without thinking of something not to be spoke of. (Montagu 1965: 1.347–52)

Montagu's writing is of interest also because it shows her awareness of the generic and representational conventions within which the Islamic Levant was usually portrayed.[7] She describes the opulence of a Sultana's dress and possessions and knows that her account will be considered embellished and too 'like . . . the Arabian tales,' and then writes of her dilemma as a 'Traveller': 'If we say nothing but what has been said before us, we are dull and we have observ'd nothing. If we tell any thing new, we are laugh'd at as fabulous and Romantic' ('Letter to Lady Mar, April 18, 1717,' in Montagu 1965: 1.347–52).[8] She reminds her correspondents that she is not known to exaggerate, but the veracity of her descriptions follows from her comparative method, that is, since her contrastive examples of English social practices are convincing, this precision extends to her account of Turkish mores too. In the same letter, she notes the presence of slaves in Turkey, but refuses to express a conventional horror at the enslavement of fellow-Christians ('you will Imagine me half a Turk,' she writes). She claims that the Turks treat them humanely and that 'their Slavery is in my Opinion no worse than Servitude all over the world.' 'Tis true that they have no wages, but they give them yearly Cloaths to a higher Value than our Salarys to any ordinary Servant.' (As can be seen in Grainger's *The Sugar-Cane*, a similar argument about plantation slavery overseas and servitude in Britain was put forward later in the century by English slave owners to justify their practices.) As an aristocrat, she has few qualms about the servitude of common people, but her claim that English employers are no less exploitative than Turkish slave owners is worth noting. Given the circumstances, it is odd that she does not mention the English slave trade, as that would have been the proper comparison, but there is no doubt about her insistence that Turkish mores have to be understood vis-à-vis parallel practices in England.[9]

A compilation of Montagu's letters was published in 1763, which means that the tone and nature of her observations on the aristocratic women she encountered in Turkey and elsewhere in her travels was known only to a few of her correspondents and others who read copies. Thus, no large claims can be made for the impact of her letters, nor did they result, when they were published, in a more empathetic understanding of gender and cultural formations vitiated by colonial warfare and competition. They are however an important instance of cross-cultural observations (limited as they were to the noble and the wealthy) that worked against the grain of reportage and historical writing. As Elizabeth Bohls suggests, Montagu turns 'aesthetics against . . . early Orientalism,' as she 'de-eroticizes and dignifies the Turkish women who earlier travelers had relentlessly objectified.' In comparison, Bohls also quotes from earlier travel writers who portray 'Turkish women as wanton or hypersexual' (Bohls 1995: 12, 29–30). Biographers and critics have offered several explanations of Montagu's difference – her being largely self-taught and hence less receptive to the 'authorities,' her emotional and intellectual bravery, which is manifested as much in her choice of husband as in the energetic exercise of her curiosity, her aristocratic identification with the riches and glamour of Turkish seraglios. We might add to these the sense that Montagu represents those few writers who, once dislocated from the cultural consensus within which other societies are experienced and described as incoherent and inferior, find paths to understanding that are unusual and refreshing. Such travelers lie athwart the developing discourse of empire, at odds with it even as they revel in some of its assumptions and rhetorical conventions. It is to another such oddity that we will now turn.

Johnson's *Rasselas*: Philosophy in an 'Oriental' Key

A generous and elevated Mind is distinguish'd by nothing more Certainly than an eminent Degree of Curiosity, nor is that Curiosity ever more agreeably or usefully employ'd, than in examining the Laws and Customs of foreign Nations.

Samuel Johnson, 'Editor's Dedication' to *Voyage to Abysinnia*
(Lobo 1735)

As literary historians have shown, the 'oriental' or 'eastern' story was a popular, literary form in the eighteenth century.[10] Such stories featured an identifiable set of narrative conventions and themes: they were most often set in putatively Islamic lands; they featured the lives of the nobility and of the powerful, and often of despotic rulers; they were fascinated by 'interned' lives, largely those of women in seraglios; and they luxuriated in the sumptuous riches of the court and of the harem.[11] They were also fascinated by the existential centrality of the act of storytelling itself: Scheherezade's tales kept her from being executed. There can no more forceful metaphor for the compulsion of stories (and indeed for the absolute power of the sultan).[12] Medieval romances in Europe had drawn on a variety of Arabic sources and story-cycles, but the particularities of such cultural translation diminished over time. Early modern travelers' tales served to revive interest in accounts of faraway places, and the rise of European holdings across the Mediterranean, India, and further south and east in Asia resulted in a surge of tales (including translations) originating from, and supposedly describing, 'oriental' lives and modes of being in the world. These were stories of monarchical and feudal worlds, but not of societies in discernible historical transition, and they were certainly not depicted as going though the changes and struggles that British or French storytellers believed energized their own societies and political systems. Indeed, one ideological effect of such fabulation was to deny a dynamic historicity to its subjects, to contain them within the repetition that was the cycle of storytelling itself.

Srinivas Aravamudan has argued that if the evolving mechanisms of the eighteenth-century domestic-realist novel produce an insular mode of representing the national subject, prose forms like the oriental tale suggest a negotiation between internal and external worlds (Aravamudan 1999: 10). Locations elsewhere are fascinating not so much for their own sake but because they allow for the apprehension of political systems, social hierarchies, kinship systems, gender relations, sexual practices, and of terms of being and happiness different from the manners and civic institutions of the developing national-imperial culture of Britain. Indeed, prose forms derived from oriental tales allowed British writers to explore existential and social issues in an idiom and a manner of proceeding not available within, or rendered illegitimate by, the cultural formations of Britain (see Caracciolo 1988). (In the second half of the eighteenth century, gothic fiction, in British locations or elsewhere, allowed similar sorts of eccentric and disturbing explorations.)

Samuel Johnson's *The History of Rasselas, Prince of Abyssinia* (1759) is an idiosyncratic contribution to this vogue, so much so that different editors have described it as a novel, a classical romance, an eastern tale, a moral comedy or satire, or, as Gwin J. Kolb does, an '"oriental moral tale" or "oriental philosophical tale" or "oriental apologue"' (Johnson 1990: xxxiv–xxxv; all references to *Rasselas* are to this edition). *Rasselas* was not Johnson's first foray into this territory. In two *Rambler* essays (nos. 204 and 205) he tells a story about Seged, the ruler of Ethiopia, although it is not quite clear why Johnson chooses that location for a story that illustrates the general maxim 'that no Man may imagine the Happiness of a Day in his own Power.' Seged is an all powerful and enormously wealthy Emperor, who decides one day that he should share in the felicity his successes have granted his subjects. Accordingly, he retires to his 'House of Pleasure' for ten days, to entertain his every desire. Each day, however, reveals to him different limits to his pleasure, till on the eighth day, his daughter Balkis develops a fatal illness. These limits to Seged's happiness, being the limits of the happiness of all men, could equally well be illustrated if told as the story of a wealthy and powerful man (or monarch) in Britain. Or perhaps not, because the point about Seged is his *absolute* power (which conception, apart from anything else, allows Johnson to indulge in a prose lush with the hyperbole and luxuriance considered appropriate to the representation of 'Eastern' absolutism). This is Seged, speaking to (and of) himself:

> Thy Throne is surrounded by Armies, numerous as the Locusts of the Summer, and resistless as the Blasts of Perdition. Thy Magazines are stored with Ammunition, thy Treasuries overflow with the Tribute of conquered Kingdoms. Plenty waves upon thy Fields, and Opulence glitters in thy Cities. Thy Nod is the Earthquake that shakes the Mountains, and thy Smile as the Dawn of the vernal Day. In thy Hand is the Strength of Thousands, and thy Health is the Health of Millions. Thy Palace is gladdened by the Song of Praise, and thy Path perfumed by the Breath of Benediction. Thy Subjects gaze upon thy Greatness, and think of Danger or Misery no more.

There are two matters of note here: the first is that the moral of the story is made more pointed by the fact that Seged, whose power – as this passage suggests – knows no limits, is not exempt from the discovery of the instability of happiness. The second is that Ethiopia and Seged allow Johnson flights of fancy, and an indulgent prose, that would be considered ridiculous were his subjects properly English.[13]

In *Rasselas*, Johnson derived crucial suggestions for locations and plot details from travel writers and historians he had read (Kolb examines Johnson's reading and sources for the Abyssinia and Egypt sections in Johnson 1990: xxvi–xxxiii). Not that Johnson's Abyssinia or his Egypt (or Imlac's foray into Mughal India) are closely observed, but in each case some attempt is made to detail distinguishing features or social practices. Further, each of the protagonists, once they escape from the Happy Valley, are fully responsive to social differences amongst the nations and people they encounter, and do not presume upon the transparency of cultural formations. For instance, we are told that Rasselas and Nekayah spend two years in Cairo learning the language so that they may best participate in life there (earlier, Imlac in Agra also learns 'the language of the country' in order to 'converse with the learned men' (Johnson 1990: 37).) In little details like this, or for instance, the more general sense of Cairo as a modern commercial and intellectual metropolis, the narrative represents faraway locations as possessed of a cultural density and historical presence usually denied them in 'oriental' tales. At times it seems as if the narrative deliberately revises crucial orientalist tropes, redoing them in familiar rather than exotic vocabularies. When Pekuah is kidnapped by the Arab chief and housed in his seraglio, her account of the women there is neither of beguiling and self-possessed beauties nor of malicious and malingering plotters (two conventional forms of representing the harem), but of women denied education, cultural exposure, and freedom, and thus reduced to dependency and trivial pursuits. (The same argument was made about British women by eighteenth-century advocates for women's education, most famously in 1792 in Mary Wollstonecraft's *A Vindication of the Rights of Women*.)

Crucial elements in *Rasselas* draw upon the dissemination of geographical and cultural information in travelogues as well as upon the vogue in oriental tales. The Happy Valley, for instance, exists because of an oppressive political system that incarcerates each potential claimant to the throne in order to prevent insurrection. One of Johnson's sources, Hiob Ludolf's *Historia Aethiopica* (1681), links Ethiopia and Turkey in the way in which they control problems in royal succession:

> The Emperors of the *Turks*, to prevent the Crimes of their Brothers, more impiously put them to death, and punish that Disloyalty which perhaps was never intended. The Ancient Kings of *Abessinia* to rid themselves of their Fears, were wont to shut up their Brothers under safe Custody, where they might abide unknown to turbulent Spirits; and so be uncapable of attempting any thing against the raigning Prince; and yet be ready to supply the want of Successors. (Ludolf 1682: 195; Johnson owned a copy)

The trappings and riches of the Happy Valley mimic descriptions of the luxuries of Ottoman courts, and differ in this regard from some of Johnson's sources, who describe the royal prison as arid and uncomfortable. Indeed, the 'atmospherics' of the tale, given that much of it transpires in Muslim lands, emphasize non-European and non-Christian modes of living.

Johnson adds to the oriental tale an unusual gravitas, indeed a philosophical seriousness, at odds with the trappings of the form. In that, he takes the trite moral or civic lessons offered in the conclusion of these tales and extends them so that the pursuit of meaning (in *Rasselas*, the 'choice of life') becomes the subject of the narrative. That Johnson was willing to imagine a group of Coptic Christians in Abyssinia exploring serious existential and geopolitical questions at a time when racist ideas about non-white peoples were actively propagated by imperialists and slave traders has led critics like Clement Hawes to celebrate Johnson's 'uniformitarian thought,' his refusal to believe that rationality and a historical sense of the world were exclusively attributes of white Europeans. Hawes argues that Johnson rejected contemporary arguments in which 'a racially exclusive notion of 'progress' was ideologically deployed to underwrite exploitation abroad,' and in doing so mounted a critique of the 'emerging equation of Enlightenment with "imperial progress"' (Hawes 1997: 119, 122, 114). There is a further dimension to Johnson's description of these Christians traveling, for the most part, in Muslim cultures, which is precisely that religious difference seems not to be an issue at all. Once the obstacles of language are overcome, the same large questions are seen to motivate the Christians travelers and their Muslim interlocutors alike. Rasselas and his party are prey to the same delusions and fears as those they encounter, and they achieve (or not) similar forms of tranquility. One response to Johnson's methods here might see *Rasselas* as an exercise in moral universalism that is inevitably Christian and Eurocentric in import (even if his protagonists are not Europeans), but, as Hawes suggests, we need instead to note that this moral and discursive equivalence refuses the human hierarchies and social distinctions advocated by contemporary colonialists.

Rasselas is not fanciful about the state of geopolitical power: when Imlac describes meeting people from northern and western Europe in Palestine, he speaks of these nations as

> now in possession of all power and all knowledge; whose armies are irresistible, and whose fleets command the remotest parts of the globe. When I compared these men with the natives of our own kingdom, they appeared almost another order of beings. In their countries it is difficult to wish for any thing that may not be obtained: a thousand arts, of which we never heard, are continually laboring for their convenience and pleasure; and whatever their climate has denied them is supplied by their commerce.

In response, Rasselas asks questions that have ever since troubled analysts of empire: 'By what means . . . are the Europeans thus powerful? or why, since they can so easily visit Asia and Africa for trade or conquest, cannot the Asiaticks and Africans invade their coasts, plant colonies in their ports, and give laws to their natural princes? The same wind that carries them back would bring us thither?' Imlac's conclusions – voiced, we will remember, by a non-European – are troubling: 'They are more powerful, Sir, than we . . . because they are wiser; knowledge will always predominate over ignorance, as man governs the other animals.' European knowledge is here species-superiority. However, Imlac cannot say why Europeans possess this exclusive knowledge, and knows only that the answer lies beyond human comprehension: 'But why their knowledge is more than ours, I know now what reason can be given, but the unsearchable will of the Supreme Being' (1990: 46–7).

Imlac returns to this topic later to praise European medicine and surgical practices, mechanical ingenuity, modes of communication, and road and bridge building techniques, deeming them all superior to any known in Abyssinia. However, he holds that these advantages do not necessarily lead to happiness: 'The Europeans . . . are less unhappy than we, but they are not happy. Human life is every where a state in which much is to be endured, and little to be enjoyed' (1990: 50). We should note that Imlac's and Rasselas's conversation is, in the first instance, about global differentials in power (Europeans 'so easily visit Asia and Africa for trade and conquest'), that is, about armed European trade and colonialism. Imlac registers this belligerence (as does Rasselas in his response), but the terms of the conversation shift away from such recognition. Imlac begins his account of European dominance by saying that they possess 'all power and all knowledge' (with the suggestion that power comes first, given that he invokes Europe's irresistible armies and commanding fleets before he elaborates on their 'thousand arts'), but then moves to a more abstract idea of knowledge – undefined, delinked from the exercise of power – as the basis for national or species superiority. Finally, it turns out that differentials in 'knowledge' are no explanation at all, given that they lie 'beyond human comprehension' and are the will of 'the Supreme Being.'

A geopolitical problem is articulated, but its resolution lies in soft-core theology. It is true that stating the issue of growing European power as a *problem* already distinguishes *Rasselas* from the reams of contemporary writing that took this dominance as natural and increasingly inevitable, rather than see it as a historical development that could bear examination and explanation. Johnson's protagonists ask historical-materialist questions, but retreat into non-materialist answers (the operations of divine will and the shared unhappiness of human life) that shift away from the implications of Imlac's opening account of the European exercise of power and the accumulation of knowledge. This rhetorical turn is not unusual, and certainly not for Johnson, and it shows how this conversation is a useful instance of the limits, or rather, the contradictions, of Johnson's anti-imperialism. The present circumstance of European dominance is stated unequivocally, its causes are sought, but it is, finally, denied a historical provenance or explanation. On the one hand, no racial or religious grounds are posited for European superiority, which makes for a pointed contrast with explanations that became commonsense over the course the eighteenth century. On the other, European 'knowledge' is contrasted with 'ignorance' elsewhere, which is deeply ironic in that Imlac and Rasselas come into contact with scholars and wise men in Cairo and other places, and are themselves representative of seekers after knowledge and human understanding. For readers today, this contradictory complexity of characterization and conversation both marks Johnson's contribution to eighteenth-century vocabularies of anti-imperialism and suggests the conceptual boundaries of his Christian humanism.[14]

This anti-imperialism and Christian universalism is on display in much of Johnson's commentary on geopolitics. A single instance must suffice here, one that will point us forward to the experiences and writing of slaves educated into English: in his 'Introduction' to *The World Displayed or a Curious Collection of Voyages and Travels*, Johnson produced this assessment of the way in which 'the power of *Europe* has been extended to the remotest parts of the world' following upon Prince Henry the Navigator's encouragement of Portuguese sailors in the fifteenth century:

> Much knowledge has been acquired, and much cruelty committed, the belief of religion has been very little propagated, and its laws have been outrageously and enormously violated. The *Europeans* have scarcely visited any coast, but to gratify avarice, and extend corruption; to arrogate dominium without right, and practise cruelty without incentive. Happy had it been for the oppressed, if the designs of *Henry* had slept in his bosom, and surely more happy for the oppressors. But there is reason to hope that out of so much evil good may sometime be produced, and that the light of the gospel will at last illuminate the sands of *Africa*, and the desarts of *America*, though its progress cannot but be slow, when it is so much obstructed by the lives of Christians. (Johnson 1759: xvi)

There is no gainsaying the historical critique of imperialism here, including the startling insight that imperialism is oppressive (differently so, to be sure) for both its victims and its perpetrators. Johnson's knowledge of past and contemporary wrongs, combined with his Tory distrust of belligerent commerce and his Christian faith, led him to condemn colonial avarice as materially and spiritually corrupt.[15] In his hope that the light of the gospel would offer a compensation for the cruelties suffered by people in Africa and in the Americas, Johnson was a precursor to the Christian abolitionists who mobilized not for the cessation of empire but for the end of the slave trade, and eventually, for the end of slavery.[16] It is to the cultural matrix of slavery and anti-slavery that we will now turn, in particular to the writing of educated slaves, who sought in the resources of English – both the language and its literature, particularly the Bible – a medium for their own experiences and their own political desires.

Phillis Wheatley: Literacy, Poetry, and Slavery

> There is now in the town of Boston a free Negro Girl, about eighteen years of age, who has been but nine years in the country, whose singular genius and accomplishments are such as not only do honour to her sex, but to human nature. Several of her poems have been printed, and read with pleasure by the public.
>
> (Benjamin Rush, *An Address to the Inhabitants of the British Settlements in America Upon Slave Keeping* (Philadelphia, 1773))[17]

A contemporary reader of Wheatley's *Poems on Various Subjects, Religious and Moral*, published in London in 1773 (after no publisher could be found in Boston, where Wheatley lived) would have to negotiate a series of prefatory materials before getting to the poems. The volume opens with an engraving in which a young and demure Phillis sits at a table pen in hand, with a sheet of paper, on which she has written some lines, before her and an unidentified volume by its side. Her eyes are cast upwards, in search for inspiration perhaps, and her left hand is raised to her chin in a further gesture of contemplation. Around the engraving runs a frame, within which is printed 'Phillis Wheatley, Negro Servant to Mr John Wheatley, of Boston.' The volume is dedicated to the Countess of Huntington, and the Preface that follows makes, in the most genteel eighteenth-century manner, its apology for publishing poems 'that were written originally for the Amusement of the Author.' The 'Importunity' of 'generous Friends' (in whose voice this preface is written) has led to their publication, and now they hope that critics will not censure their defects too severely, but will in fact recognize their merits. Apologia along these lines were to be found prefacing many volumes by women, but what follows emphasizes Wheatley's special racial status: a letter from her master that attests to the conditions under which she came to literacy in English and then to the writing of poetry. (Such attestation, we should remember, also prefaced volumes of poetry by laboring-class poets like Stephen Duck and Mary Collier.)[18]

John Wheatley's letter is addressed to Archibald Bell, the London publisher, and confirms that Phillis 'was brought from *Africa* to *America*' in 1761 when she was seven or eight years old. She was taught to read by his family, and in sixteen months could read 'the most difficult Parts of the Sacred Writings, to the great Astonishment of all who heard her.' He goes on to say that she now wishes to learn Latin and has made 'some Progress in it.' (While John Wheatley does not mention it, we might remember he named Phillis after the ship on which she was 'brought' to Massachusetts.) Next follows a notice 'To the Publick,' signed by eighteen male worthies from Boston, including the Governor, the Lieutenant-Governor, and several members of the clergy, attesting that the poems are written by Phillis, 'who was but a few Years since, brought an uncultivated Barbarian from *Africa*, and has ever since been, and now is, under the Disadvantage of serving as a Slave in a Family in this Town' (Wheatley 2001: 1–8; the portrait is reproduced on the front cover. All references to Wheatley's poems are to this edition). All this textual apparatus was considered necessary to introduce, in a proper manner, the novelty of a volume of poems by a young black slave in Boston, whose talent and piety (once they were fully vouched for) were attractive to anti-slavery and Methodist publishing circles in London. Wheatley spent five weeks in London while the book was being prepared, but returned to Boston before it was published in order to nurse her ailing mistress, teacher, and patron, Susannah. Shortly after her return, she was manumitted by her owners.

Wheatley's poems, not surprisingly, are schooled exercises in neoclassicist poetics and Christian faith. Poetic diction – that is, the idiom and tropes rendered conventional by celebrated poets like Alexander Pope or Thomas Gray – abounds, and many of her poems, in the best traditions of eighteenth-century apprentice verse, are often occasional, written to commemorate particular events or people. She wrote a surprising number of elegies on well-known and anonymous people, ranging from 'On the Death of the Rev. Mr George Whitefield' (1770) to 'On the Death of a young Lady of Five Years of Age.' Her elegies share Christian *consolatio* motifs and iconography, but are modulated to reflect the different social impact of each death. When Whitefield, one of the founders of Methodism, dies, Wheatley's verse is appropriately Miltonic in its vision:

> Behold the prophet in his tow'ring flight!
> He leaves the earth for heav'n's unmeasur'd height,
> And worlds unknown receive him from our sight.
> There *Whitefield* wings with rapid course his way,
> And sails to *Zion* through vast seas of day. (ll. 11–13)

The five-year-old Nancy's path to heaven is quieter, and suffused with a child-like wonder and even comfort (Wheatley uses the same pentameter couplet in each case, which suggests her skill at evoking an atmospherics appropriate to her subject):

> From dark abodes to fair ethereal light
> Th' enraptured innocent has wing'd her flight;
> On the kind bosom of eternal love
> She finds unknown beatitude above. (ll. 1–4)

On the whole, Wheatley's elegies are not exceptional achievements in that form; what is significant is their large number. Perhaps that should be phrased as a question: is it significant that a young slave chose to write, over and over again, poems of heavenly redemption in death, each one insisting that there is little need to mourn the transience or difficulty of life if there is a glorious afterlife, where all rest equally in the divine bosom?[19] It is reasonable to think that it cannot be otherwise, if only because, no matter how well Wheatley was treated by her owners, and introduced to elite circles at home and in London, she knew that she was a slave, and she knew that she was one of the hundreds of thousands of Africans enslaved in British America. Nor was it possible in the years before 1773 to imagine either the abolition of the slave trade, much less the end of slavery, even though Massachusetts and London saw anti-slavery activists attempt judicial and legislative reforms (and win the occasional significant victory like Lord Mansfield's 1772 judgment barring slave owners from forcibly deporting their slaves from Britain). If freedom in this life remained a forlorn hope for most slaves, redemption in a Christian afterlife remained an attractive hope for the faithful, a belief actively encouraged by the slave owners and pastors who administered to them. To claim this is not to reduce Wheatley's faith or her elegies to simple instruments of consolation, but to take seriously the conditions under which she wrote. What else could a young and educated slave offer others in their grief but graceful formal reiterations of isolation and loss, and the hope of recovery in the shared vocabulary of a religious community? And how else could she claim, or even demonstrate, a membership in that community, even as it was denied to her in law?

Wheatley's Christian poetics did not only feature metaphysical and eschatological visions, but offered her a *historical* schema with which to rationalize her enslavement and displacement.[20] In 'To the University of Cambridge, in New-England' (1767), the poet identifies herself as 'an *Ethiop*' (l. 28), and re-imagines the Middle Passage as the Israelite flight from bondage:

> 'Twas not long since I left my native shore
> The land of errors, and *Egyptian* gloom:
> Father of mercy, 'twas thy gracious hand
> Brought me in safety from those dark abodes. (ll. 3–6)

The brief 'On being brought from Africa to America' (1768), offers similar sentiments, and is worth quoting in full:

> 'Twas mercy brought me from my *Pagan* land,
> Taught my benighted soul to understand
> That there's a God, that there's a *Saviour* too:
> Once I redemption neither sought nor knew.
> Some view our sable race with scornful eye,
> 'Their colour is a diabolical die.'
> Remember, *Christians*, *Negroes*, black as *Cain*,
> May be refin'd, and join th' angelic train.

The pointed, internally dialogic quality of this poem, written by a fifteen-year-old, is a preview of the iconoclastic play that brought fame to William Blake's visions of childlike innocence and socio-historical experience.

This poem can be read as seamlessly accommodationist, as simply parroting her master's voice and religious teaching, as reducing Africa to the moral and irreligious condition defined for it by Christian slavers and colonists. But that would be a mistake, one that misses out on the poignant irony of the word 'mercy' in the opening line, and, more importantly, on the delicate ambiguity of the slave's understanding that she has been *taught* lessons in soul-making and redemption that she 'neither sought nor knew.' Lines five and six condense into a tightly rhymed couplet the full weight of the Christian racism that sees blacks as dyed in the color of the devil, damned in pigmentation as in morality. The economy and the commonsense, unembellished tone of this couplet is startling, as is the confidence with which a poet barely older than a child unflinchingly ventriloquizes the voice of those who enslave her, and who do so by deploying the same Christian vocabulary in which she seeks redemption. The penultimate line holds a similar tension in place – it appeals to, even exhorts, Christians to remember that 'Negroes,' who are 'black as *Cain*,' may still be redeemed. And yet readers of the Bible will know that Cain is 'black' because of his sin, not by his color. That being the case, might the phrase 'black as *Cain*' modify erring '*Christians*' as well as '*Negroes*,' the comma between the two words not separating these communities as much as linking them into a commonality of sin and redemption?

That Wheatley is aware of the difference a word can make to a line, and to a politics, is made clear by a variant in 'On the Death of the Rev. Mr George Whitefield.' In the earlier version, Wheatley writes:

> Take him, ye *Africans*, he longs for you,
> *Impartial Saviour* is his title due:
> Wash'd in the fountain of redeeming blood,
> You shall be sons, and kings, and priests to God. (ll. 34–7)

The poet's vision is of a Christian redemption and fellowship for slaves, rather than liberation, but even here the last line – 'sons, and kings, and priests to God' – has a social heft that does not disappear into this metaphysical promise. A different version was published in London in 1770, in which the last two lines read:

> If you will walk in Grace's heavenly Road,
> He'll make you free, and Kings, and Priests to God. (ll. 43–4)

Here, the word 'free,' which resonates in both civic and Christian registers, shows how religious aspiration enables political hope; that being the case, can we then read any articulation of transcendent freedom in Wheatley's poems, no matter how theological its inspiration or vocabulary, otherwise? The point here is simply that Wheatley's being a slave and black necessarily demands that we read her poetry differently from similar poems written by free white women or men – her social status and her moment in history resonate in her writing, rippling through its textures and shifting its meanings.

Wheatley, at one further remove than is usually the case, is a prime instance of colonial cultural education. That is, she learned elements of the same Anglo-American colonial education available to members of the family who owned and taught her. Literature was a staple of such education, as is the Bible in those contexts where proselytizing was the norm. For someone in Wheatley's position, education offered enormous benefits, made even more pointed in her case because her abilities were taken to reflect on the intellectual potential of an entire race. Such education was deeply ideological, with the glories of the colonizers' literature being a testimonial to their superiority, which is how the Bible was made available too. And yet it was an education, in a moment when education was denied to almost all slaves, and a training into culturally valued forms of expression. Wheatley's learning, and her religious faith, are those of the colonizer, but her poetics – though conventional – are not, stemming as they do from the sensibility and imagination of one enslaved for her race.[21]

Wheatley refers to her race often enough to make clear her distinction. In 'To Maecenas,' after enrolling Homer and Virgil as poetic inspirations that her 'grov'ling mind' (l. 29) can only hope to follow, she invokes Terence (a footnote says 'He was *African* by birth') and asks 'But say, ye *Muses*, why this partial grace,/ To one alone of *Afric*'s sable race' (ll. 39–40). A Roman slave who became a playwright, Terence is a particularly apt precedent, and indeed, in her knowledge, her only precursor in the Greek and Latin classical tradition. In 'An Hymn to Humanity. *To S. P. G. Esq;*' the poet emphasizes her gratitude to the addressee by asking rhetorically 'Can *Afric*'s muse forgetful prove?' (l. 31), and in 'On Recollection' (1772) she writes as a 'vent'rous *Afric*' (l. 2). Each time she announces her race the poem takes on a different historical or experiential burden, even when its vocabulary and themes are conventional and undistinguished. Thus, this ode to '*Mneme*' (Mnemosyne or memory) speaks only in moral terms of the power of memory to reward the virtuous with peace and joy and to punish sinners with reminders of their past misdeeds. However, some lines have implications not fully explored by the poem, but which give it a historical charge not at once perceptible. Lines 9–18 suggest that memory haunts not just individuals but entire collectivities. We are told that *Mneme* is the source of dreams: she 'pours/ The ample treasure of her secret stores' into 'nocturnal visions' (ll. 9–10). She also enables poetry: 'To the high-raptur'd poet gives her aid' (l. 14). More consequentially, *Mneme* also is a figure for community memory: 'The heavn'ly *phantom* paints the actions done/ By ev'ry tribe beneath the rolling sun' (ll. 17–18). This is an account of the making of communal and historical memory, an idea that is repeated in the poet's choice of collective noun in line 25:

> But how is *Mneme* dreaded by that race,
> Who scorn her warnings and despise her grace?
> By her unveil'd each horrid crime appears,
> Her awful hand a cup of wormwood bears.
> Days, years misspent, O what a hell of woe!
> Hers the worst tortures that our souls can know. (ll. 25–30)

Are we to think only of a 'race' of sinners here, a reading suggested by the 'our' of line 30, which includes the poet in that number? Or is she only testifying to her knowledge of the power of memory to torment (lines 29–30 being a couplet set off from the four lines before), leaving in place the more disturbing argument that an entire race is marked and embittered by their collective crimes?

Similar complexities mark other poems too, including those published after the 1773 collection. Wheatley's 'To a Gentleman of the Navy,' a poem published in December 1774 in the Royal American Magazine is prefaced by a reference to her as *'a young* African, *of surprising genius.'* The first eighteen lines of the poem are unmarked by her geographical origins, as Wheatley, in an overwrought Homeric compliment, describes Lieutenant Rochfort as a naval officer and poet so praiseworthy that the promise of his friendship might even have prevented the Trojan wars by distracting Paris away from Helen! These lines appeal to Calliope, the muse of epic poetry, for inspiration, but the appeal is thwarted: 'Calliope, half gracious to my prayer,/ Grants but the half and scatters half in air' (ll. 17–18). It is not clear what Calliope has denied the poet, but the poem does change tack at this point, and moves from Troy to contemporary Britain. The passage that follows invokes English nationalist verse about naval power (a prime instance of which is Pope's *Windsor-Forest*, which echoes here):

> Far in the space where ancient Albion keeps
> Amidst the roarings of the sacred deeps,
> Where willing forests leave their native plain,
> Descend, and instant, plough the wat'ry main.
> Strange to relate! With canvas wings they speed
> To distant worlds; of distant worlds the dread.
> The trembling natives of the peaceful plain,
> Astonish'd view the heroes of the main, (ll. 19–26)

The might of the British navy is here celebrated as a prelude to 'trembling natives' viewing Rochfort (and Samuel Graves, the British naval commander in Boston), both of whom are described as motivated by a 'thirst for glory' (l. 30).

However loyal a colonial subject Wheatley might have been at this time, these lines – the stuff of modern imperial epic – cannot but be a reminder that she once was one of the astonished natives who were forced to endure enslavement and the passage across the Atlantic by ships that were 'of distant worlds the dread.' The epic muse (and the conventions of imperial poetry) are invoked, and Rochfort and Graves described in their naval glory, but this vision, and this form, ceases once its geopolitical weight becomes clear. In the last section (ll. 31–40) Calliope gives way to a more personal muse, and to less belligerent and disturbing personifications of Rochfort and Graves as figures of virtue and of poetry, whose friendship and praise are all the reward the poet seeks: 'Lo! Rochfort smiles, and Graves approves my lays.' As with other lyric and odic poets of the eighteenth century, the dynamic movement, including flows, hesitations, and turns, of Wheatley's poetry are our indicators of her fears and difficulties. Clearly well tutored into the by-ways of English poetry, Wheatley could perform its conventions (and indeed its clichés), and could render its iconography and its sentiments, but they led, on more than one occasion, to a juncture where the ideology and history embedded into that poetics chafed against her being and her story. Those are the moments most rewarding to postcolonial reading, most revelatory of the lack of fit between British nationalist and neoclassicist verse and the contradictory desires of the colonial and slave subject who wrote in that tradition.

Lieutenant Rochfort responded by writing an elaborate compliment to Wheatley, which, unsurprisingly, addresses her as 'The lovely daughter of the Affric shore' (l. 8) and then goes on, most unusually, to describe Africa as 'the guilded shore, the happy land,' (l. 15), where the 'torrid heat the soul inspires;/ With strains divine and true poetic fires;' (19–20). Britain, he writes, long the home of 'lofty bards' (l. 51),

> No more can boast, but of the power to kill,
> By force of arms, or diabolic skill.
> For softer strains we quickly must repair
> To Wheatly's song, for Wheatly is the fair;
> That has the art, which art could ne'er acquire;
> To dress each sentence with seraphic fire. (ll. 57–62)

Wheatley's reply, published in the same magazine in January 1775, returns his compliments, but insists that 'that the humble Afric muse's seat' should be fixed 'At British Homer's and Sir Isaac's feet' (ll. 15–17). She picks up on Rochfort's cue (and his determinedly pastoral idiom) to claim a returning memory of Gambia as Edenic: 'Her soil spontaneous, yields exhaustless shores;/ For phoebus revels on her verdant shores.' (ll. 27–8). There is no specificity in her description, both because she had no real memories of her life there, but also because hers is a finely tuned poetic response to Rochfort, whose lines on Gambia also lack geographical specificity and are a cheerful pastiche of pastoral phrases (including an adaptation of a line from Pope's *Windsor-Forest*). In turn, Wheatley's Gambia is a bouquet of pastoral tropes and images. However, she turns aside the suggestion that nature in Britain is poorer than in Africa, or that it has lost its power to inspire poets: 'There, as in Britain's favour'd isle, behold/ The bending harvest ripen into gold!' (ll.

31–2). The problem in late-eighteenth-century Britain is not that there are no poets, but that Milton and Newton cannot easily be emulated or equaled. In the matter of poetic genealogy, Wheatley was sure she knew her place.

While Wheatley's cultural heroes are largely English, her poems do suggest an awareness of colonial estrangement. In 'To the Right Honourable William, Earl of Dartmouth . . .' (1772), Wheatley celebrates William Legge's appointment as Principal Secretary of State for the British colonies in North American and writes that 'Fair *Freedom*' now rises '*New-England* to adorn' (l. 2):

> No more, *America*, in mournful strain
> Of wrongs, and grievance unredress'd complain,
> No longer shalt thou dread the iron chain,
> Which wanton *Tyranny* with lawless hand
> Had made, and with it meant t'enslave the land. (ll. 15–19)

Wheatley writes as an American and a loyal colonial subject (there is no overt anti-colonial sentiment here) who hopes that a new colonial administrator might redress political wrongs; in the lines that follow she writes as an African and a slave who knows at first hand (rather than as political metaphors) what it means to 'dread the iron chain' and 't'enslave the land':

> Should you, my lord, while you peruse my song,
> Wonder from whence my love of *Freedom* sprung,
> Whence flow these wishes for the common good,
> By feeling hearts alone best understood,
> I, young in life, by seeming cruel fate
> Was snatch'd from *Afric*'s fancy'd happy seat:
> . . .
> Such, such my case. And can I then but pray
> Others may never feel tyrannic sway? (ll. 20–31)

This long account of the poet's enslavement and loss at the heart of this poem causes the poem's reiterated opposition of 'tyranny' and 'freedom' to take on a darker and more ironic tone. After all, the appeal for American freedoms does not include the freedom of slaves, nor did the word tyranny extend in contemporary political parlance to the bondage of slaves (except perhaps in small circles of abolitionists). But if the slave's condition is the classic political definition of unfreedom, of tyranny, then any comparison of the poet's experience with that of America suggests that emancipation – independence – is the only real solution of 'wrongs, and grievance unredress'd.'[22]

In the next few years, Wheatley's position on American grievances moved, along with her Boston circle, to the demand for independence. In October 1775, Wheatley composed a patriotic ode to George Washington, now commander of the Continental armies, and celebrated 'Columbia's scenes of glorious toils' (l. 2). She thus became one of many poets and painters who revived the figure of Columbia (after Columbus) as an icon for the political aspirations and military prowess of the thirteen colonies. Wheatley sings of Washington's army ('thick as leaves in Autumn's golden reign,/ Such, and so many, moves the warrior's train.' ll. 19–20), and of his personal 'valour' and 'virtues' (l. 27). She exhorts Washington to his duty to defeat 'whoever dares disgrace/ The land of freedom's heaven-defended race!' (ll. 31–2). Britain – once overbearing, now abject – finds a place in her poem:

> Anon Britannia droops the pensive head,
> While round increase the rising hills of dead.
> Ah! Cruel blindness to Columbia's state!
> Lament thy thirst of boundless power too late. (ll. 35–8)

There are several ironies at play in this poem. The first is linguistic and figurative: this is anti-colonial verse, but its form and idiom are precisely that of British nationalist verse, with Columbia rising where once Britannia reigned. The second is that Wheatley celebrates an army that was engulfed in a tremendous debate about whether black men should be allowed to enlist (or re-enlist, if they were free and in army service already) (relevant details of his history are available in Shuffleton 2001: 186–7). Thirdly, no state had abolished slavery, which evacuates the political claim contained in the poetic flourish that describes the colonies as the 'land of freedom's heaven-defended race.' Perhaps Washington, and her readers (the poem was published in 1776), could take at face value her patriotism, but in a climate of anti-colonial and anti-slavery mobilization (whose objectives did not always overlap), a black woman's plea for Columbia's triumph, and for improvements in 'Columbia's state,' would have worked as a reminder of an as-yet unrealized, and more uncertain, collective future.

This poem demonstrates, as I mentioned already, Wheatley's adaptation of British nationalist and imperialist iconography to her anti-colonial purposes, in which she deftly elevates Columbia into the place and status of Britannia. However, in a later poem, 'Liberty and Peace,' written in 1784 after the formal end of the war that followed the ratification of the 1783 Treaty of Paris by the US Congress, Wheatley's deployment of similar tropes and ideas endows Columbia with a more dubious imperial genealogy, even as the poem wishes for the new nation commercial success and international peace. Poets of the British Empire had harked back to Augustan Rome as a model for the rise and the decline of empire, but even more so because Augustan Rome – and the patron Maecenas – suggested the flowering of the arts, till such references became stapes of eighteenth-century neoclassicism. Many of them had grounded this comparison in the complementary notion that British international power and cultural prestige were part of the westward movement of empires and the arts. Wheatley inherits this idea (and, as it turned out, intuits the future) when she describes the victorious United States as superseding Britain: 'And new-born *Rome* shall give *Britannia* Law' (2001: 22).[23] This imperial identity nestles within a post-Independence poem that is largely about the political alliances (she thanks France and Ireland for their material support and sympathy) and battles (the burning of Charleston) that led to the survival of the colonies as an independent nation. Her vision of the future emphasizes peace and prosperity for the US, and coexistence with the British Empire. Wheatley wrote this poem in the voice of the 'prescient Muse' (l. 1); today, as the United States fights wars and stations its military across the globe, her concluding lines, which map zones of geopolitical influence and imagine 'Columbia' as the new nation whose 'swelling Sails' will spread Peace and Freedom to 'every Realm,' seem both prophetic, and sadly ironic:

> So Freedom comes array'd with Charms divine,
> And in her Train Commerce and Plenty shine.
> *Britannia* owns her Independent Reign,
> *Hibernia*, *Scotia*, and the Realms of *Spain*;
> And great *Germania's* ample Coast admires
> The generous Spirit that *Columbia* fires.
> Auspicious Heaven shall fill with fav'ring Gales,
> Where e'er *Columbia* spreads her swelling Sails:
> To every Realm shall *Peace* her Charms display,
> And Heavenly *Freedom* spread her golden Ray.

Ukawsaw Gronniosaw: Writing in Another Voice

'The Preface to the Reader,' written by the Reverend Walter Shirley, introduces *A Narrative of the Most Remarkable Particulars in the Life of James Albert Ukawsaw Gronniosaw, An African Prince, Written by Himself* (1774), in ways that bring to the fore several issues central to our understanding of the production and reception of Black writing in the late eighteenth century.[24] Shirley presents the *Narrative* as a form of Christian witnessing, with Albert an unusual witness, given his origins in Africa, his enslavement in Guinea, and his subsequent life in America and in England. Albert's importance lies in his being evidence that 'an all wise and omnipotent appointment and direction' is to be discerned in the movement of slaves from African into Christian lands (Gronniosaw 1995: 28), proof indeed that the Christian God saves even those born 'in the regions of the grossest darkness and ignorance' (1995: 27). Shirley's logic casts the slave trade in a different, indeed a divine, light here, and slavery itself becomes a necessary prelude to Christian redemption. Shirley attests to Albert's character, confirms his knowledge of the scriptures, and guarantees the moral authenticity of the *Narrative* by making clear that it was not originally designed for publication, but was written to serve the 'private satisfaction' of the young lady who acted as Albert's amanuensis:

> *This account of the life and spiritual experience of* James Albert, *was taken from his own mouth, and committed to paper by the elegant pen of a young* Lady *of the town of* Leominster, *for her own private satisfaction, and without any intention, at first, that it should be made public. But she has now been prevailed on to commit it to the press, both with a view to serve* Albert *and his distressed family, who have the sole profits arising from the sale of it; and likewise, as it is apprehended, this little history contains matter well worthy the notice and attention of every Christian reader.* (1995: 27)

Reading Shirley's certainties of faith and tone today are a reminder of just how powerfully *framed* Gronniosaw's narrative was in its entry into the world. He dictated the text, we are told; did the 'elegant pen' of the young lady simply act as recorder, or did it reshape Gronniosaw's voice into pious conventionality, if not into elegance? Gronniosaw was in his sixties then, and immured with his family in poverty. His brief account of his life closes with his reminder of the 'charitable assistance' occasionally offered them by the Christian faithful, which allows them – 'very poor pilgrims . . . traveling through many difficulties towards our heavenly home' – to subsist (1995: 53). The sales of the book are to be construed too as a species of charity. In these circumstances, how do we listen for Gronniosaw in the text, given, as his Potkay and Burr put it judiciously, that it 'is difficult to determine the degree to which the conventions and the politics of representation have sifted or indeed stifled the outrage of the earliest black writers and the range of their testimony' (1995: 1)? Evangelical Christianity, with its powerful narratives of and insistence upon witnessing and personal conversion, offered black Africans

– enslaved and free – a tenuous community, and the only self-definition, ratified by white society. Writing, then, becomes a crucial, and difficult, exercise in belonging and alienation.

This doubling has led Robert Stepto to emphasize the inextricably intertwined quests for freedom and literacy that defined Afro-American emergence from slavery, as it has led to Henry Louis Gates Jr's argument that a 'slave's texts' can only be read as 'testimony of defilement: the slave's *representation* and reversal of the master's attempt to transform a human being into a commodity, and the slave's simultaneous verbal witness of the possession of a humanity shared in common with Europeans' (Stepto 1979; Gates 1988: 128). As Gates observes, the challenge posed by the literary and publishing protocols of English to the subjectivity and language of the slave precipitates a crucial narrative topos. In a dramatic moment of misunderstanding, a slave, left alone with a book which a white master has read aloud and handled with reverence, holds it up as a divine fetish and expects it to speak to him. In doing so, he or she intuits the symbolic centrality of the printed book in confirming the power of slave traders and slave owners. This moment encapsulates both the causal connections, and the seemingly insuperable gap, between the culture of the book and the abject condition of the slave. Gates argues that the process that follows, as a few remarkable slaves become literate in their master's tongue, derives from the slave's understanding of the critical need to inscribe 'their voices in the written word' and thus into 'the text of Western letters,' in order to claim a shared humanity. Gates identifies the trope of the Talking Book – given that it is self-consciously repeated in a significant number of slave narratives – as the 'ur-trope of the Anglo-African tradition.' The Talking Book becomes a figure for the tensions between slave vernaculars and the 'literate white text,' and 'between the oral and the printed forms of literary discourse.' Slave writings explore this tension, and thus call attention to the particular conditions in which individuals learned to read and write, and then to publish (Gates 1988: 130, 131).

In Gronniosaw's case, the *Narrative* returns to his memory of himself as a newly enslaved fifteen-year-old abroad a Dutch vessel. In a first, and unusual, step towards acculturation, he remembers being grateful when his master, the ship's Captain, divests him of his childhood jewelry, and re-fashions him: 'I was now washed, & clothed in the *Dutch* or *English* manner.'[25] The Captain, he says, 'grew very fond of me, and I loved him exceedingly' (1995: 34), and these ties of affection within servitude prepare the young Gronniosaw for his impassioned encounter with his master's book:

He used to read prayers in public to the ship's crew every sabbath day; and when I first saw him read, I was never so surprised in my whole life as when I saw the book talk to my master; for I thought it did, as I observed him to look upon it, and move his lips. – I wished it would do so to me. – As soon as my master had done reading I follow'd him to the place where he put the book, being mightily delighted with it, and when nobody saw me, I open'd it and put my ear down close upon it, in great hope that it would say something to me; but was very sorry and greatly disappointed when I found it would not speak, this thought immediately presented itself to me, that every body and every thing despised me because I was black. (1995: 34)

It is important to note that at this point the young Gronniosaw and the Captain do not have a language in common; thus the voice of the book Gronniosaw hopes to hear is incomprehensible to him. But at each Sabbath reading, the book confirms his master's authority over the crew (no doubt Gronniosaw was impressed with the disciplined, perhaps reverential, attitudes with which the ship's crew listened to, and thus embodied, the power of the Captain's prayer-book or Bible) and so it is this voice of power Gronniosaw seeks to hear.

Gronniosaw's disappointed response to the book's silence focuses solely on his race: his master's favor notwithstanding, he is convinced that 'every body and every thing despised me because I was black.' The narrative does not linger upon this extraordinarily compressed and poignant insight, but it resonates with the abjection of the slave, whose alienation from people and objects is so fundamental that he can only understand it as the condition of his racial being. This moment, in which Gronniosaw is diminished by his failure to hear the book, is the most wrenching in the entire *Narrative*, far more so than his kidnapping by the Gold Coast merchant who sells him into slavery. We should also note the symptomatic irony figured here, one that structures the *Narrative*: Gronniosaw can only recover from his perceived violation by a text central to Dutch (and English) cultural practices by converting to both the religion and the culture of his masters. That process is drawn out but intense, and this section of the narrative features Gronniosaw's moral and spiritual tribulation to the exclusion of details of his life as a slave in New York.

His newest master, Mr *Freelandhouse* (now identified as an important Dutch evangelical pastor Theodorus Jacobus Frelinghuysen), arranges for his education, and his own preaching has a great impact on Gronniosaw. Even more consequentially for the form of the *Narrative*, Freelandhouse's wife gives Gronniosaw John Bunyan to read, and Bunyan's accounts of the struggle of the soul to achieve Christian faith become models for Gronniosaw's uncertain sense of himself in the world.[26] Encouraged by his tutor – 'he was greatly rejoiced to find me inquiring the way to Zion, and blessed the Lord who had worked so wonderfully for me a poor heathen' (1995: 38) – Gronniosaw's spiritual turmoil culminates in a moment of beatific joy, and he portrays himself in the vocabulary enabled by his reading of Christian texts : 'I would not have changed situations, or been any but myself for the whole world. I blest God for my poverty, that I had no worldly riches or grandeur to draw my heart from him' (1995: 39). The material condition of slavery is transformed into the spiritual bondage required of the Christian pilgrim, and Gronniosaw's *Narrative* finds its place within – and expands the subject matter of – European autobiography.

Gronniosaw's liberation into Christianity precedes his emancipation from slavery, but that follows soon as Freelandhouse, on his death-bed, gives him ten pounds and his freedom. As with a great many manumitted black men, Gronniosaw's freedom is precarious. A white man to whom he owes money threatens to sell him, and in order to avoid that fate he joins a privateer as a cook. His plans are really to find his way to England, since he was convinced by the example of Freelandhouse's evangelical friends, including the famous Methodist preacher George Whitefield, that it was home to good Christians. But before he can make his way to England, Gronniosaw becomes part of Britain's naval and military operations in the West Indies, first in St Domingo (on the island of Hispaniola) and then as part of a regiment of foot that took French strongholds in Martinique and the Spanish port of Havana. He thus joins one of the many multi-racial crews, made up of conscripts and volunteers, on board the merchant and pirate ships that built the Atlantic economy, and also participated in military expeditions that confirmed British control over sea routes and territories. Gronniosaw does not detail these exploits. He does however recall providential moments where men who had been particularly unkind to him meet untimely deaths (such divine intervention on behalf of oppressed Christians being a featured trope in conversion narratives).

Very little of Gronniosaw's shipboard or military experiences is made available, nor is there any comment on his participation in the multiracial world of sailors and soldiers (for a sense of this shipboard world, see Linebaugh and Rediker 2000). By this point, the *Narrative* confirms Gronniosaw in the persona of the unworldly Christian seeker, unable to detect deceit and trickery because of his faith in Christians everywhere. He arrives in Portsmouth and is tricked out of his money by a publican who pretends to be a good Christian. However he is rescued from his distress by the publican's sister-in-law, whom he describes as his 'Christian friend,' and who enables him to leave for London, where he hopes to meet Whitefield. Whitefield takes him in and finds him lodging, and Gronniosaw meets and befriends a silk weaver, Betty, with whom he begins to attend services. He also comes to believe that she is to be his wife, but before that can come to pass he decides to travel to Holland, in order to meet some of Mr Freelandhouse's friends, who had stated their 'curiosity to see me; particularly the gentlemen engaged in the ministry, who expressed a desire to hear my experience and examine me' (1995: 45).

In all these encounters – both benign and unpleasant – Gronniosaw's narrative jettisons the language of racial markings or racist responses altogether. As a young boy confronted by a book that refuses to talk to him, Gronniosaw cannot think of himself as anything but black, and hence despicable. Now, the primary, indeed the only, lens through which he sees himself and others is that of Christianity, with the result that his account becomes opaque to the problems of racial distinction and discrimination. There are some odd moments though. When he meets Betty, he fears that 'she should prove like all the rest I had met with at *Portsmouth* &c. and which had almost given me a dislike to all white women,' which is an odd formulation given that it was a white woman who had rescued him in his distress. (Gronniosaw had experienced Portsmouth as 'worse than *Sodom*' (1995: 44), which is not surprising, as it was, like most busy port towns, full of rowdy sailors and prostitutes attracted by their presence.) Can we sense in that blanket 'dislike to all white women' a feeling more complex than Gronniosaw's articulated fear that he had fallen amongst unchristian people in Portsmouth? And is the 'curiosity to see me' of the Dutch friends of Mr Freelandhouse a colloquialism for their desire to meet a fellow-Christian, or does the phrase contain Gronniosaw's unspoken sense that his African-ness and blackness continue to demand, and excite, visual inspection?[27] In either case, Gronniosaw does not admit to the operations of racial difference, and claims for himself only the subjectivity and self-understanding enabled by his Christian faith.

Gronniosaw is examined by a group of forty-eight Dutch Calvinist ministers whom he meets in Amsterdam once a week for seven weeks, and at the end, he notes that they were 'persuaded that I was what I pretended to be.' He withstands his extended questioning because, he believes, 'the Lord almighty was with me at that time in a remarkable manner, and gave me words, and enabled me to answer them; so great was his mercy to take me in hand a poor blind Heathen' (1995: 46).

Gronniosaw's prose (or that of his amanuensis) performs the miracle of articulation it claims, and swells into biblical cadences. The holy book had once refused to speak to him, but his Christian faith and reading now give him 'words' and a tone appropriate to the occasion. In this account, Christianity endows him with the social being denied to him by the racist world of slavery and the slave trade, and offers a way of extricating himself from its worst excesses. But – and this is of even more ideological significance – his Christianity is explicitly offered as an exculpation of the effects of slavery and the slave trade. He gets his text from Psalms 66:16, and bears witness to all that God '*hath done for my soul*' (1995: 46).

Gronniosaw works for a year in Amsterdam as butler to a rich merchant, but then returns to England to seek out Betty, whom he hopes to marry. She accepts, and they begin their lives together, and from this point on the *Narrative* becomes a hurried record of their lives, which are reasonably comfortable when either or both are employed, or wracked by poverty when they are not. Betty works among the Spitalfields weavers in London, and makes a 'very good living,' except that Gronniosaw panics when the weavers there create 'a great disturbance' (in 1765 they rioted against the importation of French silk), as he fears that he will be forced to join them. He stops Betty from weaving, looks farther afield himself for work, and moves to Colchester as a laborer. While we do not know enough about Gronniosaw in London to comment authoritatively upon his decision to distance both Betty and himself from the rioting weavers, we should note that contemporary commentators were fearful of alliances between white working-class groups and free blacks. Peter Fryer quotes the magistrate Sir John Fielding, who in *Extracts from such of the Penal Laws, as Particularly relate to the Peace and Good Order of this Metropolis* (1768) wrote that blacks, '*intoxicated with Liberty*' and '*grown refractory*,' now entered '*into Societies, and make it their Business to corrupt and dissatisfy the Mind of every fresh black Servant that comes to England*' and that they often had '*the Mob on their Side*' as they pursued their own ends (Fryer 1988: 71). Gronniosaw's decision to remove himself from Spitalfields is in keeping with his perception of himself as a good Christian, for his continued presence there would have drawn him into precisely the occasionally violent working-class alliances that would have complicated that self-representation.

This last section of the *Narrative*, from the time Gronniosaw returns to London and marries Betty, allows us an unexpected view of the unstable worlds of weavers (in Spitalfields and in Norwich) and casual or seasonal agrarian labor. Gronniosaw's trials, and those of his family, which he insists they bear with Christian fortitude and in hope of divine succor, are now those of unemployment and poverty. His master in Colchester encourages him to bring Betty and the children there, but once winter comes and Gronniosaw loses his seasonal employment, they are reduced to grinding poverty. This is not the only occasion that they starve, but each time they are in such a situation, the *Narrative* offers further proof of divine intervention as kindly people offer aid and pull them back from the brink of death. Interestingly, except for Mr Handbarrar, his employer in Colchester, no one remarks on Gronniosaw's race, and the *Narrative* registers no racial discrimination or even distinction. Scholars have documented the presence of large numbers of blacks in Britain, primarily in London and other port cities, but Gronniosaw's account is notable in losing all consciousness of color when it describes work in towns like Norwich and Kidderminster, where there would in fact have been few non-white people. His single-minded commitment to identifying only as a Christian does of course repress other modes of identification, but there is in fact another social history that is summarily enacted in Gronniosaw's 'progress' from his awareness of racial distinction to his becoming one of the many impoverished laborers and artisans in England.

As Fryer puts it, most of the 10,000 or so blacks in Britain at the turn of the nineteenth century were men, and many married white women, with the result that – over time, and in the absence of regular black immigration – their progeny, who also married other white people, lost their sense of racial distinctiveness and merged with the large number of the British poor (Fryer 1988: 235). In this way, the social history of black people in nineteenth-century Britain recapitulates Gronniosaw's personal transformation from enslaved African to immiserated British laborer. In the *Narrative*, Christian forms of self-understanding and storytelling do of course provide the mediating links that make possible this transformation, but there is no gainsaying the dense social history that frames, and occasionally finds a place within, this slave-pilgrim's progress. Gronniosaw's search for work finally leads him to Kidderminster, where the family is based when the text concludes. They live now by the fruit of Betty's loom, and by the occasional charity of people, with Gronniosaw able to contribute little because of his 'age and infirmity' (1995: 53). The *Narrative* concludes with a pious portrayal of them as 'very poor pilgrims' traveling through 'many difficulties towards our heavenly home, and waiting patiently for his glorious call, when the Lord shall deliver us out of the evils of this present world, and bring us to the everlasting glories of the world to come' (1995: 53).[28] These are the present circumstances alluded to by the Reverend Shirley in his Preface, when he explains that the book is published also *'with a view to serve Albert and his distressed family, who have the sole profits arising from the sale of it'* (1995: 27).

Wheatley and Gronniosaw, and after them John Marrant, Quobna Ottobah Cuguano and Olaudah Equiano among others, remind us of the crucial importance of reading and writing to the process of self-making for both once-enslaved Africans and free blacks in trans-Atlantic locations in the eighteenth century. The power of the book – or of literary culture in its entirety – to exclude is intuited and enacted most memorably in the trope of the talking book, but more generally in the material circumstances of their lives. In a more positive vein though, these lives also show the difficult process by which those colonized or marginalized can write themselves back into the historical or cultural accounts which deny them their humanity in the first place. Hammon's or Gronniosaw's narratives are formally constrained, as in some ways are Wheatley's poems, but these texts, and the more expansive and pointedly anti-slavery *The Interesting Narrative of the Life of Olaudah Equiano, or Gustavus Vassa, The African. Written by Himself* (London, 1789) anchor the traditions of African-American and anti-imperialist writing. It is when we think of Gronniosaw as one of the products of the slave trade whose writing (however conservative it might seem) contributed to the re-definition of political subjectivity in imperial Britain, and when we read Wheatley as having opened up the canon of British and American poetry to the experiences of non-white and enslaved subjects, that we recognize the historical force of their entry into the world of trans-Atlantic letters.

Notes

1. Robert Halsband recognizes that these letters combine features of the familiar letter (which is personal and putatively unrevised) and those of the more studied narratives 'in the form of letters, a very popular form of travel literature since the Renaissance' (Halsband 1966: 65–8).
2. The overlap between the emphases of African-American studies and colonial discourse studies has meant that Black writers like Phillis Wheatley, Ottobah Cuguano, Ignatius Sancho, and Olaudah Equiano are now taught as part of the history of trans-Atlantic literature in English.
3. Lady Mary too combined elements of various literary conventions – the romance, the oriental tale, the travelogue – to extend the familiar letter into unfamiliar territory. She did so with the cultural self-assurance of an aristocrat with many literary friends (even as literary ambition amongst women was frowned upon). Ironically, her class status was one reason why a volume of her letters was not published till after her death.
4. Letter from Adrianople, 1 April 1717, in Montagu 1965: 1. 325–30. References in Lady Mary's letters suggest that she was familiar with Richard Knolles, *The*

General History of the Turks (1603) and its continuation by Paul Rycaut, as well as with travel accounts by Jean de Thévenot, George Sandys, and Aaron Hill.

5. Some of Lady Mary's observations rebut popular misconceptions about Islam and the status of women in Turkish society: 'Our Vulgar Notion that they do not own Women to have any souls is a mistake,' she writes, and Halsband points out that this might be a precise response to Mrs Sullen's speech in George Farquhar's *The Beaux' Stratagem* (1707), where she says 'Were I born an humble Turk, where women have no soul or property, there I must sit contented' (Montagu 1965: 1.363, n. 3). Lady Mary's listing of the wealth of aristocratic Turkish women and their self-contained lives functions as a similar argument against such cultural ignorance.

6. 'Letter to Ann Thistlethwayte, April 1, 1717,' in Montagu 1965: 1. 340–4. Lady Mary took to Turkish ways in order to visit otherwise inaccessible places. She writes 'The asmak, or Turkish vail, is become not only very easy but agreeable to me, and if it was not, I would be content to endure some inconveniency to content a passion so powerfull with me as Curiosity.' 'Letter to Lady Bristol, April 10, 1718,' in Montagu 1965: 1. 396–403.

7. In a comment on Lady Mary's use of generic conventions, Billie Melman writes that 'despite the trappings of the eighteenth-century oriental tale, despite the neo-classical conventions, despite the use of the polemics of the Enlightenment, Montagu's harem . . . is in fact not dissimilar to the aristocratic household in Britain, at that time' (Melman 1992: 97). Cynthia Lowenthal argues that Lady Mary's portraits of Turkish lives are realized 'through the empowering but distorted fictional veil of romance,' which is true, but with the proviso that this 'veil' also enables her polemics against the supposedly realist claims of prior reporters on Turkey (Lowenthal 1994: 12).

8. Antoine Galland's translation, *Les Mille et une nuits, contes arabes* was published in twelve volumes in 1704–17 (cf. footnote 12).

9. Lady Mary might have owned slaves herself, as is suggested by Jonathan Richardson's 1726 portrait of her in Turkish dress with a young black liveried servant behind her. Isobel Grundy examines some contradictions in this painting in her biography (Grundy 1999: 301–4).

10. Ros Ballaster's *Fabulous Orients* emphasizes the priority of formal conventions and narrative themes over geographical or historical specificity, such that stories 'from tenth-century India, Iran, and Persia are treated as evidence' of lives lived in Turkey, Persia, or India centuries later (Ballaster 2005: 11).

11. Alain Grosrichard's *Stucture du serial* begins with this pithy observation: 'From the end of the seventeenth century and all through the eighteenth, a spectre was haunting Europe: the spectre of *despotism*' (he suggests that the term is inseparable from European accounts of the Ottoman Empire). His analysis shows that the convolutions of such writing feature a understanding that 'the heart of despotic power in the Orient, extending over vast empires, is hidden in that very place where the despot exercises his *domestic* power: in that walled space, forbidden to the gaze, saturated by sex and structured by it – the seraglio.' The seraglio – hypersexualized and hyperpoliticized – becomes 'the obligatory topos of all the accounts of travel in the Orient;' Grosrichard points out that many of them 'are alike, to the point often of repetition in the same words' (Grosrichard 1998: 3, 19, 119, 125).

12. Robert L. Mack's edition (1999) of the *Arabian Nights' Entertainments* reprints the anonymously translated English version (published between 1706 and 1721) of Antoine Galland's *Mille et une Nuits* (1704–17).

13. In a parallel instance, in *Rambler* 38, 'Mediocrity: A Fable,' Johnson argues (not surprisingly for him) that 'the middle path is the road to security' and concludes

his essay with a story of Hamet and Raschid, two shepherds on 'the plains of India.' There are no details in the story that situate these shepherds in India except the mention of the Ganges (as a river in spate). These characters could as easily have been on the banks of the Nile, or, with a change of names (Colin and Hobbinol perhaps) by the Avon. Here, it is not quite clear what Johnson derives from his Indian illustration, unless it is that 'India' allows Johnson to stage a visit from a supernatural being, 'the Genius of distribution,' who responds to the shepherds' prayers for rain in a time of drought. Greek and Roman stories were replete with sexual and other intimacies between otherworldly beings and humans, and such figuration is central to neoclassical art and literature too. However, eighteenth-century European rationalism defined its epistemological and rhetorical protocols by sidelining such paranormal fantasies into subsidiary (and vulgar) genres like tales of apparitions, the romance, or the gothic, or indeed by locating them offshore.

14. Steven Scherwatzky argues that *Rasselas* should be understood as Johnson's 'remonstrance against the political forces that fueled England's quest for empire.' War against France for control of trade and territories (later called the Seven Years' War) had been officially declared in May 1756, and Johnson challenged the belligerent mercantilism that drove this war in essays and other writing (Scherwatzky 1992: 103).

15. In Donald Green's words, Johnson defended 'the older, self-sufficient Little England against the grandiose imperial conception of England as mistress of the world's commerce, maintaining her markets by military force in every part of the world' (Green 1960: 239). For Johnson's opposition to the Seven Years' War (1756–63), and his condemnation of the racist attitudes of white colonialists more generally, see Green 1971: 37–65.

16. Evidence of the corruptions of empire from the East (involving officials of the East India Company) and the continuing brutality of the slave trade across the Atlantic encouraged various Parliamentary actions for reform. Indeed, as scholars like Nicholas Dirks have argued, such moral and political reformism became a powerful ideological justification for Empire *per se* (Dirks 2006).

17. Rush is quoted by Henry Louis Gates, Jr in Gates 1987: 68. Gates's chapter, 'Phillis Wheatley and the "Nature of the Negro"' (61–79), traces the eighteenth-century debates on slavery, race and human nature that framed Wheatley's poetry.

18. Collier is described as 'a Washer-woman, at *Petersfield* in *Hampshire*' on the title-page of *The Woman's Labour*, and the prefatory 'Advertisement' begins: 'It is thought proper to assure the Reader, that the following Verses are the real Productions of the Person to whom the Title-Page ascribes them' (Collier 1739).

19. Katherine Clay Bassard reads the elegies as evidence of poetic self-making via the 'dialogic relation' between Christianity and slavery (Bassard 1999: 58–70).

20. Sondra O'Neal, in a sensitive endorsement of Wheatley's strengths as 'a poet and as an abolitionist', writes that Wheatley (along with other early Black writers) 'found the biblical myth, language and symbol to be the most conducive vehicles for making subtle, yet effective, statements against slavery' (O'Neal 1986: 145).

21. Frank Shuffleton writes that in her 1773 collection Wheatley 'positioned herself aesthetically in terms of the Atlantic civilization of the old empire, patriotically within the context of an emergent national culture, and politically in the possibility of a new community of free people of color in New England' (Shuffleton 2001: 176).

22. In a parallel instance, the last couplet of Wheatley's 1768 poem 'To the King's Most Excellent Majesty,' a poem which celebrates George III's repeal of a colonial tax, the Stamp Act, reads: 'And may each clime with equal gladness see/ A monarch's smile can set his subjects free!' Here too, the word 'free' sets in motion divergent meanings for loyal colonists (freedom from unjust taxation), for disgruntled Americans (political independence), for slaves (emancipation).

23. This idea was articulated, *inter alia*, by George Berkeley in his 'On the Prospect of Planting Arts and Learning in America' (1726). Europe is decaying and the Muse of empire will now move across the Atlantic:

    > Westward the course of empire takes its way;
    > 　The first four acts already past,
    > A fifth shall close the drama with the day;
    > 　Time's noblest offspring is the last. (ll. 21–4)

24. Adam Potkay and Sandra Burr point out that only the 1774 imprint has the phrase 'Written by Himself' in the title. Most editions of the *Narrative* use the phrase 'as Related by Himself' (Potkay and Burr 1995: 53).

25. Gronniosaw's jewels are a sign of his royal descent. He is the grandson of the King of Baurnou (Borno, a city-state in what is now Nigeria), which grants his passage into slavery the distinction shared by fictional forbears like Oroonoko.

26. Gronniosaw's references to Bunyan do not make clear which texts he read – Potkay and Burr indicate that *Grace Abounding to the Chief of Sinners* (1666), *The Life and Death of Mr Badman* (1680), and *The Holy War* (1682) were all available in Dutch translation (Potkay and Burr 1995: 55, n. 19; 57, n. 27). In a comment on the form of autobiographies like *A Narrative of the Uncommon Sufferings and Surprizing Deliverance of Briton Hammon, A Negro Man* (1760), or Gronniosaw's *Narrative*, William L. Andrews suggests that 'editors probably solicited these stories *because* they conformed or were conformable to cultural myths and literary traditions with an already established audience appeal, such as Indian captivity or evangelical conversion narratives' (Andrews 1982: 7–8).

27. Somewhat later in the *Narrative*, Gronniosaw writes of laboring for a rich Quaker called Handbarrar, who, 'being told that a Black was at work for him, had an inclination to see me' (1995: 48). This interview does lead to higher wages.

28. This conclusion follows that of Briton Hammon's *A narrative of the uncommon sufferings, and surprizing deliverance of Briton Hammon, a Negro man* (1760). Hammon was captured by Florida Indians:

    > *And now, That in the Providence of that GOD, who delivered his Servant David out of the Paw of the Lion and out of the Paw of the Bear, I am freed from a long and dreadful Captivity, among worse Savages than they; And am return'd to my own Native Land, to Shew how Great Things the Lord hoth done for Me.* (Hammon 1760: 14)

Conclusion
'Gazing into the Future'

But now the Great Map of Mankind is unrolled at once; and there is no state of Gradation of barbarism, and no mode of refinement which we have not at the same instant under our View. The very different Civility of Europe and of China; The barbarism of Persia and Abyssinia. The erratick manners of Tartary, and of arabia. The Savage State of North America, and of New Zealand.

(Edmund Burke, complimenting William Robertson on his *History of America*)[1]

A book of this length cannot survey developments over a century of literary writing with any degree of completeness, but I have tried to show – particularly in my readings of individual texts – how the intellectual priorities of postcolonial criticism alter our understanding of the work of literature in the age of empire. Such criticism, and the map of literary history it draws, presumes that literary cultures are produced out of the international circulation of ideas, stories, and modes of representation, and that any national literary tradition defines itself via a selective foregrounding of those elements of its internationalism most conducive to its evolving sense of national difference and distinction. This was particularly important to a nation like Great Britain, whose foreign and economic policies were committed to the dominance of international trading routes and the acquisition of territories overseas. As larger sections of the population were drawn into the infrastructure of such expansion – at home and abroad – literary texts, newspapers, and magazines became crucial to imagining, debating, and coming to terms with, changing ideas of the globe and the nation. Over the course of the eighteenth century, English Literature, in all its variety, experimentation, and achievement, modeled for Britons their connections with, but also increasingly their socio-political and religious superiority to, competitor European nations and cultural formations. These competitive performances, as it were, developed alongside a more collaborative enterprise, one in which European intellectuals debated and more or less agreed upon the civilisational advantages they possessed over the peoples that populated the globe elsewhere. Nor did these discussions remain exercises in sociology; as increasing sections of the world came under European control, ideas like these were implemented in colonial governance and underwrote the moral authority arrogated to themselves by imperialists.

Any imperial culture requires the consolidation of provincial modes of being and belonging into a properly hierarchical relationship with the dominant language and culture of the national entity. While this process of nation-formation is never complete, being constantly tested and modified by its participants, a 'national' literature plays a central role in its success, not only because it more often than not performs such metropolitan dominance, but because it can serve as the basis of a national pedagogy. To read the masterworks of English literature, whether written by Englishmen and women or those from Scotland and Ireland educated into Englishness, is to learn (whether formally in school or informally within the family) how to define, and relate to, the normative values of the nation. (As the empire expanded, these masterworks also became crucial to English-language pedagogy in colonies everywhere.) If this suggests a more instrumental understanding of the functions and practices of imaginative writing than is usually acknowledged, it is because, as scholars and consumers of literature, we are often hesitant, as Edward Said put it, about defining 'the relationship between language in history and language as art' (Said 1984: xix). There is no reason why our explorations of the latter – the artistry of the work, its intimations of the ineffable or the utopian – should preclude or deny our analysis of the former, that is, the institutional and ideological effects of its production, circulation, and consumption. Further, as this book argues, both the formal and the ideological suppleness of eighteenth-century English literary writing follows from creative responses to the intensifying consciousness of empire. Thus, some of the most 'provincial' literary texts in this period – loco-descriptive poems, for instance – take the form they do in response to the more 'global' world that results from the extension of empire.

Literary Transport: to India and the South Seas

Britain's empires, formal and informal, mutated considerably over the course of this century, and it lost large sections of its first (North American) empire in 1776. However, there were signal successes elsewhere, none more consequential than those in India, where the East India Company first expanded its fortified trading operations and then, via a series of adroit political alliances and military victories, came into administrative authority (see Sen 1998). After Robert Clive's victory at Plassey (Palashi) in 1757, the Company governed, rather than simply traded in, Bengal, and from that foothold administrators developed the military, financial, and logistical infrastructure necessary to defeat local Indian rulers who opposed their interests. At the end of the Seven Years' War (1756–63), the Treaty of Paris confirmed the East India Company's dominance over its French competitors in India, who no longer posed a military threat. These developments resulted in growing parliamentary concern in England about the regulation of the Company in India, which now functioned, *de facto*, as a state. The popular press found its own objects of satire: 'nabobs,' those factors of the Company who returned to England with astonishingly large fortunes made in comparatively short stints in India. Public scandals had dogged the Company from its inception, but never more visibly than in the near-collapse in Company stocks in 1772, alongside the parliamentary enquiry into the legality of Clive's fortune. The Regulating Act of 1773 attempted to submit the Company's actions to parliamentary oversight, but in any case, India became a byword for the illegitimate spoils of empire, not only because of the questionable policies of Company administrators there but because of the pernicious influence these administrators were seen to have on parliamentary, commercial, and social practices in Britain.

While I cannot comment at any length here on either of these developments in India or in Britain, I will point to one literary text that stages this nexus. Samuel Foote's *The Nabob* (1772) confirms for us that texts do not have to travel overseas to inhabit the expanded discursive space of empire, particularly if their sense of home includes historical mutations in kinship and economic relations accelerated by the energies of trade and colonization. Even as this play is a satire of Sir Matthew Mite, the 'nabob' of the title, the plot is as concerned with shifts in class and family relations in England as it is about the source and impact of Sir Matthew's wealth. It is apprehensive too about the difficulty of separating legitimate forms of dominion and trade from the immoral practices embodied in the nabob, and it is by no means clear that the play is able to effect this separation. It features Sir Matthew Mite, who returns from Bengal with wealth enough to act upon all his *parvenu* hopes, which range from learning how to cut a fine figure in fashionable society, to buying an estate in Berkshire as well as two seats in Parliament, to seeking marriage with Sophy, the daughter of Lord and Lady Oldham. Sir Matthew is not only pretentious but also unscrupulous; he presumes upon marriage to Sophy because he has bought up a debt contracted by her father (it may well be that he advanced the money in the first place in order to effect his purposes). His methods seem to be 'Indian,' or so Lady Oldham suggests when she bemoans the fact that 'With the wealth of the east, we have, too, imported the worst of its vices.'[2] She is resentful, as an aristocrat in debt, of Sir Matthew's wealth, but the play makes clear the suspicious origins of Sir Matthew's riches.

The play revels in, and satirizes, the new idiom of exploitative commerce and governance that Sir Matthew learns in India, and squeezes into its brief compass a remarkable range of contemporary critiques of empire. References to the fraudulent methods of the East India Company abound; as Touchit, himself a corrupt gentleman from the borough of Bribe'em, puts it, English merchants 'beg to be admitted as friends, and take possession of a small spot in the country,' while promising to 'carry on a beneficial commerce with the inoffensive and innocent people,' but then 'we cunningly encroach, and fortify by little and by little, till at length, we growing too strong for the natives, we turn them out of their lands, and take possession of their money and jewels' (1974: 3. 213–14). Corruption in India encourages and renews corruption at home: when Touchit, in the name of the gentlemen of the Christian Club of Bribe'em, offers to let Sir Matthew buy the two seats they control in Parliament, Sir Matthew accepts, pleased to find, as he says, that 'the union still subsists between Bengal and the ancient corporation of Bribe'em' (1974: 3. 216). In this way, both India and England are seen to suffer at the hands of East India Company nabobs.[3] As Mr Thomas Oldham (Lady Oldham's brother, and the ethical center of the play) puts it, Sir Matthew's is 'an artful project: no wonder that so much contrivance and cunning has been an over-match for a plain English gentleman [Lord Oldham], or an innocent Indian' (3. 192–3).

However, Thomas Oldham, who has himself made money in trade, is determined not to let the public perception of the East India Company's malfeasance extend into a condemnation of all foreign commerce. He corrects his sister, Lady Oldham, when she would denounce all merchants by saying 'but there are men from the Indies, and many too, with whom I have the honour to live [on friendly terms] who dispense nobly and with hospitality here what they have acquired with honour and credit elsewhere; and, at the same time they have increased the dominions and wealth, have added virtues, too, to their country' (1974: 3. 194). He speaks for honourable traders and colonizers, and joins Lady Oldham in her attack on Sir Matthew, when she denies him marriage with Sophy, saying that she would 'rather see my child with a competence, nay, even reduced to an indigent state, than voluptuously rioting in pleasures that derive their source from the ruin of others.' Sir Matthew defends himself by reminding her that people like him have given Britain 'dominion and wealth,' but Thomas Oldham rejects his claim: 'I could wish even that fact was well founded, Sir Matthew,' he says, but your 'riches . . . by introducing a general spirit of dissipation, have extinguished labour and industry, the slow, but sure source of national wealth' (1974: 3. 233).

Both Thomas Oldham's critique of Sir Matthew and his defense of English colonists and traders are of a piece with the domestic drama afoot. Thomas Oldham wishes to marry his son to Sophy (the cousins desire each other), a match that Lady Oldham has discouraged because Thomas Oldham's money is tainted by the '*counting-house*,' that is, by his trade as a merchant (1974: 3. 193). However, once he rescues Lord Oldham by discharging his debt, Thomas asks for, and is granted, Sophy for his son. As Daniel O'Quinn argues, Thomas's financial and legal acumen bests Sir Matthew, and his benevolent plans to bring the lovers together enacts 'an accommodation between the commercial classes and the aristocracy, which secures the financial power of the former and the historical legitimacy of the latter.'[4] That is, even as English ways are preserved from the predatory Sir Matthew, they change to reflect new arrangements of domestic and international power. Foote's play, then, is not only a satire of the East India Company nabob and of the vices he imports from 'the East,' but a more complex staging of historical shifts underway in class alliances in England in the wake of eighteenth-century commercial and colonial developments. Sir Matthew's corruption connects Bengal and Bribe'em, but that is only an egregious subset of the more transformatory social and economic links between 'the Indies' and Britain embodied in Thomas Oldham and the future he arranges for Sophy and his son.

If India, and the trade it made possible with China and and southeast Asia, became the centerpiece of the British Empire in the nineteenth century, another part of this empire, the islands of the South Pacific including Australia and New Zealand, also became prominent in public awareness in the 1760s and 1770s. In three voyages, James Cook and the botanists and illustrators who sailed with him brought news of land masses and peoples unknown or little known in Europe. On his first voyage (1768–71), Cook sailed to Tahiti, circumnavigated and mapped the coastline of New Zealand, went ashore in eastern Australia, and returned to England after landing on, re-naming, and claiming on behalf of the crown 'Possession Island' in the Torres Strait. Cook's second voyage (1772–6) took him on a route parallel to Antarctica in search of the fabled landmass of *Terra Australis incognita*, whose existence he debunked. (He stopped at Tahiti to replenish supplies and took on board a young man called Omai, whose subsequent presence in London created a sensation.) Cook's third voyage (1776–9) led to disaster: after returning Omai to Tahiti, Cook surveyed the west coast of North America on a fruitless search for the Northwest Passage, and then, after becoming the first European to encounter Hawaii (which he named the Sandwich Islands), he was killed in a skirmish with Hawaiians when he returned to repair a ship. Apart from the territories he claimed on behalf of Britain, Cook's voyages added enormously to European knowledge of the South Pacific. Cook himself produced very accurate navigational charts and maps of islands. On the first voyage Joseph Banks and two other botanists collected a variety of flora and fauna to be cultivated in England but also for inclusion in the Linnaean classificatory system then being developed (Banks's subsequent fame led him to be elected President of the Royal Society in 1778) (Gascoigne 1998). The painter William Hodges sailed on the second voyage and his paintings of Tahiti and other islands became the basis for engravings in books, and contributed to the iconography of pastoral beauty that excited European attention for the next century and more.[5]

The South Seas had had their moment of great notoriety in Britain early in the eighteenth century. Travelogues then had fueled interest in the potential of the South Sea Company (founded in 1711), and thus contributed to the inflation and bursting of the South Sea Bubble. As Jonathan Lamb, Vanessa Smith, and Nicholas Thomas, the editors of *Exploration and Exchange*, point out, between 1680 and 1720, bucca-neers like William Dampier, Lionel Wafer, and Woodes Rogers followed Spanish treasure galleons into the South Sea (the oceans to the south and west of the isthmus of Panama), and published accounts of their exploits that 'blurred the difference between truth and falsehood, as well as between nothing and something' (Lamb, Smith, Thomas 2000: 6). This play between fact and fiction also galvanized the early novel: Jonathan Swift's *Gulliver's Travels* (1726) draws upon Dampier's *A New Voyage Round the World* (1697–1703) and *A Voyage to New Holland* (1703), and Daniel Defoe drew upon reports of the South Seas in both his com-mercial journalism and in *Robinson Crusoe*. The South Seas remained the space of ambition and fantasy, where English mariners hoped to raid Spanish fleets on the route from Manila to Acapulco, as was the case with Admiral George Anson's voyage around the world (1740–4). However, it was Cook's extended voyages that made details of these vast spaces available to Europeans, and inaugurated the continuing contact that led to white settler colonies, and the domination of indigenous peoples, in Australia and New Zealand

After Cook's first voyage, part of this attention followed from the brouhaha surrounding the publication of John Hawkesworth's compilation (in effect, re-writing) of journals kept by botanists, illustrators, and ship's captains like Samuel Wallis (who first went ashore in Tahiti in 1767), Banks, and Cook. When Hawkesworth's *An Account of the Voyages Undertaken by the Order of His Present Majesty for Making Discoveries in the Southern Hemisphere* (London, 1773) appeared, it was attacked for Hawkesworth's narrative technique (he wrote largely in the first person, as if he was there), his representation of Polynesian sexual activities (all recorded in the journals he consulted), and his less-than-charitable views of human behavior in the face of uncertainty and fear. Hawkesworth's *Account*, and the acrimonious debate that followed, remind us that narratives of the Pacific encounter, like other travelogues, were necessarily caught up in the cultural, intellectual, and political dynamics of eighteenth-century empire. That is, no commentaries on the behavior of Britons or Europeans in these seas, or on the communities of people they came into contact with, or on the landscapes they observed, could fail to 'concern themselves . . . with various alternatives to civility: isolation, mutiny, cannibalism, infanticide, paradise, utopia, romance, voluptousness,' nor avoid experiencing a range of emotions or moods 'whose mildest manifestation is reverie or curiosity, and whose most turbulent is frenzy' (Lamb, Smith, Thomas 2000: xvi). The civil English self, schooled into a particular understanding of the proper forms of human conduct and community, intuits its limits and its contradictions in these contact zones.[6] The way forward, the preservation of the self, lies in forceful action, and also in the consolations offered by a religious cosmology and a historical sociology that confirms – perhaps after initial stutters – the superior morality, civic organization, and technological skills of commercial society.

This account of Pacific exploration in the late eighteenth century does no more than gesture towards oceans and land masses that were, over the next century, to become part of the British Empire. The Maori in New Zealand and the Aboriginal peoples of Australia suffered the brunt of settler assaults, as had, in previous centuries, Caribs and Indians in South America and Native Americans in North America. For Britons, including transported criminals and poor laborers, these lands became spaces for economic rehabilitation and personal reinvention, and English writers took note of these developments. One instance, from Charles

Dickens' wonderful novel *Great Expectations* (1861), will have to suffice here. The money that transforms its hero Pip from (potentially) a rural blacksmith to a London gentleman comes from Abel Magwitch, a criminal transported to Australia. Pip knows nothing of this, and in that ignorance – and in his anger and chagrin when he finds out – Dickens models an important relation between English gentility and colonial resources. Magwitch is no nabob, but he too finds in the colonies possibilities denied him at home, and if he is not able to remake himself on his return to England, he finds in Pip a vital surrogate. The criminal, or the stock breeder (which Magwitch becomes), in the colonies, is father to the gentleman at home – Dickens does not belabour the point, it is made with an imaginative precision that is worth remembering.[7]

I will close this book with a different instance of the place of the South Seas in literary performance, one that turns not on forgetting but on the transformation of colonial history into a vision of poetic transcendence. This poem suggests not only the energizing links between the literary imagination and the founding moments of modern European empire, but also sublates that history into its idiom of poetic transport and self-discovery. In 1816, John Keats read Chapman's translation of Homer's *Illiad* and *Odyssey* (first published in 1616) with great pleasure, exclaiming over passages he found particularly moving. That same night he wrote, 'On First Looking into Chapman's Homer,' a sonnet which has since become a well-known model of poetic epiphany. The structuring vocabulary of the sonnet is that of land-holding, or rather of realms discovered (in poetry) and thus transformed into property. The sonneteer imagines Apollonian bards as poets who make available to their readers 'realms of gold,' 'many goodly states and kingdoms,' and 'many western isles.' We are not told where these are – they might refer to the Mediterranean contexts of early Greek expansion (if we take 'bards in fealty to Apollo' to refer to classical Greek poets alone) or, if, if we take Apollonian inspiration to be available to poets more generally, the reference might extend to the Atlantic context of early modern exploration:

> Much have I traveled in the realms of gold,
> And many goodly states and kingdoms seen;
> Round many western islands have I been
> Which bards in fealty to Apollo hold.
> Oft of one wide expanse had I been told
> That deep-browed Homer ruled as his demesne;
> Yet did I never breathe its pure serene
> Till I heard Chapman speak out loud and bold . . .

In line 6, the word 'demesne' is striking because its archaism (and anachronism) locates Homer within a medieval tradition of Anglo-Germanic law in which the word signifies possession rather than ownership.[8] However, the 'demesne'/ 'serene' rhyme rapidly refines this image of poet as property-holder into a more immaterial, even sublime, form of poetic power, one in which the Homeric domain is characterized as aspiration, as the 'pure serene' that transports a sensitive reader.

The sestet does not so much turn away from this vocabulary of discovery and possession as extend it into modern specificity: Keats provides two analogies for the effect of Chapman's translation, one cosmological, in which the wonder he feels is like that of a 'watcher of the skies' who views the motion of an unknown planet, and the other geopolitical, that features the astonishment of Spanish conquistadors when they viewed the Pacific:

Then felt I like some watcher of the skies
When a new planet swims into his ken;
Or like stout Cortez when with eagle eyes
He stared at the Pacific – and all his men
Looked at each other with a wild surmise –
Silent, upon a peak in Darien.

The poem does not say so, but the new planet might well be Uranus, discovered in 1781 by Sir William Herschel. The eagle-eyed Spaniard, 'stout Cortez,' seems a stand-in for Vasco Núñez de Balboa, whose Indian guides led his 1513 expedition across the isthmus of Panama to view (and claim in the name of his sovereign) the South Seas.[9] Keats's choice of conquistadors – Cortez instead of Balboa – will continue to be debated, but it remains clear that his model for sublime discovery and elevation in poetry derives from the history and geography of the European conquest of the Americas. His poetics might feature the anxious belatedness of a young poet reading the masters who came before, but its concluding, and most powerful, metaphor derives from the originary moments of colonization. Balboa, and Cortez after him, saw a vision not only of oceanic vastnesses, but, as it turned out, of European dominance; this is the legacy that allows Keats his vision of poetic possibility. He reads Homer and must reach for startling cosmological and geopolitical analogies in order to comprehend fully the transport and the challenge he felt; or is it that the power of the latter, of the modern world of astronomy and empire, provides models for the expansiveness of literary subjectivity and ambition that the young poet now traces back via Chapman to Homer?[10] We now recognise the fecundity with which poets and other writers engaged with contemporary British power across the globe, and also that they derived a great deal of creative energy from the world made available to them by empire. Keats's sonnet contains entire worlds: those linked by Homeric seaways, but most pressingly, those that swam into his ken as a result of European colonization across the Atlantic between the sixteenth and the eighteenth centuries. The poet gazes, like Cortez, into history. Keats was far from the only writer who marveled at the 'realms of gold' that literary texts made available, nor was he the only one whose work reflected on the process by which the world was transmuted into art. His sonnet enacts, and reveals, the artistic stakes involved when writing engages with, and is produced within, the history of modern empires, and he finds in this conjunction a model of poetic sublimity of great and lasting power.

Postcolonial critics explore that conjunction too, and our analyses both recognize the particular condensed power of the literary artifact, its power to move and to elevate, and examine the even more consequential ways in which such creativity gains its ambition and its coordinates from historical, cultural, and institutional circumstances. Keats's sonnet, as I have suggested briefly, performs the rhetorical finesse – of history but aesthetically and subjectively removed from it – that is one of the most powerful artistic capacities of literary writing in the age of empire and aggressive nationalism. Its realm of gold is so finely crafted that it shimmers over, rather than is weighted down by, the legacy of conquest and colonization which encourages it to extend its imaginative horizons to that point in the historical and geographical distance where conquistadors in the New World saw even wider seas to traverse and to make their own. Homer knew this world of epic ambition and war, but on a far more limited scale; Chapman saw, as did those around him in early seventeenth-century England, that the paths to international power lay across the oceans. We might argue that Keats arrived late to this vision, and that he no longer had to work out the messy details that concerned many writers in seventeenth- and eighteenth-century Britain. Certainly the wide reaches of empire had become for him – and for many other Britons in the nineteenth century – the contemporary geopolitical and cultural condition. By this time, Great Britain was inescapably a product of its imperial history, its economic, political, and social energies inseparable from its commitment to empire. Not surprisingly, writing of all kinds – including the varieties we include in our histories of English Literature – played a dynamic role in this process of world-making. And it is that dynamism, one that resonates forcefully into our present moment, that our critical work continues to chart.

Notes

1. Burke, Letter to Dr William Robertson, 9 June 1777 (Burke 1961: 3. 351).
2. Foote 1974: 3. 193. (References to the play are given by volume and page number.)
3. This is how John Bee's prefatory 'Remarks' describe the impact of nabobs:

   [in Sir Matthew] we discern a villain of higher aim and deeper stamp, who, returning to his native soil, laden with ill-gotten pelf, applies it to the annoyance, the ruin of his neighbours. By this means, the features of *country life* were totally changed in some parts, and the commercial superseded the landed interest, by the corrupt return of M. P.'s to seats so obtained. (1974: 3.181)

4. O'Quinn 2005: 66. O'Quinn offers a persuasive reading of *The Nabob* within the context of parliamentary debates about the functioning of East India Company officials accused of enriching themselves at the cost of Company stockholders and of the Indians they governed in Bengal (2005: 43–73).
5. Hodges's skills led him to India in 1780, and his paintings of landscapes, monuments, and people exhibited at the Royal Academy set the tone for many subsequent representations of India. He also published an illustrated travelogue, *Travels in India During the Years 1780, 1781, 1782, and 1783* (1793). (See Tobin 2005: 117–67, and Tobin 1999.)
6. For an insightful reading of the modes in which ship's captains like Cook were meant to embody these civilities (their 'moral economy'), see Neill 2003: 296–308.
7. For a more elaborate, though parallel instance, Adam Hochschild (in a chapter entitled 'The Great Forgetting') writes of the determined speed at which Belgians repressed the atrocities they had committed in the Congo, including causing the deaths of millions of Congolese. Hochschild also remarks on many ornate buildings and monuments in Brussels, either built or renovated to their present splendor with profits from their colony: 'the blood spilled in the Congo, the stolen land, the severed hands, the shattered families and orphaned children, underlie much that meets the eye' (Hochschild 1998: 293).
8. The first definition the *OED* offers is: 'In Germanic, including English, law, the primary idea in relation to property is *possession*, not *ownership* (= Roman *dominium*), as we now understand it. Hence, derivatives of L. *dominium* and *proprietas* became in mediæval law chiefly or even exclusively associated with possession.'
9. For a rebuttal of the critical convention that sees an error in Keats's naming of Cortez where Balboa might seem appropriate, see Charles Rzepka, '"Cortez – or Balboa, or Somebody Like That": Form, Fact, and Forgetting in Keats's "Chapman's Homer" Sonnet,' in *Keats-Shelley Journal*, 51 (Rzepka 2002): 35–75. Rzepka also reminds us that as a schoolboy Keats was a great reader of travelogues and histories.
10. In addition to his translations, George Chapman wrote several plays on contemporary themes, including *Eastward Ho* (1605) with Ben Jonson and John Marston, whose satire of activities in London extends across the ocean to Virginia. He also celebrated Sir Walter Raleigh's exploits in the Caribbean in *De Guiana, Carmen Epicum* (1596). Gold is a repeated motif in the latter, and Guiana offers Elizabeth (if she will support Raleigh) the wealth that will allow England international power. Chapman is important too for Keats as a crucial step in the literary genealogy that Keats indicates here – he 'Englishes' Homer, while preserving his sublimities, thus confirming the idea of *translatio studii* that was so important to the early formation of English Literature and to the self-conception of young poets reading Greek and Latin literature.

Bibliography

Adams, Percy G. (1983), *Travel Literature and the Evolution of the Novel*, Lexington: The University Press of Kentucky.

Addison, Joseph, Richard Steele, et al. [1711–14] (1945), *The Spectator*, ed. G. Gregory Smith, 4 vols, London: J. M. Dent.

Alpers, Paul (1979), *The Singer of the Eclogues*, Berkeley: University of California Press.

Anderson, Benedict [1983] (1991), *Imagined Communities: Reflections on the Origin and Spread of Nationalism*, London: Verso.

Anderson, Howard, Philip B. Daghlian, and Irvin Ehrenpreis (eds) (1966), *The Familiar Letter in the Eighteenth Century*, Lawrence: University of Kansas Press.

Andrews, William L. (1982), 'The First Fifty Years of the Slave Narrative, 1760–1810', in John Sekora and Darwin T. Turner (eds), *The Art of Slave Narrative*, Macomb: Western Illinois University Press, pp. 6–24.

Aravamudan, Srinivas (1999a), 'In the Wake of the Novel: The Oriental Tale as National Allegory', *Novel* 33: 1, 5–31.

— (1999b), *Tropicopolitans: Colonialism and Agency, 1688–1804*, Durham: Duke University Press.

— (2005), 'Fiction/Translation/Transnation: The Secret History of the Eighteenth-century Novel', in Paula R. Backscheider and Catherine Ingrassia (eds), *A Companion to the Eighteenth-Century English Novel and Culture*, London: Blackwell, pp. 48–74.

Aubin, Penelope, trans. Pétis de la Croix's *The History of Genghizcan the Great, First Emperor of the Antient Moguls and Tartars; in Four Books: Containing His Life, Advancement and Conquests; with a short History of his Successors to the present Time; the Manners, Customs and Laws of the Antient Moguls and Tartars; and the Geography of the vast Countries of Mongolistan, Turquestan, Capschac, Yugurestan, and the Eastern and Western Tartary. Collected from several Oriental Authors, and European Travellers; whose Names, with an Abridgement of their Lives, are added to this Book*, London: 1722.

Backscheider, Paula (1993), *Spectacular Politics: Theatrical Power and Mass Culture in Early Modern England*, Baltimore: Johns Hopkins University Press.

Backscheider, Paula R. and Catherine Ingrassia (eds) (2005), *A Companion to the Eighteenth-Century English Novel and Culture*, London: Blackwell.

Ballaster, Ros (1992), 'New Hystericism: Aphra Behn's *Oroonoko*: The Body, the Text and the Feminist Critic', in Isobel Armstrong (ed.), *New Feminist Discourses: Critical Essays on Theories and Texts*, London: Routledge, pp. 283–96.

— (2005), *Fabulous Orients: Fictions of the East in England 1662–1785*, Oxford: Oxford University Press.

Barker, Francis, Peter Hulme, and Margaret Iversen (eds) (1998), *Cannibalism and the Colonial World*, Cambridge: Cambridge University Press.

Barrell, John (1983), *English Literature in History 1730–80: An Equal, Wide Survey*, London: Hutchinson.

Basker, James G. (1991), 'Scotticisms and the Problem of Cultural Identity in Eighteenth-Century Britain', *Eighteenth Century Life* 15: 1 & 2, 81–95.

Bassard, Katherine Clay (1999), *Spiritual Interrogations*, Princeton: Princeton University Press.

Batchelor, Robert (2006), 'On the Movement of Porcelains', in John Brewer and Frank Trentmann (eds), *Consuming Cultures, Global Perspectives: Historical Trajectories, Transnational Exchanges*, Oxford: Berg, pp. 95–122.

Bayly, C. A. (1994), 'The British Military-Fiscal State and Indigenous Resistance, India 1750–1820', in Lawrence Stone (ed.), *An Imperial State at War: Britain from 1689–1815*, London: Routledge, pp. 322–54.

Beckles, Hilary McD. (1989), *White Servitude and Black Slavery in Barbados, 1627–1725*, Knoxville: University of Tennessee Press.

Been, Anita Cavagnaro (2004), *Animals and Authors in the Eighteenth-Century Americas*, Providence: John Carter Brown Library.

Behn, Aphra [1688] (1993), *The Widow Ranter*, ed. Aaron R. Walden, New York: Garland Publishing.

— [1688] (1996), *The Widow Ranter*, in Janet Todd (ed.), *The Works of Aphra Behn*, 7 vols, London: William Pickering, vol. 7, pp. 285–354.

— [1688] (1997), *Oroonoko: or the Royal Slave. A True History*, ed. Joanna Lipking, New York: W. W. Norton.

Blair, Hugh [1783] (2005), *Lectures on Rhetoric and Belles Lettres*, ed. Linda Ferreira-Buckley and S. Michael Halloran, Carbondale: Southern Illinois University Press.

Bogel, Fredric V. (1990), *The Dream of My Brother: An Essay on Johnson's Authority*, English Literary Studies Monograph, 47, British Columbia: University of Victoria.

Bohls, Elizabeth A. (1995), *Women Travel Writers and the Language of Aesthetics, 1716–1818*, Cambridge: Cambridge University Press.

Bond, Donald F. (ed.) (1965), *The Spectator*, 5 vols, Oxford: Clarendon Press.

Boswell, James [1791] (1980), *Life of Johnson*, ed. R. W. Chapman, Oxford: Oxford University Press.

Bowie, Karin (2007), *Scottish Public Opinion and the Anglo-Scottish Union 1699–1707*, Woodbridge: The Boydell Press.

Boyle, Robert (1692), *General Heads for the Natural History of a Country, Great or Small; Drawn out for the Use of Travellers and Navigators*, London.

Brantlinger, Patrick (1996), *Fictions of State: Culture and Public Credit in Britain, 1694–1994*, Ithaca: Cornell University Press.

Brewer, John (1983), 'Commercialization and Politics', in Neil McKendrick, John Brewer, and J. H. Plumb (eds), *The Birth of a Consumer Society: The Commercialization of Eighteenth-century England*, London: Hutchinson, pp. 197–264.

— (1989), *Sinews of Power: War, Money and the English State, 1688–1783*, London: Unwin Hyman.

Brewer, John and Roy Porter (eds) (1993), *Consumption and the World of Goods*, London: Routledge.

Brewer, John and Susan Staves (eds) (1995), *Early Modern Conceptions of Property*, London: Routledge.

Brewer, John and Frank Trentmann (eds) (2006), *Consuming Cultures, Global Perspectives: Historical Trajectories, Transnational Exchanges*, Oxford: Berg.

Brotton, Jerry (1997), *Trading Territories: Mapping the Early Modern World*, London: Reaktion Books.

— (2002), *The Renaissance Bazaar: From the Silk Road to Michaelangelo*, Oxford: Oxford University Press.

Brown, Laura (1985), *Alexander Pope*, London: Basil Blackwell.

— (1993), *Ends of Empire: Women and Ideology in Early-Eighteenth-Century English Literature*, Ithaca: Cornell University Press.

Burke, Edmund (1961), *The Correspondence of Edmund Burke*, ed. George H. Guttridge, 3 vols, Chicago: University of Chicago Press.

Bush, M. L. (2000), *Servitude in Modern Times*, London: Polity.

Cain, P. J. and A. G. Hopkins (2002), *British Imperialism: 1688–2000*, 2nd edn, London: Longman.

Canny, Nicholas (1988), *Kingdom and Colony: Ireland in the Atlantic World 1560–1800*, Baltimore: Johns Hopkins University Press.

— (2001), *Making Ireland British 1580–1650*, Oxford: Oxford University Press.

Caracciolo, Peter L. (ed.) (1988) *The Arabian Nights in English Literature*, London: Macmillan Press.

Carey, Daniel (2006), 'Travel, Geography, and the Problem of Belief: Locke as a Reader of Travel Literature', in Julia Rudolph (ed.), *History and Nation*, Lewisburg: Bucknell University Press, pp. 97–136.

Carlyle, Alexander (1860), *Autobiography of the Rev. Dr Alexander Carlyle*, ed. J. H. Burton, Edinburgh: Blackwood and Sons.

Chaudhuri, Mita (2000), *Interculturalism and Resistance in the London Theater, 1660–1800: Identity, Performance, Empire*, Lewisburg: Bucknell University Press.

Clare, Janet (2002), *Drama of the English Republic, 1949–60*, Manchester: Manchester University Press.

Cole, Lucinda (1995), '*The London Merchant* and the Institution of Apprenticeship', *Criticism*, 37:1, 57–85.

Colley, Linda (1992), *Britons: forging the nation, 1707–1837*, New Haven: Yale University Press.

Collier, Mary (1739), *The Woman's Labour*, London.

Coughlan, Patricia (1990), '"Cheap and common animals": The English Anatomy of Ireland in the Seventeenth Century', in Thomas Healy and Jonathan Sawday (eds), *Literature and the English Civil War*, Cambridge: Cambridge University Press, pp. 205–23.

Crawford, Rachel (2002), *Poetry, Enclosure, and the Vernacular Landscape, 1700–1830*, Cambridge: Cambridge University Press.

Crawford, Robert (1992), *Devolving English Literature*, Oxford: Clarendon Press.

— (ed.) (1998), *The Scottish Invention of English Literature*, Cambridge: Cambridge University Press.

Cronin, Anthony (1982), *Heritage Now: Irish Literature in the English Language*, Dingle: Brandon.

Dabydeen, David (1985), 'Eighteenth-century English Literature on Commerce and Slavery', in David Dabydeen (ed.), *The Black Presence in English Literature*, Manchester: Manchester University Press, pp. 26–49.

Davenant, William [1656–9] (1973), *The Siege of Rhodes, Parts 1 and 2*, Ann-Marie Hedbäck (ed.), *Studia Anglistica Upsaliensia* 14, Uppsala: Acta Universitatis Upsaliensis.

Davis, Leith (2004), 'At "Sang About": Scottish Song and the Challenge to British Culture', in Leith Davis, Ian Duncan, and Janet Sorensen (eds), *Scotland and the Borders of Romanticism*, Cambridge: Cambridge University Press, pp. 188–203.

Davis, Leith, Ian Duncan, and Janet Sorensen (eds) (2004), *Scotland and the Borders of Romanticism*, Cambridge: Cambridge University Press.

Defoe, Daniel (1697), *An Essay on Projects*, London.

Defoe, Daniel [1719] (1972), *The Life and Strange Surprizing Adventures of Robinson Crusoe, of York, Mariner . . . Written by Himself*, ed. J. Donald Crowley, Oxford: Oxford University Press.

Dirks, Nicholas B. (2006), *The Scandal of Empire: India and the Creation of Imperial Britain*, Cambridge: Harvard University Press.

Dixon, Peter (1991), *Oliver Goldsmith Revisited*, Boston: Twayne Publishers.

Doody, Margaret Anne (1985), *The Daring Muse: Augustan Poetry Reconsidered*, Cambridge: Cambridge University Press.

Doody, Margaret Anne (1998), *The True History of the Novel*, London: Fontana Press.

Dryden, John (1987), *Poems: The Works of Virgil in English 1697*, ed. William Frost and Vinton A. Dearing, Berkeley: The University of California Press.

Duncan, Ian (2004), 'The Pathos of Abstraction: Adam Smith, Ossian, and Samuel Johnson', in Leith Davis, Ian Duncan, and Janet Sorensen (eds), *Scotland and the Borders of Romanticism*, Cambridge: Cambridge University Press, pp. 38–56.

Edney, Matthew W. (1997), *Mapping an Empire: The Geographical Construction of British India, 1765–1843*, Chicago: Chicago University Press.

Ellis, Markman (2005), *The Coffee-House: A Cultural History*, London: Phoenix.

— (ed.) (2006), *Eighteenth-Century Coffee-House Culture*, 4 vols, London: Pickering & Chatto.

Erskine-Hill, Howard (1983), *The Augustan Idea in English Literature*, London: E. Arnold.

Felsenstein, Frank (1995), *Anti-Semitic Stereotypes: A Paradigm of Otherness in English Popular Culture, 1660–1830*, Baltimore: Johns Hopkins University Press.

Felsenstein, Frank (1999), *English Trader, Indian Maid: Representing Gender, Race, and Slavery in the New World*, Baltimore: Johns Hopkins University Press.

Ferguson, Adam [1767] (1966), *An Essay on the History of Civil Society*, ed. Duncan Forbes, Edinburgh: Edinburgh University Press.

Ferguson, Margaret (1991), 'Juggling the Categories of Race, Class and Gender: Aphra Behn's *Oroonoko*', *Women's Studies* 19: 159–82.

Ferguson, Niall (2003), 'The Empire Slinks Back', *The New York Times Magazine*, 27 April 2003, pp. 52–9.

Fisher, Michael H. (1996), *The First Indian Author in English: Dean Mahomed (1759–1851) in India, Ireland, and England*, Delhi: Oxford University Press.

Foote, Samuel [1772] (1974), *The Nabob; A Comedy, In Three Acts*, in Jon Bee (ed.), *The Works of Samuel Foote*, 3 vols, New York: Georg Olms Verlag, vol. 3, pp. 178–237.

Fryer, Peter (1988), *Staying Power: The History of Black People in Britain*, London: Pluto Press.

Fuller, Mary (1995), *Voyages in Print: English Travel to America 1576–1624*, Cambridge: Cambridge University Press.

Gascoigne, John (1998), *Science in the Service of Empire: Joseph Banks, the British State and the Uses of Science in the Age of Revolution*, Cambridge: Cambridge University Press.

Gates, Jr, Henry Louis (1987), *Figures in Black: Words, Signs, and the 'Racial' Self*, New York: Oxford University Press.

— (1988), *The Signifying Monkey: A Theory of Afro-American Literary Criticism*, New York: Oxford University Press.

Gibbons, Luke (2004), *Gaelic Gothic: Race, Colonization, and Irish Culture*, Galway: Arlen House.

Gilmore, John (2000), *The Poetics of Empire: A Study of James Grainger's* The Sugar-Cane, London: Athlone Press.

Goldsmith, Oliver (1928), *The Collected Letters of Oliver Goldsmith*, ed. Katherine C. Balderston, Cambridge: Cambridge University Press.

— (1966), *Collected Works*, ed. Arthur Friedman, 5 vols, Oxford: Clarendon Press.

— (1969), *The Poems of Gray, Collins and Goldsmith*, ed. Roger Lonsdale, London: Longman.

Goldstein, Laurence (1977), *Ruins and Empire: The Evolution of a Theme in Augustan and Romantic Literature*, Pittsburgh: University of Pittsburgh Press.

Grainger, James (1764), *An Essay on the more common West-India Diseases; and the Remedies which that Country itself produces. To which are added Some Hints on the Management, &c. of Negroes*, London.

Grainger, James [1765] (2000), *The Sugar-Cane*, in John Gilmore, *The Poetics of Empire: A Study of James Grainger's* The Sugar-Cane, London: Athlone Press.

Green, Donald. J. (1960), *The Politics of Samuel Johnson*, New Haven: Yale University Press.

— (1971), 'Samuel Johnson and the Great War for Empire', John H. Middendorf (ed.), *English Writers of the Eighteenth Century*, New York: Columbia University Press, pp. 37–68.

Green, Martin (1980), *Dreams of Adventure, Dreams of Empire*, London: Routledge and Kegan Paul.

Greig, J. Y. T. (ed.) (1932), *The Letters of David Hume*, 2 vols, Oxford: Clarendon Press.

Gronniosaw, Ukawsaw [1774] (1995), *A Narrative of the Most Remarkable Particulars in the Life of James Albert Ukawsaw Gronniosaw, An African Prince, Written by Himself*, in Adam Potkay and Sandra Burr (eds), *Black Atlantic Writers of the Eighteenth Century: Living the Exodus in England and the Americas*, London: Macmillan, pp. 27–53.

Grose, John Henry (1766), *Voyage to the East Indies*, London.

Grosrichard, Alain [1979] (1998), *The Sultan's Court: European Fantasies of the East*, trans. Liz Heron, London: Verso.

Grove, Richard (1995), *Green Imperialism: Colonial Expansion, Tropical Island Edens and the Origins of Environmentalism, 1660–1860*, Cambridge: Cambridge University Press.

Grundy, Isobel (1999), *Lady Mary Wortley Montagu*, Oxford: Oxford University Press.

Habermas, Jürgen [1962] (1989), *The Structural Transformation of the Public Sphere: An Inquiry into a Category of Bourgeois Society*, trans. Thomas Burger and Fredrick Lawrence, Cambridge: Polity.

Hakluyt, Richard (1598–1600), *The Principal Navigations, Voyages, Traffiques and Discoveries of the* English Nation, *made by Sea or over-land, to the remote and farthest distant quarters of the Earth, at any time within the compasse of these 1600 yeres*, London.

Halsband, Robert (ed.) (1965), *The Complete Letters of Lady Mary Wortley Montagu*, 3 vols, Oxford: Clarendon Press.

— (1966), 'Lady Mary Wortley Montagu as Letter-Writer', in Howard Anderson, Philip B. Daghlian, and Irvin Ehrenpreis (eds), *The Familiar Letter in the Eighteenth Century*, Lawrence: University of Kansas Press, pp. 49–70.

Hammon, Briton (1760), *A Narrative of the Uncommon Sufferings, and Surprizing Deliverance of Briton Hammon, a Negro Man*, Boston.

Harris, Bernard (1984), 'Goldsmith in the Theatre', in Andrew Swarbrick (ed.), *The Art of Oliver Goldsmith*, London: Vision and Barnes and Noble, pp. 144–67.

Hattox, Ralph S. (1985), *Coffee and Coffeehouses: The Origins of a Social Beverage in the Medieval Near East*, Seattle: University of Washington Press.

Hawes, Clement (1997), 'Johnson and Imperialism', in Greg Clingham (ed.), *The Cambridge Companion to Samuel Johnson*, Cambridge: Cambridge University Press, pp. 114–26.

— (2005), *The British Eighteenth Century and Global Critique*, New York: Palgrave Macmillan.

Healy, Thomas and Jonathan Sawday (eds) (1990), *Literature and the English Civil War*, Cambridge: Cambridge University Press.

Hechter, Michael (1978), *Internal Colonialism: the Celtic Fringe in British National Development, 1536–1966*, London: Routledge and Kegan Paul.

Hochschild, Adam (1998), *King Leopold's Ghost: A Story of Greed, Terror, and Heroism in Colonial Africa*, Boston: Houghton Mifflin.

Hodges, William (1793), *Travels in India During the Years 1780, 1781, 1782, and 1783*, London.

Hoppit, Julian (2000), *A Land of Liberty? England 1689–1727*, Oxford: Oxford University Press.

Hulme, Peter (1986), *Colonial Encounters: Europe and the Native Caribbean, 1492–1797*, London: Methuen.

Hulme, Peter and Ludmilla Jordanova (eds) (1990), *The Enlightenment and its Shadows*, London: Routledge, 1990.

Hume, David (1752), *Political Discourses*, Edinburgh.

— (1932), *The Letters of David Hume*, ed. J. Y. T. Greig, 2 vols, Oxford: Clarendon Press.

— [1741–2] (1987), *Essays Moral, Political, and Literary*, ed. Eugene F. Miller, Indianapolis: Liberty Classics.

Hunter, J. Paul (1990), *Before Novels: The Cultural Contexts of Eighteenth-Century English Fiction*, New York: W. W. Norton.

Hutner, Heidi (2001), *Colonial Women: Race and Culture in Stuart Drama*, Oxford: Oxford University Press.

Jago, Richard (1784), *Poems, Moral and Descriptive*, London.

Johnson, Samuel (1759), 'Introduction' to *The World Displayed or a Curious Collection of Voyages and Travels*, compiled by Christopher Smart, Oliver Goldsmith, and Samuel Johnson, 20 vols (1759–61), London, vol. 1, pp. iii–xxii.

— (1971), *The Complete English Poems*, ed. J. D. Fleeman, London: Allen Lane.

— (1990), *Rasselas and Other Tales*, ed. Gwin J. Kolb, New Haven: Yale University Press.

Kamps, Ivo and Jyotsna Singh (eds) (2001), *Travel Knowledge: European 'Discoveries' in the Early Modern Period*, New York: Palgrave.

Kaul, Suvir (1990), 'Why Selima Drowns: Thomas Gray and the Domestication of the Imperial Ideal', *PMLA* 105, 223–32.

— (1992), *Thomas Gray and Literary Authority*, New Delhi: Oxford University Press.

— (1994), 'Treating Literary Symptoms: Colonial Pathologies and the *Oroonoko* Fictions of Behn, Southerne, and Hawkesworth', *Eighteenth-Century Life* 18, 80–96.

— (2000), *Poems of Nation, Anthems of Empire: English Verse in the Long Eighteenth Century*, Charlottesville: University of Virginia Press.

— (2003), 'Mercantile Gothic: The Case of Lillo's *The London Merchant*', in Sambuddha Sen (ed.), *Mastering Western Texts*, New Delhi: Permanent Black, pp. 116–34.

— (2008), 'On Intersections Between Empire, Colony, Nation, and Province in Eighteenth-century British Poetry', *The Eighteenth-Century Novel* 6–7, 121–51.

Keen, Paul (1999), *The Crisis of Literature in the 1790s: Print Culture and the Public Sphere*, Cambridge: Cambridge University Press.

Keynes, John Maynard (1950), *A Treatise on Money*, 2 vols, London: Macmillan.

Kiernan, Victor [1969] (1995), *The Lords of Human Kind: European Attitudes to Other Cultures in the Imperial Age*, London: Serif.

Kindersley, Jemima (1766), *Letters from the Island of Teneriffe, Brazil, the Cape of Good Hope, and the East Indies*, London.

Klein, Lawrence E. (1995), 'Property and Politeness in the Early Eighteenth-century Whig Moralists: The Case of the *Spectator*', in John Brewer and Susan Staves (eds), *Early Modern Conceptions of Property*, London: Routledge, pp. 221–33.

Knapp, Louis M. (1949), *Tobias Smollett: Doctor of Men and Manners*, Princeton: Princeton University Press.

Kramnik, Jonathan Brody (1998), *Making the English Canon: Print-Capitalism and the Cultural Past, 1700–1770*, Cambridge: Cambridge University Press.

Lach, Donald F. (1965–), *Asia in the Making of Europe*, Chicago: University of Chicago Press.

Lach, Donald F. and Edwin J. Van Kley (2000), 'Asia in the Eyes of Europe: The Seventeenth Century', in Anthony Pagden (ed.), *Facing Each Other: The World's Perception of Europe and Europe's Perception of the World*, Aldershot: Ashgate, pp. 243–60.

Lamb, Jonathan, Vanessa Smith, and Nicholas Thomas (eds) (2000), *Exploration and Exchange: A South Seas Anthology 1680–1900* (Chicago: University of Chicago Press).

Landa, Louis [1971] (1980), 'Pope's Belinda, The General Emporie of the World, and the Wondrous Worm', *Essays in Eighteenth Century English Literature*, Princeton: Princeton University Press, pp. 178–98.

Langford, Paul (1989), *A Polite and Commercial People: England 1727–1783*, Oxford: Clarendon Press.

Ligon, Richard (1673), *A True and Exact History of the Island of Barbadoes*, London.

Lillo, George [1731] (1965), *The London Merchant*, ed. William H. McBurney, Lincoln: University of Nebraska Press.

Linebaugh, Peter (1992), *The London Hanged: Crime and Civil Society in the Eighteenth Century*, Cambridge: Cambridge University Press.

Linebaugh, Peter and Markus Rediker (2000), *The Many-Headed Hydra: Sailors, Slaves, Commoners, and the Hidden History of the Revolutionary Atantic*, Boston: Beacon Press.

Lobo, Jerome (1735), *A Voyage to Abyssinia by Father Jerome Lobo. With a Continuation of the History of Abyssinia, and Fifteen Dissertations, by Mr Le Grand. From the French*, trans. Samuel Johnson, London.

Lonsdale, Roger (ed.) (1969), *The Poems of Gray, Collins and Goldsmith*, London: Longman.

Loomba, Ania (2002), '"Break her will, and bruise no bone sir": Colonial and Sexual Mastery in Fletcher's *The Island Princess*', *Journal of Early Modern Cultural Studies* 2:1, 68–108.

Loomba, Ania, Suvir Kaul, Antoinette Burton, Matti Bunzl, and Jed Esty (eds) (2005), *Postcolonial Studies and Beyond*, Durham: Duke University Press.

Low, Anthony (1985), *The Georgic Revolution*, Princeton: Princeton University Press.

Lowenthal, Cynthia (1994), *Lady Mary Wortley Montagu and the Eighteenth-Century Familiar Letter*, Athens: University of Georgia Press.

Ludolf, Hiob [1681] (1682), *Historia Aethiopica*, in J. P. Gent (trans.), *A New History of Ethiopia*, London.

MacBurney, Willam H. (1963), *Four Before Richardson: Selected English Novels, 1720–27*, Lincoln: University of Nebraska Press.

McCormack, W. J. (1984), 'Goldsmith, Biography and the Phenomenology of Anglo-Irish Literature', in Andrew Swarbrick (ed.), *The Art of Oliver Goldsmith*, London: Vision and Barnes and Noble, pp. 168–94.

McHugh, Roger and Maurice Harmon (1982), *A Short History of Anglo-Irish Literature*, Dublin: Wolfhound Press.

McIntosh, Carey (1998), *The Evolution of English Prose, 1700–1800: Style, Politeness, and Print Culture*, Cambridge: Cambridge University Press.

Mack, Robert L. (ed.) (1999), *Arabian Nights' Entertainments*, Oxford: Oxford University Press.

McKendrick, Neil (1983), 'Commercialization and the Economy', in Neil McKendrick, John Brewer, and J. H. Plumb (eds), *The Birth of a Consumer Society: The Commercialization of Eighteenth-century England*, London: Hutchinson, pp. 9–196.

McKendrick, Neil, John Brewer, and J. H. Plumb (1983), *The Birth of a Consumer Society: The Commercialization of Eighteenth-century England*, London: Hutchinson.

Mackie, Erin (1997), *Market à la Mode: Fashion, Commodity, and Gender in THE TATLER and THE SPECTATOR*, Baltimore: Johns Hopkins University Press.

— (ed.) (1998), *The Commerce of Everyday Life: Selections from THE TATLER and the Spectator*, New York: Bedford/St Martin's.

McLeod, Bruce (1999), *The Geography of Empire in English Literature 1580–1745*, Cambridge: Cambridge University Press.

McNeil, David (1990), *The Grotesque Depiction of War and the Military in Eighteenth-Century English Fiction*, Newark: University of Delaware Press.

Mancall, Peter C. (2007), *Hakluyt's Promise: An Elizabethan's Obsession for an English America*, New Haven: Yale University Press.

Mandeville, Bernard [1714] (1970), *The Fable of the Bees*, ed. Philip Harth, London: Penguin.

Markley, Robert (2005), '"I have now done with my island, and all manner of discourse about it": Crusoe's *Farther Adventures* and the Unwritten History of the Novel', in Paula R. Backscheider and Catherine Ingrassia (eds), *Companion to the Eighteenth-Century English Novel*, London: Blackwell, pp. 25–47.

Markley, Robert (2006), *The Far East and the English Imagination, 1600–1730*, Cambridge: Cambridge University Press.

Marshall, P. J. and Glyndwr Williams (1982), *The Great Map of Mankind: British Perceptions of the World in the Age of Enlightenment*, London: Dent and Sons.

Matar, Nabil (1999), *Turks, Moors, and Englishmen in the Age of Discovery*, New York: Columbia University Press.

— (2003), 'Introduction', in Daniel J. Vitkus (ed.), *Piracy, Slavery, and Redemption: Barbary Captivity Narratives from Early Modern England*, New York: Columbia University Press, pp. 1–54.

— (2005), *Britain and Barbary 1589–1689*, Gainesville: University Press of Florida.

Maurer, Shawn Lisa (1998), *Proposing Men: Dialectics of Gender and Class in the Eighteenth-Century English Periodical*, Stanford: Stanford University Press.

Mayer, Robert (1997), *History and the Early English Novel: Matters of fact from Bacon to Defoe*, Cambridge: Cambridge University Press.

Meek, Ronald (1976), *Social Science and the Ignoble Savage*, Cambridge: Cambridge University Press.

Melman, Billie (1992), *Women's Orients: English Women and the Middle East, 1718–1918*, London: Macmillan.

Montagu, Mary Wortley (1965), *The Complete Letters of Lady Mary Wortley Montagu*, ed. Robert Halsband, 3 vols, Oxford: Clarendon Press.

Moore, Daffyd (2003), *Enlightenment and Romance in James MacPherson's* The Poems of Ossian: *Myth, Genre, and Cultural Change*, Burlington: Ashgate.

Neill, Anna (2003), 'South Seas Trade and the Character of Captains', in Felicity Nussbaum (ed.), *The Global Eighteenth Century*, Baltimore: Johns Hopkins University Press, pp. 296–308.

Nussbaum, Felicity (ed.) (2003), *The Global Eighteenth Century*, Baltimore: Johns Hopkins University Press.

O'Brien, Karen (1997), *Narratives of Enlightenment: Cosmopolitan History from Voltaire to Gibbon*, Cambridge: Cambridge University Press.

O'Neal, Sondra (1986), 'A Slave's Subtle War: Phillis Wheatley's Use of Biblical Myth and Symbol', *Early American Literature* 21: 2, 144–66.

O'Quinn, Daniel (2005), *Staging Governance: Theatrical Imperialism in London, 1770–1800*, Baltimore: Johns Hopkins University Press.

O'Sullivan, Donal (2001), *Carolan: The Life and Times and Music of an Irish Harper*, Cork: Ossian Publications.

Olaniyan, Tejumola (1992), 'The Ethics and Poetics of a "Civilizing Mission": Some Notes on Lillo's *The London Merchant*', *English Language Notes* 29:4, 33–48.

Oldham, John, "David's Lamentation for the Death of Saul and Jonathan, Paraphras'd" (1677), in *The Works of Mr John Oldham, together with his remains* (1710), London.

— (1684), *Poems and Translations. By the Author of* The Satyrs upon the Jesuits, London.

Orr, Bridget (2001), *Empire on the English Stage 1660–1714*, Cambridge: Cambridge University Press.

Pack, Richardson (1719), 'The Praise of Sulpitia', in Richardson Pack, *Miscellanies in Prose and Verse*, 2nd edn, London.

Pagden, Anthony (ed.) (2000), *Facing Each Other: The World's Perception of Europe and Europe's Perception of the World*, Aldershot: Ashgate.

Palmer, Patricia (2001), *Language and Conquest in Early Modern Ireland: English Renaissance literature and Elizabethan imperial expansion*, Cambridge: Cambridge University Press.

Percy, Thomas (1763), *Five Pieces of Runic Poetry: Translated from the Icelandic Language*, London: R & J Dodsley.

Philips, John [1708] (2001), *Cyder. A Poem in Two Books*, ed. John Goodridge and J. C. Pellicer, Cheltenham: The Cyder Press.

Pinkerton, John (ed.) (1781), *Scottish Tragic Ballads*, London.

Pittock, Murray G. H. (1994), *Poetry and Jacobite Politics in Eighteenth-Century Britain and Ireland*, Cambridge: Cambridge University Press.

Plumb, J. H. (1983), 'Commercialization and Society', in Neil McKendrick, John Brewer, and J. H. Plumb (eds), *The Birth of a Consumer Society: The Commercialization of Eighteenth-century England*, London: Hutchinson, pp. 265–334.

Pocock, J. G. A. (1985), 'Virtues, Rights, and Manners: A Model for Historians of Political Thought', in J. G. A. Pocock, *Virtue, Commerce, and History: Essays on Political Thought and History, Chiefly in the Eighteenth Century*, Cambridge: Cambridge University Press, 37–50.

Pope, Alexander (1940), *The Rape of the Lock and Other Poems*, ed. Geoffrey Tillotson, London: Methuen.

— (1961), *Pastoral Poetry and An Essay on Criticism*, ed. E. Audra and Aubrey Williams, London: Methuen.

Porter, David (2001), *Ideographia: The Chinese Cipher in Early Modern Europe*, Stanford: Stanford University Press.

Potkay, Adam and Sandra Burr (eds) (1995), *Black Atlantic Writers of the Eighteenth Century: Living the Exodus in England and the Americas*, London: Macmillan.

Pratt, Mary Louise (1992), *Imperial Eyes: Travel Writing and Transculturation*, London: Routledge.

Raven, James (1992), *Judging New Wealth: Popular Publishing and Responses to Commerce in England, 1750–1800*, Oxford: Clarendon Press.

Richetti, John [1969] (1992), *Popular Fiction before Richardson: Narrative Patterns 1700–1739*, Oxford: Clarendon Press.

Roach, Joseph (1996), *Cities of the Dead: Circum-Atlantic Performance*, New York: Columbia University Press.

Roberts, Andrew (2006), *A History of the English-Speaking Peoples Since 1900*, London: Weidenfeld and Nicholson.

Robertson, John (1995), 'Empire and Union: Two Concepts of the Early Modern European Political Order', in John Robertson (ed.), *A Union for Empire: Political Thought and the British Union of 1707*, Cambridge: Cambridge University Press, pp. 3–36.

Rudolph, Julia (ed.) (2006), *History and Nation*, Lewisburg: Bucknell University Press.

Rzepka, Charles (2002), '"Cortez – or Balboa, or Somebody Like That": Form, Fact, and Forgetting in Keats's "Chapman's Homer Sonnet"', *Keats-Shelley Journal* 51: 35–75.

Said, Edward (1984), 'Foreword' to Raymond Schwab, *The Oriental Renaissance: Europe's Rediscovery of India and the East, 1680–1880*, trans. Gene Patterson-Black and Victor Reinking, New York: Columbia University Press.

St Clair, William (2004), *The Reading Nation in the Romantic Period*, Cambridge: Cambridge University Press.

Sayre, Gordon (1997), *Les Sauvages Américains: Representations of Native Americans in French and English Colonial Literature*, Durham: University of North Carolina Press.

Scanlan, Thomas (1999), *Colonial Writing and the New World, 1583–1671*, Cambridge: Cambridge University Press.

Scherwatzky, Steven (1992), 'Johnson, *Rasselas*, and the Politics of Empire', *Eighteenth-Century Life* 16: 3, 103–13.

Schiebinger, Londa (2004), *Plants and Empire: Colonial Bioprospecting in the Atlantic World*, Cambridge: Harvard University Press.

Schiebinger, Londa and Claudia Swan (eds) (2005), *Colonial Botany: Science, Commerce, and Politics in the Early Modern World*, Philadelphia: University of Pennsylvania Press.

Scott, Walter (1825), *Lives of the Novelists*, 2 vols, Paris: A. & W. Galignani.

Sekora, John (1977), *Luxury: The Concept in Western Thought, Eden to Smollett*, Baltimore: Johns Hopkins University Press.

Sen, Sudipta (1998), *Empire of Free Trade: The East India Company and the Making of the Colonial Marketplace*, Philadelphia: University of Pennsylvania Press.

Shammas, Carole (1993), 'Changes in English and Anglo-American Consumption from 1550–1800', in John Brewer and Roy Porter (eds), *Consumption and the World of Goods*, London: Routledge, pp. 177–205.

Shapiro, James (1996), *Shakespeare and the Jews*, New York: Columbia University Press.

Sheridan, Richard B. (1985), *Doctors and Slaves*, Cambridge: Cambridge University Press.

Shevelow, Kathryn (1989), *Women and Print Culture: The Construction of Femininity in the Early Periodical*, London: Routledge.

Shuffleton, Frank (2001), 'On Her Own Footing: Phillis Wheatley in Freedom', in Vincent Carretta and Philip Gould (eds), *Genius in Bondage: Literature of the Early Black Atlantic*, Lexington: University Press of Kentucky, pp. 175–89.

Siskin, Clifford (1998), *The Work of Writing: Literature and Social Change in Britain, 1700–1830*, Baltimore: Johns Hopkins University Press.

Smart, Christopher [1752] (1949), *The Hop-Garden*, in Norman Callan (ed.), *The Collected Poems of Christopher Smart*, 2 vols, London: Routledge and Kegan Paul, vol. 1, pp. 142–61.

Smollett, Tobias [1748] (1999), *Roderick Random*, ed. Paul-Gabriel Boucé, Oxford: Oxford University Press.

Snader, Joe (2000), *Caught Between Worlds: British Captivity Narratives in Fact and Fiction*, Lexington: University Press of Kentucky.

Sorensen, Janet (2000), *The Grammar of Empire in Eighteenth-Century British Writing*, Cambridge: Cambridge University Press.

Spengemann, William C. (1984), 'The Earliest American Novel: Aphra Behn's *Oroonoko*', *Nineteenth-Century Fiction* 38: 4, 384–414.

Statt, Daniel (1995), *Foreigners and Englishmen: The Controversy over Immigration and Population, 1660–1760*, Newark: University of Delaware Press.

Stepto, Robert B. (1979), *From Behind the Veil: A Study of Afro-American Narrative*, Urbana: University of Illinois Press.

Stewart, Susan (1991), *Crimes of Writing: Problems in the Containment of Representation*, New York: Oxford University Press.

Stone, Lawrence (ed.) (1994), *An Imperial State at War: Britain from 1689–1815*, London: Routledge.

Swarbrick, Andrew (ed.) (1984), *The Art of Oliver Goldsmith*, London: Vision and Barnes and Noble.

The Case of the Royal African Company of England (1730), London.

Thomson, James [1726–30] (1981), *The Seasons*, ed. James Sambrook, Oxford: Clarendon Press.

— (1986), *Liberty, The Castle of Indolence, and Other Poems*, ed. James Sambrook, Oxford: Clarendon Press.

Tibullus, (1990) *Elegies*, ed. and trans. Guy Lee, with Robert Maltby, Leeds: Francis Cairns.

Tobin, Beth Fowkes (1999), *Picturing Imperial Power: Colonial Subjects in Eighteenth-Century British Painting*, Durham: Duke University Press.

— (2005), *Colonizing Nature: The Tropics in British Arts and Letters, 1760–1820*, Philadelphia: University of Pennsylvania Press.

Trumpener, Katie (1997), *Bardic Nationalism: The Romantic Novel and the British Empire*, Princeton: Princeton University Press.

Turley, Hans (2004), 'Protestant Evangelicalism, British Imperialism, and Crusonian Identity', in Katherine Wilson (ed.), *A New Imperial History: Culture, Identity, and Modernity in Britain and the Empire, 1660–1840*, Cambridge: Cambridge University Press, pp. 176–96.

Turner, Michael E. (1980), *English Parliamentary Enclosure: Its Historical Geography and Economic History*, Folkestone: Dawson.

Vitkus, Daniel J. (ed.) (2003), *Piracy, Slavery, and Redemption: Barbary Captivity Narratives from Early Modern England*, New York: Columbia University Press.

Warner, William B. (1998), *Licensing Entertainment: The Elevation of Novel Reading in Britain, 1684–1750*, Berkeley: University of California Press.

Watt, Ian (1957), *The Rise of the Novel*, London: Chatto and Windus.

Watts, Issac (1715), *Divine Songs Attempted in Easy Language for the Use of Children*, London.

Weinbrot, Howard (1978), *Augustus Caesar in Augustan England: The Decline of a Classical Norm*, Princeton: Princeton University Press.

Wheatley, Phillis (2001), *Complete Writings*, ed. Vincent Carretta, New York: Penguin.

Wheeler, Roxanne (2000), *The Complexion of Race: Categories of Difference in Eighteenth-Century British Literature*, Philadelphia: University of Pennsylvania Press.

— (2005), 'Racial Legacies: The Speaking Countenance and the Character Sketch in the Novel', in Paula R. Backscheider and Catherine Ingrassia, *A Companion to the Eighteenth-Century English Novel and Culture*, London: Blackwell, pp. 419–40.

Williams, Raymond (1961), *The Long Revolution*, New York: Columbia University Press.

Wilson, Kathleen (1994), 'Empire of Virtue: The Imperial Project and Hanoverian Culture c. 1720–1785', in Lawrence Stone (ed.), *An Imperial State at War: Britain from 1689–1815*, London: Routledge, pp. 128–64.

— (ed.) (2004), *A New Imperial History: Culture, Identity, and Modernity in Britain and the Empire, 1660–1840*, Cambridge: Cambridge University Press.

Wiseman, Susan J. (1990), '"History digested": Opera and Colonisation in the 1650s', in Thomas Healy and Jonathan Sawday (eds), *Literature and the English Civil War*, Cambridge: Cambridge University Press, pp. 189–204.

Wolfe, John (1598), 'To the Reader', in John Hvighen Van Linschoten, *His Discours of Voyages into ye Easte & West Indies*, London.

Wycherley, William [1676] (1979), *The Plain Dealer*, ed. James L. Smith, London: Ernest Benn.

Yadav, Alok (2004), *Before the Empire of English: Literature, Provinciality, and Nationalism in Eighteenth-Century Britain*, New York: Palgrave Macmillan.

Young, Edward (1728), *Ocean. An Ode*, London.

Zaret, David (2000), *Origins of Democratic Culture: Printing, Petitions, and the Public Sphere in Early-Modern England*, Princeton: Princeton University Press.

Further Reading

Adams, Percy G. (1983), *Travel Literature and the Evolution of the Novel*, Lexington: The University Press of Kentucky. Accounts for the wealth of travelogues that fed into the novel.

Aravamudan, Srinivas (1999), *Tropicopolitans: Colonialism and Agency, 1688–1804*, Durham: Duke University Press. A sophisticated analysis of intellectual and critical issues important to colonial discourse studies.

Ballaster, Ros (2005), *Fabulous Orients: Fictions of the East in England 1662–1785*, Oxford: Oxford University Press. A reminder of the importance of stories of and from the 'East' in the cultural imaginary of England.

Brewer, John (1989), *Sinews of Power: War, Money and the English State, 1688–1783*, London: Unwin Hyman. An important discussion of the infrastructure of an imperial state.

Brown, Laura (1993), *Ends of Empire: Women and Ideology in Early-Eighteenth-Century English Literature*, Ithaca: Cornell University Press. Argues that empire provides the ideological horizon for discussions of women and of femininity.

Crawford, Robert (1992), *Devolving English Literature*, Oxford: Clarendon Press. On the importance of Anglo-Scottish relations in the making of 'English' literature.

David Dabydeen (ed.) (1985), *The Black Presence in English Literature*, Manchester: Manchester University Press. Calls attention to black figures, both marginal and central, in literary texts and art.

Dirks, Nicholas B. (2006), *The Scandal of Empire: India and the Creation of Imperial Britain*, Cambridge: Harvard University Press. Shows how the scandalous cupidity of East India Company officials in India and in Britain helped legitimize empire.

Goldstein, Laurence (1977), *Ruins and Empire: The Evolution of a Theme in Augustan and Romantic Literature*, Pittsburgh: University of Pittsburgh Press. A still relevant statement about the iconic importance of ruins to the imperial imagination.

Grove, Richard (1995), *Green Imperialism: Colonial Expansion, Tropical Island Edens and the Origins of Environmentalism, 1660–1860*, Cambridge: Cambridge University Press. Argues that the origins of modern botany and ecological management lie in colonial policies and practices.

Hechter, Michael (1978), *Internal Colonialism: The Celtic Fringe in British National Development, 1536–1966*, London: Routledge and Kegan Paul. An early statement about the systematic – and colonial – underdevelopment of England's peripheries.

Hulme, Peter (1986), *Colonial Encounters: Europe and the native Caribbean, 1492–1797*, London: Methuen. A sweeping account of Caribbean encounters as Europeans established their trans-Atlantic dominance.

Kaul, Suvir (2000), *Poems of Nation, Anthems of Empire: English Verse in the Long Eighteenth Century*, Charlottesville: University of Virginia Press. A survey of eighteenth-century English poetry that claims empire mattered to these poets.

Kiernan, Victor [1969] (1995), *The Lords of Human Kind: European Attitudes to Other Cultures in the Imperial Age*, London: Serif. Describes the racial and other forms of cultural arrogance that marked European contact with peoples elsewhere.

Lach, Donald F. (1965–), *Asia in the Making of Europe*, Chicago: University of Chicago Press. A monumental, and yet unfinished, cataloguing of archives and texts that describe the creative interaction between Asia and Europe.

Lamb, Jonathan (2001), *Preserving the Self in the South Seas 1680–1840*, Chicago: Chicago University Press. Traces the violence and vulnerability that defined European explorers in their encounters with peoples and places in the South Seas.

McLeod, Bruce (1999), *The Geography of Empire in English Literature 1580–1745*, Cambridge: Cambridge University Press. Argues that important forms of literary production are derived from the imaginative coordinates of empire.

Markley, Robert (2006), *The Far East and the English Imagination, 1600–1730*, Cambridge: Cambridge University Press. Traces the imagined and real engagement between the Far East and Britain.

Nussbaum, Felicity (1995), *Torrid Zones: Maternity, Sexuality and Empire in Eighteenth-Century English Narratives*, Baltimore: Johns Hopkins University Press. Shows that domestic norms of sexuality and family relations mutated in response to the challenges and prospects of empire.

— (ed.) (2003), *The Global Eighteenth Century*, Baltimore: Johns Hopkins University Press. Essays that demonstrate the global concerns, and imperial persuasions, of literary texts and cultural forms.

Orr, Bridget (2001), *Empire on the English Stage 1660–1714*, Cambridge: Cambridge University Press. Theatre as it stages, and meditates upon, imperial relations.

Sorensen, Janet (2000), *The Grammar of Empire in Eighteenth-Century British Writing*, Cambridge: Cambridge University Press. Examines the role played by linguistic relations and language pedagogy in the making of writerly codes.

Sussman, Charlotte (2000), *Consuming Anxieties: Consumer Protest, Gender, and British Slavery, 1713–1833*, Stanford: Stanford University Press. Traces the links between colonialism and consumer protests, figurations of gender, and the slave trade.

Tobin, Beth Fowkes (2005), *Colonizing Nature: The Tropics in British Arts and Letters, 1760–1820*, Philadelphia: University of Pennsylvania Press. On the ideological representation of tropical landscapes and ecologies in art and literature.

Trumpener, Katie (1997), *Bardic Nationalism: The Romantic Novel and the British Empire*, Princeton: Princeton University Press. A wide-ranging survey of colonial themes in novels.

Wheeler, Roxann (2000), *The Complexion of Race: Categories of Difference in Eighteenth-Century British Literature*, Philadelphia: University of Pennsylvania Press. Argues that crucial features of literary and social-scientific classification were derived from the urgencies of empire.

Yadav, Alok (2004), *Before the Empire of English: Literature, Provinciality, and Nationalism in Eighteenth-Century Britain*, New York: Palgrave Macmillan. Argues that feelings of cultural provinciality – vis-à-vis Europe – define literary culture in this period.

Index

Adams, Percy G., 62
Addison, Joseph, 84–95, 101, 108
    Spectator essays, 27, 84, 85,
        87–108
Andrews, William L., 154n26
Aravamudan, Srinivas, 34n52, 68,
    79, 83n26, 127
Aubin, Penelope, 63–4, 67, 80n4,
    81n6

Backscheider, Paula, 46
Ballaster, Ros, 25, 34n53, 152n10
Barrell, John, 33n50, 116n16n22
Bassard, Katherine Clay, 153n19
Batchelor, Robert, 30n23
Bayly, C. A., 89
Beckles, Hilary McD., 28n3
Behn, Aphra, 24, 26, 27, 49, 64, 67,
    78
    The Widdow Ranter, 50–5
Blair, Hugh, 32n41, 94–5,
    119n43n44
Bohls, Elizabeth A., 126
Bond, Donald F., 115n13
Boyle, Robert, 13–14
Brantlinger, Patrick, 31n34
Brewer, John, 33n47
Brotton, Jerry, 29n12
Brown, Laura, 90
Burke, Edmund, 155
Burr, Sandra, 144, 154n24n26
Bush, M. L., 114n1

Campbell, John, 8–12
Carey, Daniel, 12
Caribbean, 14–18, 19, 22, 24, 36,
    68–78, 84, 86, 98, 101
Carlyle, Alexander, 95
Chaudhuri, Mita, 59n10
China, 6–7, 14, 62, 110, 155, 159
chinoiserie, 14, 30n20n23, 86, 91,
    109
Clare, Janet, 57n1, 58n2n5
coffeehouses, 4, 92, 101, 106,
    115n9n14
Colley, Linda, 31n27
Collier, Mary, 134, 153n18
colonialism *see* empire
consumerism, 11–12, 15, 20,
    30n23n24, 84–95, 109, 156
Coughlan, Patricia, 31n29
Crawford, Robert, 20, 83n27,
    117n27

Davenant, William, 36–7, 39
    The History of Sir Francis Drake,
        37–9
    The Siege of Rhodes, 39–47, 51
Defoe, Daniel, 22, 29n18, 33n46,
    34n52, 160
    Robinson Crusoe, 22, 67–78
Dirks, Nicholas B., 153n16
Doody, Margaret Anne, 55, 61, 80n1
Drake, Sir Francis, 15, 26, 36–9, 69,
    89

Dryden, John, 26
 Amboyna, 47–8
Duncan, Ian, 97

East India Company, 16, 47, 81n13,
 89, 153n16, 157–9
Edney, Matthew W., 29n16
empire, 1–6, 16–21, 26–8, 35–40,
 44–6, 54–5, 83n24, 85, 88,
 91–3, 108–12, 121–7, 131–3,
 143, 155–64
Enlightenment, 20, 27, 33n47, 80n3,
 84, 108–13, 130

Felsenstein, Frank, 32n37
Ferguson, Adam, 112–13
Fisher, Michael H., 29n14
Foote, Samuel, *The Nabob*, 157–9
France (and the French), 15–16, 18,
 24, 31n27, 39, 41, 49, 56, 63,
 69, 77, 91, 103, 105–6, 108,
 111, 124, 127, 143, 147, 149,
 157
Fryer, Peter, 149, 150

Gates, Jr., Henry Louis, 145
Gibbons, Luke, 31n30
Goldsmith, Oliver, 26, 33n48, 86
Grainger, James, 24, 125
Great Britain, making of, 3–7, 15–27,
 55–7, 62, 83n22, 85–7, 95–8,
 108–10, 124, 127, 155–7,
 159–62
Green, Donald. J., 153n15
Green, Martin, 78
Gronniosaw, Ukawsaw, 27, 121, 122
 A Narrative, 143–51
Grose, John Henry, 29n14
Grosrichard, Alain, 152n11
Grove, Richard, 30n22
Grundy, Isobel, 152n9

Hakluyt, Richard, 6, 29n15, 31n28
Halsband, Robert, 151n1, 152n5
Hammon, Briton, 151, 154n26n28
Harris, John, 8–12

Hawes, Clement, 33n45, 130
Hechter, Michael, 62
Hedbäck, Ann-Marie, 58n2n4
Hochschild, Adam, 165n7
Hodges, William, 160
Hoppit, Julian, 31n33
Hulme, Peter, 69, 72, 82n17
Hume, David, 110–12
Hunter, J. Paul, 61, 67

India, 7, 14, 16, 27, 57, 61, 110, 113,
 127, 129, 153n13, 156–9
Ireland (and the Irish), 3–5, 15–18,
 22, 36, 49, 55, 62, 79, 85, 100,
 103, 143, 156

Johnson, Samuel, 27, 33n45, 95,
 119n42
 Rasselas, 120, 122, 126–33

Keen, Paul, 19
Keynes, John Maynard, 81n13
Kiernan, Victor, 33n48
Kindersley, Jemima, 29n14
Klein, Lawrence E., 78
Kley, Edwin J. Van, 29n10
Knapp, Louis M., 116n20
Kramnik, Jonathan Brody, 88

Lach, Donald F., 29n10
Lamb, Jonathan, 160, 161
Langford, Paul, 90–1
Ligon, Richard, 64–7
Lillo, George, 24, 56–7
Linschoten, John Hvighen Van, 6
Locke, John, 12–13
Lowenthal, Cynthia, 152n7
Ludolf, Hiob, 129
luxury, 85, 89, 96, 108–13

MacBurney, Willam, 81n6
McIntosh, Carey, 32n41, 95
McKendrick, Neil, 85, 114n7
Mackie, Erin, 92
McLeod, Bruce, 31n36, 33n46,
 83n22n23

Mancall, Peter C., 29n15
Mandeville, Bernard, 34, 114n2
Markley, Robert, 29n11, 47, 83n23
Matar, Nabil, 29n13, 81n14
Maurer, Shawn Lisa, 115n11
Mayer, Robert, 81n12
Meek, Ronald, 116n18
Melman, Billie, 152n7
Montagu, Mary Wortley, 27, 120, 122, 123–6
Mughals, 6–7, 16, 46, 62, 108, 110, 129

Neill, Anna, 165n6

O'Brien, Karen, 119n44
O'Neal, Sondra, 153n20
O'Quinn, Daniel, 57, 159
Orr, Bridget, 39, 52
Ottomans, 6–7, 37, 39–46, 62, 108, 110, 120, 124–6, 129

Pittock, Murray G. H., 31n32
Plumb, J. H., 85, 115n14
Pocock, J. G. A., 57
Pope, Alexander, 21–2, 134, 139, 140
postcolonial criticism, 1–5, 22–6, 44, 46, 53–5, 61–2, 64, 121, 140, 155, 164
Potkay, Adam, 144, 154n24n26
print culture, 8, 17–22, 27, 85–95, 145

Raven, James, 114n4
Richetti, John, 34n51
Roach, Joseph, 54
Roberts, Andrew, 28n1
Robertson, John, 32n38
Robertson, William, 44, 155
Roman empire, 5, 35, 39, 51, 109, 113, 118n37, 119n42, 138, 143
Royal Society, 8, 13, 160
Rzepka, Charles, 165n9

Said, Edward, 156
St Clair, William, 33n43
Sayre, Gordon, 30n21
Scanlan, Thomas, 31n28
Scherwatzky, Steven, 153n14
Schiebinger, Londa, 34n54
Scotland (and the Scots), 3–5, 15–22, 27, 36, 54, 55, 62, 79, 84–5, 94–113, 143, 156
Scott, Walter, 79
Sekora, John, 108–9
Seven Years' War, 16, 153n14, 157
Shammas, Carole, 30n24
Shapiro, James, 31n27
Shevelow, Kathryn, 87
Shuffleton, Frank, 153n21
Siskin, Clifford, 20
slavery, 11, 14, 19, 24, 42, 64–7, 69–74, 78, 86, 89, 95–101, 104–8, 111, 120–2, 124–6, 130–51
Smith, Adam, 20, 32n41, 34n50, 84, 94–5
Smith, Vanessa, 160
Smollett, Tobias, 83n27, 84
    Roderick Random, 95–108
Snader, Joe, 80n5
Sorensen, Janet, 28n4, 97
South Sea Company (and 'South Sea Bubble'), 57, 59n15, 60n17, 89, 160
Staves, Susan, 33n47
Steele, Richard, 27, 78, 84
    Spectator essays, 27, 84, 85, 87–108
    'Yariko and Inkle', 27, 65–7
Stepto, Robert B., 145

Thomas, Nicholas, 160, 161
Thomson, James, 19
translatio imperii et studii, 5
travelogues, 6–14, 21, 26, 36, 64, 94, 129, 160–1, 165n9
Turley, Hans, 83n23
Turner, Michael E., 83n22

Virgil, 5, 35, 138
Vitkus, Daniel J., 80n5

Warner, William B., 83n25
Watt, Ian, 82n16
Watts, Issac, 32n37
Wheatley, Phillis, 27, 121–2, 151
    Poems, 133–43
Wheeler, Roxanne, 79, 118n39

Williams, Raymond, 32n40
Wilson, Kathleen, 115n10
Wiseman, Susan J., 37
Wycherley, William, 49, 54

Yadav, Alok, 32n41
Young, Edward, 33n42

Zaret, David, 32n39